Born in the U.S.A.

Also by Jim Cullen

*The Art of Democracy: A Concise History of
Popular Culture in the United States*

The Civil War in Popular Culture: A Reusable Past

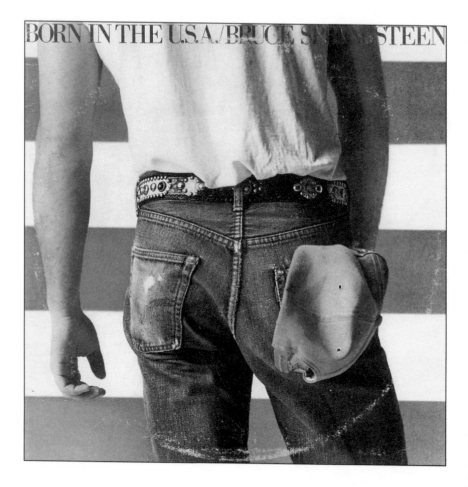

Born in the U.S.A.

Bruce Springsteen
and the American Tradition

Jim Cullen

HarperCollins*Publishers*

HarperCollins books may be purchased for educational, business, or sales promotional use. For information please write: Special Markets Department, HarperCollins Publishers, Inc., 10 East 53rd Street, New York, NY 10022.

FIRST EDITION

Designed by Joseph Rutt

Library of Congress Cataloging-in-Publication Data

Cullen, Jim, 1962–
    Born in the U.S.A. : Bruce Springsteen and the American tradition / by Jim Cullen. — 1st ed.
        p.   cm.
    Includes index.
    ISBN 0-06-018780-8
    1. Springsteen, Bruce—Criticism and interpretation.   I. Title.
ML420.S77C85   1997
782.42166'092—dc21   97-2416

97 98 99 00 01 ❖/RRD 10 9 8 7 6 5 4 3 2 1

For Gordon Anderson Sterling,

who listens

If my work was about anything, it was about the search for identity, for personal recognition, for acceptance, for communion, and for a big country. I've always felt that's why people come to my shows, because they *feel* that big country in their hearts.

—Bruce Springsteen in *The Advocate*,
a gay and lesbian magazine, 1996

CONTENTS

INTRODUCTION

A Big Country

Bruce Springsteen has the night off. It is late October 1980, and he is in Denver, on tour to support his new album *The River*. Restless, he leaves his hotel room, hops in a car, and goes driving. After cruising the city for a while, he decides to go to the movies. He has just bought some popcorn when he is recognized by a fan, who asks him if he would like to sit with him and his sister. Springsteen agrees.

Ironically, the feature that night is *Stardust Memories*, Woody Allen's bitter lament on the cost of fame. "Jesus, I don't know what to say to ya," Springsteen later recalls the man saying. "Is this the way it is?" He replies, "No, I don't feel like that so much."

Emboldened, the fan invites Springsteen to go home with him and his sister to meet their parents. Again, Springsteen agrees. The three arrive shortly after 11 P.M. to find the parents watching television and reading a newspaper. "Hey, I got Bruce Springsteen here," the son explains. "Aw, g'wan," they say. Exasperated, he goes to his room and returns with an album cover to show that Springsteen is the same person as the man in the picture. Convinced and excited, they bid him to stay for a meal. He spends the next two hours there, eating and talking with them, before the fan gives him a ride back. "I felt so good that night," Springsteen later recalls.

Like most fans to whom he has spoken in his music, I have never met Bruce Springsteen. But like most, I feel as if I know him. Perhaps as important, I feel as if he knows *me*—or, at any rate, the person I would like to be: trusting, generous, happy to enjoy the company of others. But our relationship, such as it is, is not simply a matter of imagined mutual admiration. The truth is, I don't often feel trusting, generous, or happy to enjoy the company of others. But I want to. Springsteen appeals to me—the word "appeals" connoting an attraction *to* him as well as a challenge *from* him—not simply because he does seem to be such a person, but, more important, because his songs show me people with difficulties similar to my own, their successes and failures revealing what's at stake in becoming (or not becoming) the people we hope to be. "My job is I search for the human things in myself, and I turn them into notes and words," Springsteen has said. "And then, in some fashion, I help people hold on to their own humanity—if I'm doing my job right."

Obviously, I'm not the only one to feel that he does good work. Indeed, in the course of writing this book I have been deeply impressed by the breadth and depth of Springsteen's impact on American culture even outside the often insular world of rock and roll music. In her 1994 memoir *Prozac Nation* and in other work, the Harvard-educated Elizabeth Wurtzel evokes a compelling Springsteen whose songs plumb the depths of clinical depression with unusual empathy and insight. In her 1985 novel

In Country, novelist Bobbie Ann Mason describes a Springsteen whose periodic appearances on television and radio thrill and console the fourteen-year-old Kentuckian Samantha Hughes, whose father died in Vietnam before she was born ("Somehow there was a secret knowledge in his songs, as though he knew exactly what she was feeling.") Even more lighthearted Springsteen fans suggest a powerful bond between performer and audience. In the 1986 film *Back to School,* the millionaire-turned-undergraduate Rodney Dangerfield empties a room full of students waiting to register for courses by having his chauffeur stand outside with a sign that falsely suggests Springsteen is in a nearby limousine.

But if Springsteen strikes me as very much a man of his time, I have been even more impressed by the way his life and work resonate with some of the most important themes and figures in American history. Many of us know that his work represents the latest chapter in a story that includes Woody Guthrie, Elvis Presley, and Bob Dylan. But that work becomes even more striking when juxtaposed, simply and clearly, with that of figures ranging from Mark Twain to Martin Luther King Jr. In this book, I make a series of such comparisons in an effort to open windows on American history and its ongoing possibilities.

It may seem odd, even absurd, to compare a rock and roll singer with the likes of Twain or King. Indeed, public figures ranging from William Bennett to Bill Clinton have tended to see popular culture generally as more of a problem in American life than as a source of insight or opportunity. But I have undertaken this inquiry in the faith that a democratic culture depends on a willingness to take seemingly modest people and ideas seriously, whether at the polls or in a studio. Actually, American intellectuals from Ralph Waldo Emerson to John Dewey have argued that our way of life depends precisely on this faith; it is one reason why, for example, the great psychologist and pragmatic philosopher William James was such a fan of Walt Whitman. Looked at in this light, one could even argue that Springsteen is a *more* important artist than Whitman, who, while unquestionably speaking *for* the people, never managed to speak *to* the people on the kind of scale that Springsteen has for twenty-five years. The point here, in any case, is less about ranking important figures in American life than in seeking a living community of people and ideas who can deepen and broaden our sense of who we are—and who we can be.

Born in the U.S.A. is not a biography. Instead, it explores a series of myths, symbols, and words in American culture, and the ways in which Springsteen's music clarifies, revises, and reinterprets them. Chapter 1, for example, revisits a well-publicized moment in recent history: Ronald Reagan's invocation of Springsteen while running for reelection in 1984. Reagan, of course, is an icon in his own right, the embodiment of modern conservative Republicanism. What his use of Springsteen—and Springsteen's response—reveals, however, is an alternative conservatism, and republicanism, that I believe is far closer to the vision of the Founding Fathers and successors like Abraham Lincoln.

If chapter 1 is about Springsteen's musical politics, chapter 2 focuses on his musical aesthetics. Here I argue that Springsteen is the direct heir of a republican artistic tradition that was articulated by Emerson, received its first clear expression in Whitman, and was carried through a lineage that includes Twain, Dylan, and countless other creators of American popular culture. I pay special attention to a series of works inspired by John Steinbeck's 1939 novel *The Grapes of Wrath*, including Springsteen's 1995 album *The Ghost of Tom Joad*.

The next three chapters investigate a set of powerful American myths, defined here as widely held beliefs that cannot empirically be confirmed or denied. Chapter 3 explores the American Dream (or, more accurately, a series of American *Dreams*), with a particular focus on two contemporaries—Presley and King—whose lives dovetail and diverge in illuminating ways. Illuminating as well have been Springsteen's efforts to come to terms with their shared legacies of integration and the important differences between them.

Chapter 4 deals with what was described in the nineteenth century as "Manifest Destiny" and which has been more recently called "Victory Culture." This belief in effortless national success, and an assumption of the American way of life as a continental (and later global) blessing was severely challenged by the American experience in the Vietnam War, an experience Springsteen sought to make sense of in "Born in the U.S.A." The song represents a rare and important effort to accept and incorporate limits and defeat into our national story, and in so doing to recognize (and mitigate) the price paid by those, living and dead, mangled by the myth.

Chapter 5 looks at the work ethic, a Puritan ideal whose decline has been lamented for hundreds of years, but especially since the Industrial Revolution. A close look at Springsteen's work reveals, however, a parallel tradition: the play ethic. Shaped by specifically American traditions and influenced by the work ethic, it represents a less common sensibility, but a vibrant—and essential—one.

The last two chapters of the book examine two broader kinds of identity that suffuse any definition of national character. The subject of chapter 6 is manhood and the ways in which Springsteen's depictions of growth from boy to man reflect and comment upon the tremendous social changes wrought by the women's movement, which made some of its most important gains during the years Springsteen came of age. Springsteen's exploration of male friendship, heterosexual romance, and parenthood document the resiliency and utility of older models of masculinity as well as the possibility and efficacy of change.

The final chapter of the book deals with religion. A lapsed, even apostate, Catholic, Springsteen's religious upbringing has nevertheless shaped his work in important—and increasingly apparent—ways. In one sense, his Catholicism is a kind of foil for his republicanism; in another, it enlivens and extends what was originally a decisively Protestant ideal, in effect enlarging what the subtitle of this book denotes as "the American tradition."

I will confess to some uneasiness about that title, in large measure because of my deeply held commitment to pluralism—to American *traditions*. But as the assistant editor for this project pointed out to me, pluralism is itself the heart of a unified vision of national identity: *e pluribus unum*. In a big country, there is something positively liberating about seeking common ground. Something worth finding, nurturing, and preserving. That's why I wrote this book.

ONE

The Good Conservative
On the Trail of Springsteen and Reagan

September 19, 1984, was a typical day on the campaign trail for Ronald Reagan. The president spent the morning in the Democratic stronghold of Waterbury, Connecticut. There, as elsewhere, he read prepared remarks, but added some local color—in this case, invoking the spirit of John F. Kennedy, who had visited Waterbury in 1960. "Even though it was the fall, it seemed like springtime, those days. I see our country today and I think it is springtime for America once again," he told the crowd. "And I think John Kennedy would be proud of you and the things you believe in." Reagan, of course, had supported Richard Nixon in that election.

The president then proceeded to the affluent suburban town of Hammonton, New Jersey, in the southern part of the state. There, he praised Italian-American voters. "You are what America is all about," he told them. "You didn't come here seeking streets paved with gold. You didn't come here asking for welfare or special treatment." And as in Waterbury, Reagan also cited a local favorite. "America's future rests in a thousand dreams inside our hearts. It rests in the message of hope so many young people admire: New Jersey's own Bruce Springsteen. And helping you make those dreams come true is what this job of mine is all about."

Actually, the Reagan camp had hoped to have Springsteen by the President's side in Hammonton. Though attempts to recruit rock stars Billy Joel and John Cougar Mellencamp failed, Michael

GREAT COMMUNICATOR: Springsteen performs in Washington, D.C., August 1985.

BANNER YEAR: President Reagan on tour in New Jersey, October 1984.

Jackson had recently appeared with Reagan at the White House in an anti-drunk-driving campaign. And six days earlier, after attending a Springsteen concert, conservative columnist George Will had written a glowing review that echoed dominant Republican campaign themes. "I have not got a clue about Springsteen's politics, if any," Will wrote, "but flags get waved at his concerts while he sings songs about hard times. He is no whiner, and the recitation of closed factories and other problems always seems punctuated by a grand, cheerful, affirmation: 'Born in the U.S.A.!'"

The office of presidential handler Michael Deaver contacted Springsteen's promoter, who relayed the request to appear with Reagan. Springsteen's agent declined on behalf of his client, saying he was unavailable for any outside appearances during his tour. Springsteen's people thought that was the end of the matter—until Reagan invoked Springsteen anyway. The President's press aide could not immediately tell reporters what Reagan's favorite

Springsteen song was, although the *Los Angeles Herald-Examiner* reported an aide as saying that Reagan listened to Springsteen's records all the time.

It's not hard to see why Reagan's campaign regarded Springsteen as a useful political asset. Since 1972, when he released his first album, Springsteen had built a steadily growing audience that peaked with the release of *Born in the U.S.A.* in June of 1984. The album sold 20 million copies in the United States and 10 million more abroad, making him a superstar. But much of Springsteen's appeal stemmed from a refusal to act like one. His legendary concerts, for example, were extraordinary in their length and in Springsteen's desire to give his fans more than mere money could buy. Such generosity was also evident in his songs, which depicted the hopes and fears of the ethnic working class from which he emerged with a clarity and empathy that had appealingly moral overtones.

This ethnic working-class constituency was the keystone of Reagan's electoral coalition, the bloc that turned the Republicans into the nation's governing party in the 1980s. So the attempt to appropriate Springsteen's appeal was more than routine political window dressing; it reflected a broader strategy that had precipitated a major political realignment. Among other tactics, this strategy involved stoking the resentments of working-class whites uneasy about black gains since the Civil Rights movement, and capitalizing on the ill will generated by white liberals who had regarded the working class with suspicion, if not outright hostility, since the sixties. This strategy also involved championing religious and patriotic causes the American left had largely abandoned in the wake of the Vietnam War.

Springsteen's good-guy image and unabashed patriotism, then, seemed to make him a perfect fit for the Reaganites. Indeed, given the extent to which the Republican Party had appropriated God and Country by 1984, it seemed possible to fit some of the best ideas and traditions of American history under a GOP banner

(George Will's column on Springsteen is a case study of this process in action). As far as they were concerned, Springsteen was a conservative Republican that fall.

Many people, even those with only a passing familiarity with Springsteen's music, regarded this effort to capture Springsteeen as, at best, misguided. More committed fans reacted with outrage. Springsteen's biographer Dave Marsh later wrote that Will's column "was such a perversion of what Springsteen was trying to communicate that it constituted an obscenity." Few in the years since would have reason to disagree.

In a very real way, however, both Will and Reagan were right: Springsteen really was, and is, a conservative as well as a republican. But he's not a conservative republican (lowercase "c" and "r") in the Reagan sense of the term. Rather, he's the conservator of an older, more resonant republicanism that shaped and built a nation.

ORIGINAL REPUBLICANS

It is essential to such a government that it be derived from the great body of the society, not from an inconsiderable proportion, or a favored class of it; otherwise, a handful of tyrannical nobles, exercising their oppressions by a delegation of powers, might aspire to the rank of republicans, and claim for their government the honorable title of republic.
—JAMES MADISON, "THE FEDERALIST PAPERS"

Popular legend associates Bruce Springsteen with the board-walk town of Asbury Park, New Jersey, but he actually hails from nearby Freehold. The town's origins date back to the American Revolution, when George Washington fought the British to a draw in 1778 at the Battle of Monmouth, and the very word "Freehold" is redolent with Jeffersonian associations. A "freeholder" typically referred to a person who owned a relatively small piece of land farmed for family use. Such people lived in marked contrast to plantation owners who controlled vast estates; urban workers or tenant farmers who worked on land they did not own; or slaves who owned neither land nor their own labor. Freeholders were the repository of the fondest hopes of Jefferson and like-minded Founding Fathers. They considered such small, independent producers, who literally had a stake in the nation's fortunes, as those most likely to rule themselves responsibly and avoid the twin tyrannies of autocracy and mob rule.

The issue was how to achieve such a balance. While the United States could never be a democracy in the purest, ancient Greek sense of the term—even in its infancy, the nation was too big to give every citizen a role in decision making—the Founders crafted, under conditions of great difficulty, a *representative* democracy in which leaders would be elected to the most important positions of responsibility.

The name the Founding Fathers gave to their philosophy of representative democracy was republicanism. Even in its earliest incarnations in the mid-eighteenth century, republicanism was never a tightly formulated philosophy of airtight consistency. Still, however diffuse its sources and meanings, republican ideas were instrumental in the formulation of a series of discrete propositions that were of decisive importance to Franklin, Washington, Jefferson, Adams, Madison, and Hamilton, uniting them under one intellectual umbrella. These propositions included:

- the idea of government as deriving from the consent and wishes of the people (as opposed to large private interests);

- an assertion of the necessity of (nonsectarian) civic virtue on the part of those in authority;

- an assumption that power tends to corrupt those who have it, requiring vigorous checks and balances;

- a view of governing as a form of (temporary) service undertaken for the good of the society as a whole;

- the faith that legitimate authority is earned, not conferred, and that the best will rise to prominence on the strength of achievement, not birth;

- the premise that however great those achievements, all are still accountable to the same laws, and have the same rights to life, liberty, and the pursuit of happiness. This is the specific meaning of the Declaration's proclamation that "all men are created equal."

All of this may seem like common sense (even if it has proved extraordinarily difficult to incorporate into the everyday life of our government). But it only *became* common sense over a relatively long period of time and after a good deal of conflict. Indeed, the very title of Thomas Paine's 1776 manifesto *Common Sense* excited the American colonists in their struggle with Great Britain because Paine told them that the things they valued (equality, self-determination, etc.) were not important to their English masters, for whom "common" was a pejorative term. The Founders, by contrast, assumed that (at least white) Americans were truly human and as such had what they called "the moral sense," i.e., the ability to know right from wrong, good from evil, and thus to make sensible choices at the polls and elsewhere.

The moral sense is crucial to an allegory formulated by Jefferson that goes to the heart of the republican philosophy. It goes like this: "State a moral case to a ploughman and a professor; the former will decide as well, and often better than the latter, because he has not been led astray by artificial rules." The plowman and the professor (here you can substitute "congressman," "administrator," or even "boss") are equal in their ability to grasp what is right and what should be done in a given situation. They are not equal in terms of their talents and achievements. The professor is the best-equipped person to *organize* and *execute* a policy, but not to single-handedly *decide* what that policy should be. This is the model, for example, that governs the armed forces, a professional institution headed by the president, a civilian.

Figuratively speaking, Jefferson assumed that the nation would be governed by professors—what he and other republicans more commonly called "natural aristocrats." By dint of effort, a plowman might become a professor, in the process improving himself and providing a fresh, rotating stock of political leadership. This potential for improvement was precisely what made "natural" aristocrats natural, in contrast to old-world aristocrats, who received hereditary titles without having to earn them and in so doing were "unnatural." Jefferson hoped and believed that plowmen would become professors. But he did not want the nation to be led by plowmen.

Although in many ways attractive, republican ideology was not without philosophical weaknesses and practical problems. The most obvious from a Jeffersonian perspective was that in the most literal sense the future of the nation did not belong to plowmen. Even before he became president, the industrial future of the nation was becoming clear to rivals like Alexander Hamilton, whose advocacy of a strong central government proved in the long run more practical than Jefferson's agrarianism. If the republican dream of a truly representative democracy were to have lasting validity, his vision would have to be extended to include factory workers, slaves, and women. And these were all projects that would ultimately require government to overcome the resistance of private interests.

Republicanism faced two major challenges in the decades before the Civil War. The first was the unexpected and powerful growth through the 1850s of the institution of slavery. Not willing to rely solely on its obvious financial benefits for plantation owners, pro-slavery advocates—who had forced Founders like Jefferson into a reluctant compromise with the peculiar institution—became increasingly interested in providing a social, political, and even scientific rationale for it, which ranged from proto-Darwinian explanations of white supremacy to revisionist interpretations of the American Revolution that denied equality not only to African Americans, but also to many varieties of white citizens, such as immigrants. By seeking to limit the growth of equality and social mobility, and in denying the universal moral sense of the populace, such doctrines sought to sidestep, if not actually reject, the intellectual foundations of republicanism.

So when varied factions of a fragmenting American political landscape came together in 1854 to form a new political party, the name they chose for themselves—Republican—represented a conscious act of rededication to the original creed even as they sought to extend it. Not all the factors impelling the Republicans to act were laudable; a hate and fear of black people whom they wanted to contain within the South motivated at least as many members as did a conviction that slavery was morally wrong. For other Republicans, slavery posed a purely economic problem, potentially preventing small producers in Northern states required to pay their workers from competing with larger ones in Southern states who did not. (This basis of opposition to slavery was not unlike recent resistance to the North American Free Trade Agreement, which pits relatively well-paid American workers against foreign ones paid slave wages.) But whatever its justification, the Republican effort to expand equality as well as opportunity in the 1850s and 60s represented the last, best hope for a government by and for all the people. *This* Republican Party, far more than its subsequent incarnations, was the party of Abraham Lincoln.

The other major challenge to republican principles came from capitalism itself. In many ways, of course, capitalism was consonant with republicanism; the right to hold and augment one's private property has always been a matter of basic consensus in American political culture. The problem, which became unmistakably apparent in the second half of the nineteenth century, was that unrestrained capitalism increasingly encroached on a number of other cherished republican principles. The independent farmer or mechanic, once viewed as the necessary, even inevitable result of constitutional democracy, was now more likely to be a cog in an industrial machine, with little opportunity for advancement.

Moreover, the march of industrialization was matched by comparable revolutions in finance and management. The effect was the creation of elite and managerial classes espousing cults of expertise to justify their control of politics and the economy. Being able to vote for president meant relatively little when your boss could buy the candidate of his choice, and when he made all the rules in the company town in which you were forced to live.

Despite—or because of—such co-optation, a variant republican faith remained alive after the Civil War. In general, this lowercase republicanism was dominated by the upper-case Republicanism at voting booths and picket lines. Nevertheless, it was the source of the language, symbols, and traditions for a variety of movements in American life, among them the labor movement, populism, and the New Deal. These and other movements varied widely in their power, geographic locus, and ideological thrust. But all fought entrenched privilege, valorized individual aspiration and achievement, and looked toward a truly representative government (as opposed to one dominated by the railroad and banking interests that sprang up after 1870) as the best means for securing such aims. Just as important, these movements gradually expanded the definition of "the people" to include those, like blacks and women, prevented from becoming full citizens.

Nevertheless, by the time Bruce Springsteen was born in Freehold in 1949, the town was not exactly a Jeffersonian paradise. Now overwhelmingly industrial, Freehold was largely the home of migrant Southerners and white ethnics whose livelihoods were tied to a rug mill, a 3M factory, a Nestlé's chocolate plant, or various smaller companies. Freehold's population was largely lower working class, and it was racially segregated, literally, by the railroad tracks that ran through it. Anyone living there then or now could be forgiven for wondering whether the republicanism of Jefferson, Hamilton, or Lincoln had any relevance whatsoever to their lives.

But it did, and an anecdote Springsteen told during his European tour of 1981 makes clear just how thoroughly, if largely unconsciously, Springsteen had absorbed—and sought to extend—the republican tradition:

> I started reading this book [Allan Nevins's and Henry Steele Commager's] *History of the United States,* and it seems things weren't the way they were meant to be—like the way my old man was living, and his old man, and the life that was waiting for me—that wasn't the original idea. But even if you find those things out, it's so hard to change those things. It wasn't until I started listening to the radio, and I heard something in those singers' voices that said there was more to life than what my old man was doing and the life that I was living. And they held out a promise, and it was a promise that every man has a right to live his life with some decency and some dignity. And it's a promise that gets broken every day in the most violent way. But it's a promise that never, ever dies, and it's always inside of you.

This is, of course, a somewhat simplified and romantic notion of American history. But it is not without its truth, especially when one considers the prominent place of "the pursuit of happiness" in the original republican vision. Nor is it surprising that this would be the moral Springsteen would extract from Nevins and Commager; first published in 1942, the book was a nationalist manifesto meant to draw an implicit contrast between the United

States and Nazi Germany by emphasizing the pluralist, egalitarian elements in our history.

It was in this culture of the thirties, even more than his own culture of the sixties, that Springsteen would find a spiritual home. What makes the thirties near and dear to the heart of republicans like Springsteen is the way the period celebrated the common man. No one was better at it than Franklin Delano Roosevelt, who, along with Eleanor Roosevelt, understood, and compellingly spoke for, working people.

The key to FDR's credibility was the egalitarian spirit that animated his administration's efforts. "If all our people have work and fair wages and fair profits, they can buy the products of their neighbors and business is good," he said in a fireside chat in 1933. "But if you take away the wages and the profits of half of them, business is only half as good. It doesn't help much if the fortunate half is very prosperous—the best way is for everybody to be reasonably prosperous." A half century later, Springsteen would voice a similar idea at the start of his video for "Born to Run": "Remember, nobody wins unless everybody wins."

This is not a sentiment usually regarded as a force that drives economics and politics, both of which are often understood to be controlled by self-interest and rational calculation. But self-interest is not always obvious, and rationality is not always the basis for human behavior, as much as some might like it to be. In fact, what is "rational" or "realistic" at any given moment is subject to change. Roosevelt himself made this point. "I have no sympathy with the professional economists who insist things must run their course and that human agencies have no influence on economic ills," he continued in the same fireside chat. "One reason is that I happen to know that professional economists have changed their definition of economic laws every five or ten years for a very long time." Under such circumstances, fidelity to an ideal like equity is no less—and may even be more—practical than a claim of "realism."

Nevertheless, even one willing to accept the real role of ideas and attitudes in American life could plausibly ask why FDR should be held up as the true voice of the common man when Ronald Reagan—the son of an alcoholic shoe salesman—was a more authentic plowman than the patrician FDR ever was. Given his celebrated skills as the "Great Communicator," the undeniable appeal of Reagan's paeans to freedom, and his decisive electoral successes, is not Reagan a republican Republican?

Perhaps. There is no doubt about Reagan's humble beginnings. And the freedom he celebrated is justly prized by most Americans. The issue is whose interests Reagan ultimately represented, and here there are real doubts about his democratic commitments. Whatever else he might have been, Reagan was not the kind of man to argue that "nobody wins unless everybody wins." It was more his style to praise people, like those Italians in Hammonton, for not expecting anything from their government.

Bruce Springsteen was no politician. Nor did he seem to know very much about his republican inheritance. But there was something about having his name invoked in the middle of Reagan's campaign speech that he knew was wrong. The question was how to respond.

THIS LAND IS *YOUR* LAND

They basically tried to co-opt every image that was American, including me. I wanted to stake my own claim to those images, and put forth my own ideas about them.
—BRUCE SPRINGSTEEN ON
REAGAN-ERA REPUBLICANS, 1995

Springsteen had just finished a four-night run in Philadelphia, about forty miles southeast of Hammonton, on the day of Reagan's campaign swing into New Jersey. He made no immediate reply to the speech. Springsteen had always been diffident about taking public political positions. In 1980, for example, he had been the only performer who refused to sign a statement opposing the proliferation of nuclear power plants at the "No Nukes" benefit concerts at New York's Madison Square Garden, a decision that was less an indication of his feelings than an uneasiness about public declarations. Instead, he performed a song, "Roulette," he had written after the Three Mile Island disaster in 1979, depicting the anger and anxiety of a man whose family is forced to flee its home.

As news of the Reagan speech spread, however, interest in and speculation about Springsteen's reaction intensified. As the *Christian Science Monitor* reported, Springsteen had become "the first popular singer to be recruited by the President of the United States as a character reference." Fans and observers alike could be forgiven for wondering how Springsteen felt about the speech, and what his response might reveal about him or his music.

ONE FOR THE GIPPER: "Wealth, passing through the hands of the few, can be made a much more potent force for the elevation of our race than if distributed in small sums to the people themselves," industrialist Andrew Carnegie wrote in 1889.

The night after Reagan's speech, Springsteen played in Pittsburgh. He made no public comment at this point, either. But when he learned that Ron Weisen, president of the United Steelworkers of America Local 1397 of Homestead, Pennsylvania, sought a meeting with him, Springsteen agreed.

The fact that Springsteen would meet with a union official from Homestead, Pennsyl-

NOT WORKING: Striking mill workers view the idled Carnegie Steel Company in Homestead, Pennsylvania, in the aftermath of the unilateral 20 percent pay cut imposed by management in 1892. Almost a century later, Springsteen's work would intersect with this pivotal event in labor history.

vania, in the aftermath of Reagan's speech is rich with historical irony. Homestead, very much like Freehold, evokes a Jeffersonian vision of small yeomen tilling the land; indeed, Abraham Lincoln had signed the Homestead Act of 1862 with the explicit idea of extending Jefferson's legacy. Within a generation, however, Lincoln's Republican successors presided over the emergence of a Darwinian industrial order that turned Homestead into a steel town inhabited by factory laborers producing steel at the behest of, and with enormous profits for, the millionaire Andrew Carnegie.

In a very real sense, Carnegie is the father of the trickle-down economics Ronald Reagan would later champion. In "Wealth," his 1889 manifesto celebrating the individual capitalist, Carnegie described an ideal state "in which the surplus wealth of the few will become, in the best sense, the property of many, because it is administered for the common good; and this wealth, passing through the hands of the few, can be made a much more potent force for the elevation of our race than if distributed in small sums to the people themselves."

While Carnegie was more generous than many of his fellow robber barons—as the libraries he built attest—he claimed complete freedom to run what he considered his business in his own way. By the late 1880s, many workers at the Carnegie Steel Company in Homestead belonged to the Amalgamated Iron, Steel and Tin Workers, the largest and most powerful union in the American Federation of Laborers, or AFL. The union won a strike in 1889 that resulted in higher pay for skilled workers than for those of neighboring mills, and wages for unskilled laborers (many of them immigrants from southern and eastern Europe) pegged to that of the craftsmen. Carnegie considered this unacceptable. After three years of labor tension, he took a vacation in Scotland and designated his associate, Henry Clay Frick, to announce a 20 percent wage cut and the company's unwillingness to negotiate with a union. Knowing that the workers would reject such terms, Frick simultaneously prepared for a strike by ordering the construction around the factory of a wooden stockade with holes for rifles and barbed wire on top. When the local government refused to assign police to work on management's behalf—as government almost always did until Franklin Roosevelt became president—Frick brought in a private security force. This force tried to reach the factory by boat under cover of darkness, but was met with gunfire by striking workers, and the subsequent battle resulted in the deaths of ten strikers and three security guards. The governor of Pennsylvania called in 8,000 National Guardsmen to restore order (corporations increasingly pressured state and local governments to perform such work, realizing that decentralized authority was easier to control than federal power). Within months, the company cut wages and blacklisted union leaders, and the Amalgamated was broken not only at Carnegie's Homestead factory, but at every major steel company in the nation. It would be over forty years before the federal government, as part of the New Deal, finally required companies to recognize the rights of workers to organize unions to seek better pay and working conditions.

Almost a century after the Homestead strike, Ron Weisen, whose local had formed a successful food bank that helped hundreds of laid-off workers, was one of the more dissident voices in the United Steelworkers union. Weisen opposed concessions to management regarded as inevitable by other union leaders. There is no record of what transpired at Weisen's meeting with Springsteen. But it seems clearly to have aided Springsteen in formulating a response to Reagan.

On the night of September 22, 1984, Springsteen played his third concert in Pittsburgh. In the middle of his first set, he paused to address the audience. "The President was mentioning my name the other day, and I kinda got to wondering what his favorite album musta been. I don't think it was the *Nebraska* album," he said, referring to his 1982 collection of songs in the vein of Woody Guthrie. "I don't think he's been listening to this one." With that, Springsteen began singing "Johnny 99."

To say, as one magazine story at the time did, that "Johnny 99" is a song about "an unemployed auto worker who gets drunk and kills someone" is accurate in that it summarizes the song and conveys the unlikelihood that it's the kind of song Ronald Reagan would ever listen to, never mind celebrate, on the campaign trail. But as is the case with so many of Bruce Springsteen's songs, "Johnny 99" is more than a catchy pop tune. It also tells a story, replete with characters, narrative, action, and a moral.

"Johnny 99" is a stark, simple piece of music; the only instruments are an acoustic guitar, a harmonica, and Springsteen's voice. He begins the song by yodeling—an eerie, melancholy wail. This wail, an act of musical homage, conjures up the ghost of Jimmie

Rodgers, the beloved "Singing Brakeman" of Mississippi who left the railroad to become the first major country and western singer in the 1920s. Even before he's said a word, then, Springsteen connects his story to a great working-class musical tradition.

> *Well they closed the auto plant in Mahwah late last month*
> *Ralph went lookin' for a job but he couldn't find none*
> *He came home too drunk from mixin' Tanqueray and wine*
> *He got a gun shot a nightclerk now they call him Johnny 99*

The clarity of this scene stems from both its particularity and its archetypal quality. The Mahwah, New Jersey, auto plant had been one of the largest in the country before labor and quality control problems shut it down around the time Springsteen wrote the song in 1982. The basic plot elements here—unemployment, alcoholism, easy access to guns, and the fatal results of combining them—are all too recognizable, and could have happened in Homestead, Pennsylvania, in the 1880s about as easily as in Mahwah, New Jersey, in the 1980s.

As with crime novels, however, the murder is only the beginning of the story:

> *Down in the part of town where you hit a red light you don't stop*
> *Johnny's wavin' his gun around and threatenin' to blow his top*
> *When an off-duty cop snuck up on him from behind*
> *Out in front of the club Tip Top they slapped the cuffs on*
> *   Johnny 99*

Seemingly almost offhand details in the song give it resonance. The fact that Johnny's rage unfolds in a dangerous part of town calls attention to the social forces that serve as a backdrop for, and perhaps shape, his actions. The very name of the club, the "Tip Top," suggests instability; it's a short step from the "tip" to "fall," and "top" suggests substantial height (like that between productive worker and displaced madman). It's also seemingly incidental—but very revealing—that it's an "*off-duty*" policeman who finally intervenes at the scene, suggesting a sense of responsibility that is more than official or contractual.

Conversely, subsequent verses depict the grimly mechanical nature of the legal process. Johnny is tried, convicted, and sentenced to ninety-nine years in jail (hence his nickname). Despite such summary justice, there is little order in the court; a fistfight breaks out in the courtroom, Johnny's girlfriend must be dragged out of it, and his mother makes a passionate plea for mercy. None of this makes any difference. But when Johnny is given a chance to have a say, he makes clear that he is not the only one on trial:

> *Now judge I got debts no honest man can pay*
> *The bank was holdin' my mortgage and they was takin' my*
>   *house away*
> *Now I ain't sayin' that makes me an innocent man*
> *But it was more 'n all this that put that gun in my hand*

As he himself admits, Johnny is responsible for his crime. But he also implicates the CEO of the auto company, the board of the bank, and state and federal regulators, *i.e.*, anyone who helped create a situation in which people are saddled with debts they cannot honestly repay. The exploitative company stores of the post–Civil War South; the misleading railroad company brochures luring homesteaders onto the arid plains; the unenforced Civil Rights statutes in the wake of thousands of lynchings—this is an old story in American life, and one that has been far more common than the Donald Trumps, Lee Iacoccas, or Ronald Reagans of the world would care to admit.

Such abuses constitute a working definition of anti-republicanism: action without accountability. Contemporary conservatives are fond of pointing out the need for personal responsibility in everyday life. They typically have less to say about collective responsibility, and the evils that occur when people are encouraged to think only of themselves and their families (or their shareholders). When that happens—and one might say that the core argument of Springsteen's music in songs like "Johnny 99" is that it happens far too often—the system isn't working. The frighteningly angry unemployed oil worker of "Seeds" (released on *Live 1975–85*) offers a concise encapsulation of the problem to a businessman passing through an oil field: "Well big limousine long shiny and black/You don't look ahead and you don't look back." Doing either, he implies, would result in a significant change of direction.

CHOOSING THE BOSS

I appropriate to myself very little of the demonstrations of respect with which I have been greeted. I think little should be given to any man, but that it should be a manifestation of adherence to the Union and the Constitution.

—President-elect Abraham Lincoln,
Trenton, New Jersey, February 21, 1861

In 1834, the twenty-five-year-old Abraham Lincoln launched his second race for the Illinois state legislature (he had lost his first two years earlier). Lincoln was running as a Whig, which meant that he was opposed to the policies of the highly popular president, Andrew Jackson, and was firmly committed to the "American system" of government-sponsored projects like the roads, canals, and railways championed by his hero, Senator Henry Clay of Kentucky. Such positions were difficult to hold in highly Democratic Illinois (which would remain so until Lincoln's election to the presidency in 1860). But even people skeptical of Lincoln's politics seemed to like him personally; in his last race, he had won 277 out of the 300 votes cast in his hometown of New Salem.

This time out, Lincoln decided to campaign more directly, eschewing speeches and statements of principles in favor of a more personal approach. On one such excursion, he made a pitch to about thirty men who were harvesting grain in a field. When some grumbled that they would never vote for a man who was ignorant of field work, he reputedly responded, "Boys, if that is all, I am sure of your votes." Taking a farming implement and holding it with ease, he led the harvesters on one full round of the field. "The boys was satisfied," an observer later said, "and I don't think he lost a vote in the crowd." Lincoln won a seat in the legislature handily.

This story demonstrates how, in the most literal, Jeffersonian sense of the word, Lincoln staked his appeal to the voters on his bona fide credentials as a plowman, one who would later become our greatest professor of republican democracy. Yet even as he made this gesture—in fact, even as Jefferson was formulating his maxim—the terms of that maxim were changing. Lincoln left the countryside for the towns and cities of Illinois. And if Andrew Jackson, the dominant president of Lincoln's youth, was metaphorically a plowman with little interest in becoming a professor, Lincoln's own successors would increasingly be professors having ebbing contact with plowmen—neither the literal ones who still ranged across the nation's interior, nor the figurative ones who sowed the seeds of the nation's industrial growth in the cities.

As this gap began to widen, a new word was introduced to describe those who increasingly controlled the nation's fate: "boss." The term, of Dutch origin, had racial as well as class overtones. Journeymen apprentices had been supervised by a figure known as a master workman, but "master" was increasingly perceived as too closely associated with black slaves against whom white workers measured themselves. "Boss," meanwhile, emphasized the authority of a man in charge—and, perhaps, the less meritocratic basis of that authority, now less commonly earned by moving up the ranks than by being designated by a banker or a manager.

Despite the material realities implied in such linguistic changes, however, memory of—and belief in—the original republican vision has survived. To this day, and with varying degrees of success, political candidates emphasize their common touch to voters. This happens across party lines, as well it should, not only because Democrats and Republicans boast men and women of modest origins, but also because a successful politician in a democracy *should* have a common touch. Of course, by the time most run for office they are rarely humble folk; while he desperately needed a salary when he campaigned for office in 1834, Lincoln was a wealthy railroad lawyer when he ran for the presidency in 1860. Nevertheless, humble origins (or, in the case of someone like Franklin Delano Roosevelt, experience in adversity) often play a positive role in building leadership stature.

Such plowman-like qualities are relevant in a more broadly cultural and social sense as well. Indeed, they can explain one of the seemingly strange aspects of Bruce Springsteen's career, i.e., why this supposed champion of the working class has been tagged with the nickname of "the Boss." It is a tag, moreover, that Springsteen loathes. "I hate being called Boss," he has said. During a 1985 rendition of "Rosalita (Come Home Tonight)," he went so far as to change the lyrics to make his point: "You can call me lieutenant, honey, but don't ever call me boss." He's rarely resisted the name actively, however, perhaps because he doesn't want to alienate his fans, or perhaps because he recognizes the limits on his power to influence the way in which he's perceived. Or maybe he hopes that the nickname will just go away.

It might. But probably not. The reason has less to do with a collective misreading of who Springsteen is—in a very literal way, he really *is* a boss who provides a livelihood for an organization that includes band members, managers, and roadies—than with the fact that he is an embodiment of the republican values woven into his constitution. In an updated version of the Jeffersonian maxim, Springsteen represents what a "boss" should be: One of us. But better.

TWO

Republican Character

SPRINGSTEEN AND THE AMERICAN ARTISTIC TRADITION

By February 1842, when he arrived in New York to deliver a series of lectures on "The Times" at the New York Society Library, thirty-eight-year-old Ralph Waldo Emerson was well on his way to becoming the preeminent man of letters in American history. In essays like "Nature," "The American Scholar," and "Self-Reliance," he outlined a vigorous, pragmatic philosophy suitable for a democratic society. "Books are for a scholar's idle times," he told audiences, in a line typical of his inversion of the conventional wisdom. "Foolish consistency is the hobgoblin of little minds," he said. "A man is a god in ruins."

The descendant of a long line of Boston ministers, Emerson had been one himself before he—a Boston Brahmin if ever there was one—left the pulpit to gain literary fame. So by breeding and accomplishment he was well-connected socially, and on this New York trip he had the pleasure of meeting with some of the most important figures of his day: editor and poet William Cullen Bryant; editor and future presidential candidate Horace Greeley; and Henry James Sr., father to the novelist Henry James and the philosopher William James (who, as the founder of an Emersonian-influenced American school of pragmatism, met the Sage of Concord as a two-month-old infant).

On March 5, Emerson gave a lecture titled "The Poet," a version of which was published two years later and became one of his most celebrated essays. The topic was a familiar one. For over fifty years, American intellectuals had looked to the day when a distinctively national culture would emerge. The United States had clearly achieved *political* independence, but its *artistic* independence was proving more elusive. For thinkers like Emerson, the nation's culture seemed polarized between an infatuation with European writers like Sir Walter Scott on the one hand and vulgar American dreck, like the dime novel *Confessions of a Free Love Sister*, on the other.

In "The Poet," however, Emerson told his audience that art is not as much about formal technique as it is about the ability of the artist, in strong, clear language, to reveal beauty in the unlikeliest of places. "Readers of poetry see the factory-village and the railway, and fancy that the poetry of the landscape is broken up by these; for these works of art are not yet consecrated in their reading," he explained. Later, he flatly stated that, "I look in vain for the poet I describe."

That poet was in the audience. Not that Emerson could have been expected to know that. His name was Walter Whitman, and he was a twenty-three-year-old journalist reviewing the lecture for *The Aurora*, a New York newpaper he edited. Young Whitman, still over a decade away from publishing his first book of poems, liked what he heard. "The lecture was one of the richest and most beautiful compositions, both in its manner and style, we have ever heard anywhere, at any time," he wrote.

It's not surprising that the newspaperman and fledgling writer of free verse would find Emerson's pronouncements attractive. Far more than Emerson himself, Whitman would be intimately familiar with the rhythms of the factory-village and the railway. A Long Island farm boy who had come to the big city, he spent countless hours walking the streets of New York, talking to—and, more important, listening to—the shipbuilders, firemen, and even the gang members who roamed the city. When, thirteen years later, he finally published the first edition of *Leaves of Grass*, he described a world Emerson could only theorize about:

> *The clean-hair'd Yankee girl works with her sewing-machine or*
> *in factory or mill,*
> *The paving-man leans his two-handed rammer, the reporter's*
> *lead flies swiftly over the note-book, the sign-painter is*
> *lettering blue with gold,*
> *The canal boy trots on the tow path, the book-keeper counts at his*
> *desk, the shoemaker waxes his thread,*
> *The conductor beats time for the band and all the performers*
> *follow him,*
> *The child is baptized, the convert is making his first professions,*
> *The regatta is spread on the bay, the race is begun (how the white*
> *sails sparkle!)*
> *. . . And of these one and all I weave a song of myself.*

In the most literal of terms, Walt Whitman was a representative democrat, depicting ordinary people in ordinary language while finding the music, drama, and beauty ("sparkle!") of their lives. And his identification with them was total.

To put it somewhat differently, Whitman was the first great republican artist of American history. If the *politics* of republicanism is *representative* democracy, then the *art* of republicanism is *representational* democracy. Whitman was a master at distilling the popular culture of his time and demonstrating its expressive possibilities in a society struggling to realize both freedom and equality in life and art.

Bruce Springsteen is a direct inheritor of this republican artistic tradition. When, in "Growin' Up," he sings, "I found the key to the universe in the engine of an old parked car," he unwittingly fulfills Emerson's prescription in "The Poet" of finding transcendental meaning in the stuff of everyday life. When, in "Jungleland," he sings, "We'll meet beneath this giant Exxon sign/That brings this fair city light," he carries forth the Whitmanic tradition of a working-class romanticism that endows ordinary objects with grandeur. But Emerson and Whitman aren't the only forebears one can hear in Springsteen's music. They all belong to a broad, and varied, republican tradition.

SIMPLE GIFTS

The message of the great poets to each man and woman are,
Come to us on equal terms, Only then can you understand us,
We are no better than you, What we enclose you enclose,
What we enjoy you may enjoy.
—WALT WHITMAN, PREFACE TO THE 1855 EDITION OF
Leaves of Grass

"Thunder Road," which opens *Born to Run*, is one of Springsteen's "monologue" songs. While "Johnny 99," with its cast of characters and omniscient narrator, unfolds like a short story, "Thunder Road" is largely an oration by one character to another, as in a play. After some initial lines that establish the setting, "Thunder Road" becomes one such monologue:

The screen door slams
Mary's dress waves
Like a vision she dances across the porch while the radio plays
Roy Orbison singing for the lonely
Hey that's me and I want you only
Don't turn me home again
I just can't face myself alone again

The only instruments preceding and accompanying these words are harmonica and piano, which help set the scene (the harmonica in particular lends an air of yearning comparable to that of the lyrics). It's notable that Springsteen opens an unabashedly rock album like *Born to Run* with basic, acoustic instruments. This strategy, combined with pastoral images (the screen door, the porch, the dress waving in the breeze) gives the song a timeless quality, as if the scene described here could be unfolding in the 1920s as easily as the 1970s.

The sole detail that anchors this tableau in a particular historical moment is the reference to Roy Orbison (whose "Only the Lonely" reached number two on the *Billboard* pop chart in June of 1960). "Only the lonely know the way I feel tonight," Orbison begins, instantly creating a community of the emotionally disenfranchised. Springsteen's decision to have the lines ending in "lonely" and "only" rhyme reinforces the narrator's identification with the song—and Springsteen's debt to Orbison.

But perhaps the most salient quality of the song is its simplicity. To make the point in a reductive but useful way: virtually every word in the above-quoted passage is two syllables or less. The only (related) exceptions are "radio" and "Orbison," both of which go a long way toward giving the scene immediacy. By using only the most basic diction and the most active verbs—"slams," "waves," "dances"—Springsteen conjures up a vivid, resonant picture of a relationship in motion. At the same time, this sense of motion is coupled with a lack of resolution, hinted at through the repeated use of the word "again" to indicate that these people have been here before. This time, however, our narrator intends for things to turn out differently.

> *Don't run back inside*
> *Darling you know just what I'm here for*
> *So you're scared and you're thinking that maybe you ain't that*
> *   young anymore*
> *Show a little faith, there's magic in the night*
> *You ain't a beauty, but hey you're alright*
> *And that's alright with me . . .*

These lines point toward a corollary to the simplicity of "Thunder Road": frankness. This is a man who knows what the woman he's addressing is thinking, and he says so. And he doesn't pull any punches by telling her she's something she's not. But the potential brutality of his honesty is offset by both his vulnerability—he has, after all, been "turn[ed] home" by her at least once—and his confidence (his command to "Show a little faith" is delivered with the power of a Baptist preacher).

The simplicity and frankness of "Thunder Road" place it squarely in the republican tradition. The components of that tradition were first hinted at by the American revolutionary Royall Tyler in his 1787 play *The Contrast*, which pitted foreign pretense against native simplicity. The former was represented by the pretentious, Anglophilic New Yorker Dimple and his valet, Jessamy; the latter by Colonel Manly (the name speaks volumes) and his servant Jonathan. Tyler's prologue makes his aim for the play clear:

> *Exult each patriot heart!—this night is shewn*
> *A piece, which we may fairly call our own;*
> *Where proud titles of "My Lord! Your Grace!"*

To humble "Mr." and plain "Sir" give place.
Our Author pictures not from foreign climes
The fashions, or follies of the times;
But has confin'd the subject of his work
To the gay scenes—the circles of New-York

The clear hero of Tyler's play was Colonel Manly. But in an important sense, the future belonged to Jonathan, whose unpretentiousness, skill, decency—and, in subsequent incarnations, independence—became the model for pop culture icons ranging from Davy Crockett to John Wayne. Springsteen himself, in his frequent use of words like "Mister" and "Sir" in his own songs—e.g., "Mister, I ain't a boy" in "The Promised Land"—carries forward the plainspoken themes and language advocated by Tyler.

Meanwhile, the quest for a native idiom "which we may fairly call our own" became the central preoccupation for American intellectuals through Emerson's generation. In fact, there was a group of journalists known as the "Young Americans" in the 1840s whose work was premised on rejecting the claim of John Quincy Adams and other writers for elite publications that literature, "in its nature, must be aristocratic." Whitman, himself part of the Young America movement, described its goals: "The art of art, the glory of expression and the sunshine of the light of letters is simplicity," he explained in his first preface to *Leaves of Grass*. "Nothing is better than simplicity."

Whitman viewed simplicity as the core of American art because he saw it as the core of American life. So did other observers. "In America, where the privileges of birth never existed and where riches confer no particular rights on their possessors, men unacquainted with one another are very ready to frequent the same places and find neither peril nor advantage in the free interchange of their thoughts," Alexis de Tocqueville noted in *Democracy in America*, his classic study of early nineteenth-century American society. "If they meet by accident, they neither seek nor avoid intercourse; their manner is therefore natural, frank, and open; it is easy to see that they hardly expect or learn anything from one another, and that they do not care to display any more than conceal their position in the world."

It was this stylistic as well as material reality of equality in American life, equality that avoided pretense and embraced directness, that shaped the literary aesthetics of writers like Tyler, Emerson, and Whitman. They recognized a living tradition of simplicity in the society they lived in, and it was one they tried to sustain and extend. If the reality of substantial equality receded in the excesses of the Gilded Age, their values survived nonetheless.

The main avenue of transmission for their tradition to Springsteen was not poetry or theater, however, but the way both were captured in vernacular music in the hundred years preceding the arrival of rock and roll in the 1950s. Springsteen's most obvious ancestor is Stephen Foster, whose songs about everyday life won him enormous popularity in the years preceding and following the Civil War. Listened to today, his work often sounds quaint. But there can be no mistaking its immediacy or accessibility for millions of listeners, as the very title of the rough-hewn but evocative "Hard Times Come Again No More" attests. "While we seek mirth and beauty/And music light and gay/There are frail forms fainting at the door," Foster wrote, in lines that suggest a class-conscious literal edge as well as a more metaphorical one. (The power, drama, and durability of "Hard Times" is apparent in the respective folk and rock readings of the song performed by Mare Winningham and Jennifer Jason Leigh in the 1995 film *Georgia.)*

A good deal of Foster's appeal drew on his familiarity with black musical traditions, traditions that more than any other have made American music truly American. The cornerstone of black music, in turn, has been simplicity. This is not to say that African-American music lacks complexity, as any listener of the songs of

Duke Ellington and Billy Strayhorn would instantly know. But they and others built their work on foundations laid by generations of nameless slave singers, musicians, and composers who made music communally and without the benefit of conservatory training. As such, it was designed to be easily appreciated even as it remained the repository of more subtle artistry.

Indeed, it may be less accurate to say that the best American popular music *is* simple than that it *seems* simple. Sometimes such complexities are a matter of making virtuosic performance seem easy, like the phrasing of a Billie Holiday song. Other times it's a matter of veiled meanings residing in apparently innocuous words or delivery. Take, for example, the slave standard "Blue-Tail Fly":

Ole Massa gone, now let him rest
Dey say all t'ings am for de best
I nebber forget till de day I die
Ole Massa an' dat blue-tail fly

Most of us know this song from its chorus: "Jimmy crack corn, I don't care . . . Massa's gone away." What we may not have realized (much in the same way we may not realize that the childhood song "Ring Around the Rosy" is a song about the bubonic plague) is that "Blue-Tail Fly" is sung from the point of view of a slave celebrating the death of a master. In such a context, the clichéd condolence that things are for the best takes on an ironic sting as deadly as that of a disease-carrying insect.

It would be foolish to suggest that the textured simplicity of such art can be attributed to the republican theorizings of Emerson or even Whitman. The point here is precisely the opposite: that the black and white musical streams from which Springsteen later drew were broadly consonant with republican aesthetics—in large measure because acute republicans like Whitman, a devotee of popular music, were so attuned *to* them, and thus influenced *by* them.

These are the broadest, loosest, outlines of Springsteen's musical heritage. But one can make direct connections as well. Woody Guthrie, for example, fused Whitman's democratic poetics with Foster's vernacular music, and became a major influence on Bob Dylan. Dylan, in turn, directly influenced Springsteen in the most obvious of ways. Compare, for example,

> *Once upon a time you looked so fine*
> *Threw the bums a dime in your prime*
> *Didn't you?*

in Dylan's 1965 hit single "Like a Rolling Stone" to

> *Madman drummers bummers*
> *And Indians in the summer*
> *With the teenage diplomat*
> *In the dumps with the mumps*
> *As the adolescent pumps*
> *His way into his hat*

in Springsteen's "Blinded by the Light," from his debut album of 1973. Despite the obvious contrast in tone (Dylan's caustic, Springsteen's jubilant), there is clear continuity in the way both use simple words, romanticize the ordinary, and play with the inherent musicality of language.

These are precisely the same tendencies Whitman exhibited in "Song of Myself."

> *The smoke of my own breath,*
> *Echoes, ripples, buzz'd whispers, love-root, silk-thread, crotch*
> *and vine*
> *My respiration and inspiration, the beating of my heart, the*
> *passing of blood and air through my lungs . . .*

The differences here are clear, the most obvious being the lack of a rhyme scheme (for the most part, Whitman considered rhyme stultifying convention—except, in a case like "respiration and inspiration" when it represented a kind of syncopated freedom). But one can plainly see here the same exuberant cataloging at work, the same musicality, the same density achieved by piling on images. Above all, the language is similarly simple and arrestingly accessible.

By the time of "Thunder Road," however, Springsteen began moving away from dense simplicity to a more streamlined form. In so doing, he achieved a different kind of density, one attained not by clusters of many words but by compressing a few. A very good illustration of this point can be made with "Hungry Heart," Springsteen's first hit single:

> *I met her in a Kingstown bar*
> *We fell in love I knew it had to end*
> *We took what we had and ripped it apart*
> *Now here I am down in Kingstown again*
> *Everybody's got a hungry heart . . .*

Like "Blue-Tail Fly," "Hungry Heart" has such a catchy, buoyant tune that it's easy to overlook the complexities lurking within it. "We fell in love I knew it had to end" encapsulates not only an entire relationship but also the fatalism of the man who entered into it (but can't quite leave it behind, either). Moreover, it does so with ten monosyllabic words, none more than four letters long. Economy of expression was never exactly Whitman's strong suit. But within a few years of releasing his first record, Springsteen had mastered it.

Whatever its nuances, of course, simplicity is not a uniquely American value. Leo Tolstoy espoused it in his short stories about Russian peasants; it is central to the aesthetics of the poetical tradition of haiku in Japan. But nowhere has simplicity informed a living social and political tradition to the degree that it has in the United States. Here, simplicity was not only a matter of style, a philosophical school, or a religious aspiration. It was also a material reality.

MOVING ASPIRATIONS

Camerado! I give you my hand!
I give you love more precious
*   than money*
I give you myself before
*   preaching or law;*
Will you give me yourself? will
*   you come travel with me?*
Shall we stick by each other as
*   long as we live?*

—Walt Whitman

Will you walk with me out on
*   the wire?*
'Cause baby I'm just a scared and
*   lonely rider*
But I gotta know how it feels
I wanna know if love is wild, I
*   wanna know if love is real*
Can you show me?

—Bruce Springsteen

"Thunder Road" is not only a typical Springsteen song in its simplicity, but also showcases one of his favorite images and symbols: driving a car.

. . . Roll down the window
And let the wind blow back your hair
Well the night's bustin' open
These two lanes will take us anywhere
We got one more chance to make it real
To trade in these wings on some wheels
Climb in back
Heaven's waiting down on the tracks . . .

There are two romances being portrayed here: one between two people, and the other between those people and the road. And while there is a happy, carefree element to these romances, there is an element of risk, too. As this man later tells a woman named Mary, "The door's open/But the ride it ain't free."

In a republican country, there are no free rides ("You pay your money and you play your part," Springsteen sings in "Hungry Heart," another song about inner restlessness). That notwithstanding, Americans were taking "one last chance" for "heaven" long before there were cars—and, for that matter, long before there were roads. From the very beginning, moving has been a very big part of our national drama. Happiness, Jefferson said, must be *pursued.*

One of the signal characteristics of republicanism has been mobility: plowmen becoming professors. In the cultural realm of republicanism, however, mobility is represented much more literally. Moving—for a buck, for a dream, or simply for the sake of moving—is one of the great themes of American art.

In large measure, this is because moving has been a great fact of American life, not only for heroic figures like Daniel Boone or Lewis and Clark, but for ordinary citizens as well. De Tocqueville noted this, too. "In the United States a man builds a house in which to spend his old age, and he sells it before the roof is on; he plants a garden and lets it just as the trees are coming into bearing; he brings a field into tillage and leaves other men to gather the crops; he embraces a profession and gives it up; he settles in a place, which he soon afterwards leaves to carry his changeable longings elsewhere," he wrote in 1840. The "changeable longings" is a nice touch; it's as if de Toqueville is suggesting that desires are like luggage you pack according to some shifting internal thermometer. In most classic American romances with travel, people move not so much as a result of external constraints (as in Russia or Ireland), but rather out of an inner compulsion: however logical or irrational, it simply feels better to be on the move.

In art and life, the means of transportation have varied widely, from covered wagons to the aptly named information superhighway. Natty Bumppo, the hero of James Fenimore Cooper's Leatherstocking saga, traversed Indian trails from upstate New York to the Great Plains. Herman Melville's characters wandered the globe in navy vessels and whaling ships. The Beats went west in any old jalopy they could find, traversing the continent for no apparent reason other than because it was there.

Huck Finn hopped on a raft to get away from his unhappy home life, and later, to help his friend Jim escape from slavery. But the appeal of moving was also more basic:

> I never felt easy till the raft was two mile below there and out in the middle of the Mississippi. Then we hung up our signal lantern, and judged that we was free and safe once more . . . We said there warn't no home like a raft, after all. Other places do seem so cramped up and smothery, but a raft don't. You feel mighty free and comfortable on a raft.

For Huck, the journey matters far more than the destination. His creator agreed. "When I was a boy, there was but one permanent ambition among my comrades in our villages on the west bank of the Mississippi River. That was, to be a steamboatman," Mark

Twain wrote in 1875. His "permanent ambition," in other words, was permanent impermanence. A century later, Springsteen would express a similar idea in "Growin' Up," when he sang of finding the key to the universe in a car (which is more or less what the narrator of "Thunder Road" does as well). For Springsteen's alter egos, no less than Twain's, the essence of freedom is movement.

And yet movement is more often than not accompanied by an air of uncertainty, even anxiety. Cooper's Leatherstocking can never get far enough away from the encroaching civilization he wants to escape. For Huck and (especially) Jim, staying still is not simply uncomfortable, but dangerous, and only in moving can they still their restlessness. In Jack Kerouac's *On the Road*, one suspects that Neal Cassidy and company can't stop moving even if they want to; the amphetamines they pop seem less the source of their nervous energy than a reflection of it. These characters are always anxious to leave where they've been, but never really know where they're going.

Even the ebullient Whitman displays not-so-quiet desperation. He ends his paean to movement, "Song of the Open Road," on a note of uncertainty, assertions giving way to questions (see page 34).

Compare this finale to Springsteen's "Born to Run," a piece of music one could legitimately call his own "Song of the Open Road." Both show the same combination of confidence, vulnerability, and excitement, all set within a context of movement. But this is only the middle of the song. Unlike Whitman, Springsteen ends his biker's song of the road not with questions, but with assertions:

> *Together Wendy we'll live with the sadness*
> *I'll love you with all the madness in my soul*
> *Someday girl, I don't know when*
> *We're gonna get to that place where we really wanna go*

And we'll walk in the sun
But 'til then, tramps like us
Baby we were born to run

Love is a universal experience. But "Born to Run" is truly an American love song. The assertion that one *will* walk in the sun; the assumption that one can make it happen through sheer force of will; the insistence on *movement*, be it ship, stagecoach, railroad, or motorcycle to get there—these are sentiments the first Pilgrim or the most recent immigrant would recognize. It is in this sense that one can speak of "Born to Run," like "Thunder Road," as a republican love song.

GREAT DEFEATS

Have you heard that it is good to gain the day?
I also say it is also good to fall, battles are lost in the same
spirit in which they are won.
—WALT WHITMAN, "SONG OF MYSELF"

Five years after "Thunder Road," Bruce Springsteen released another song, "The River," in which a man tells a story about himself and his wife—who, not coincidentally, is named Mary. The two met in high school, when she was seventeen, and consummated their romance.

Then I got Mary pregnant
And man that was all she wrote
And for my nineteenth birthday
I got a union card and a wedding coat
We went down to the courthouse
And the judge put it all to rest
No wedding day smiles, no walk down the aisle
No flowers no wedding dress

It's all downhill from here. The man gets a job with a construction company, but loses it during a recession. The love he and Mary share dries up like the river they used to drive to and swim in during their courting days. "All them things that seemed so important/Well mister they vanished right into the air," he explains. "Now I act like I don't remember/Mary acts like she don't care." But they *do* remember and care. That's why the song is so sad.

"The River" is a song about the way poor judgment, personal failure, and bad luck ruin individual lives, and is not overtly a social statement. But there is yet another sense in which republicanism animates the song. The key to this is a word that sounds sentimental but is actually quite demanding: *caring*. Politically speaking, a good republican looks at a situation like the one described by "The River" and asks whether there's anything that can or should be done in the public realm. Culturally speaking, a good republican avoids labeling people with abstractions (like one of Ronald Reagan's favorites, "welfare queen") and sees them as individuals with rich private lives—a habit of thought, which if practiced assiduously in the private realm, is likely to have ramifications in the public realm. The best republican artists are those who connect particular lives with a larger community; to use the language of Emerson, they pierce "rotten diction and fasten words again to visible things."

Because a republican government places high expectations on its people, and because those expectations are often not met, the characteristic stance of republican art is often protest. This does not mean it should take the form of propagandist sloganeering. On the contrary, it usually means putting public issues in private terms. When Mark Twain critiqued slavery in *The Adventures of Huckleberry Finn*, he did so not through the use of abstract symbols, or tightly reasoned argument, but rather through depicting the anguish of a young boy torn between the immoral legal code by which he was raised and loyalty to his fugitive friend. ("All right then, I'll *go* to hell," he concludes, casting his lot with Jim.)

Whitman adopted a similar strategy. In his first edition of *Leaves of Grass* in 1855, he describes a scene that is both profoundly personal and political:

> *The runaway slave came to my house and stopt outside*
> *I heard his motions crackling the twigs of the woodpile*
> *Through the swung half-door of the kitchen I saw him limpsy*
> *   and weak*
> *And went where he sat on a log and led him in and assured him*
> *And brought water and fill'd a tub for his sweated body and*
> *   bruis'd feet . . .*

For the poet no less than Huck Finn, aiding a fugitive slave is a federal offense. While the scene described here is somewhat archetypal, even generic, specific details like the crackling twigs and half-door of the kitchen give the scene particularity and immediacy.

Later in the same poem, Whitman goes even farther in representing a fugitive:

> *I am the hounded slave, I wince at the bite of dogs,*
> *Hell and despair are upon me, crack and again the crack of*
> *   marksmen*
> *I clutch the rails of the fence, my gore dribs, thinn'd with ooze of*
> *   my skin*
> *I fall on the weeds and stones . . .*

Upon hearing Whitman's poetry aloud for the first time, the ex-slave and abolitionist lecturer Sojourner Truth asked who wrote it, but then added, "Nevermind the man's name—it was God who wrote it, he chose the man—to give his message."

Springsteen's own embrace of this facet of the republican tradition was largely instinctive, relying less on the conscious emulation of older models (most of which came to him through movies and records) than on careful observation of the world in which he grew up. But by the late seventies and early eighties—the years when

"The River" and "Hungry Heart" were being written—he did begin seeking out kindred spirits.

Perhaps the most important was Dylan's hero, Woody Guthrie. As much as any artist in American history, Guthrie bridged the cultural and political strands of republicanism, fusing populist themes with vernacular language. The most celebrated example is "This Land Is Your Land," his love song to America. Generations of schoolchildren have sung this virtual national anthem unaware that it was penned by a Communist sympathizer, or that Guthrie wrote it as a response to what he perceived as the smug piety of Irving Berlin's "God Bless America." Along with lyrics celebrating the redwood forest and Gulf Stream waters, Guthrie also included lyrics about people on relief lines, and high walls with "private property" signs. Far from an innocuous folk song, "This Land Is Your Land" was written as a pointed statement about who the fruits of this nation really belonged to: everyone.

Guthrie first came to the mature Springsteen's attention on November 5, 1980, the day after Ronald Reagan had been elected to the presidency. He was given a copy of journalist Joe Klein's biography of Guthrie, where he learned about the history of "This Land Is Your Land"—and incorporated it into his repertoire (his version appears on *Live 1975–85)*. Springsteen later recorded "I Ain't Got No Home," Guthrie's mournful meditation on homelessness, and "Vigilante Man," his attack on mob justice, for *A Vision Shared,* a 1988 tribute album to Guthrie and Leadbelly organized by the Smithsonian.

More importantly, Guthrie informed Springsteen's own work. Nowhere is this influence more obvious than on *Nebraska,* whose stark acoustic songs evoke Guthrie's dust bowl ballads. Just as Guthrie's "Pretty Boy Floyd," his ballad of a populist bank robber, depicts a topsy-turvy world in which economic equity is a form of crime, Springsteen songs like "Johnny 99" and "Highway Patrolman" (in which a policeman allows his brother to escape the law) protest a

BOUND FOR GLORY: Woody Guthrie's "Tom Joad" forms a musical bridge between John Steinbeck's *The Grapes of Wrath* and Springsteen's *The Ghost of Tom Joad.*

country that imposes on its people debts no honest man can pay. While not all these people are blameless—the narrator of "Nebraska" is a mass murderer—most are forced to shoulder the burden for sins not of their own making. The motorist narrator of "State Trooper" speaks for many when he says, "License, registration, I ain't got none/But I got a clear conscience about the things that I done."

Yet what's perhaps most surprising about so many of these people is not their sense of anger or disillusionment, but rather the tenaciousness with which they hold on to their dreams. "Everything dies baby, that's a fact/But maybe everything that dies someday comes back," asserts the narrator of "Atlantic City," a sentiment particularly striking within the context of the civic corruption described in the song. On "Reason to Believe," the song that closes *Nebraska,* Springsteen catalogs a series of deaths and abandonments experienced by ordinary people, who respond by simply getting on with their lives.

Their reasons for believing have a religious character, but they have a political one as well. A republican government does not depend on perfection, but it does depend on the possibility—and, sooner or later, the reality—of improvement. Though severely stretched, Americans' faith in the republican social contract has never been broken—even when, in the eyes of some, it should have been.

TOM JOAD'S CHILDREN

*The nonchalance of boys who are sure of a dinner, and would
disdain as much as a lord to do or say aught to conciliate one,
is the healthy attitude of human nature.*
—RALPH WALDO EMERSON, "SELF-RELIANCE"

*I'll be in the way kids laugh when they're hungry and they
know supper's ready.*
—TOM JOAD, PROTAGONIST OF JOHN STEINBECK'S (AND
JOHN FORD'S) *The Grapes of Wrath*

On March 3, 1940, Woody Guthrie appeared at New York's
Forrest Theater in a benefit performance for what was billed as
"The John Steinbeck Committee for Agricultural Workers."
Steinbeck's novel *The Grapes of Wrath*, chronicling the mass migra-
tion of displaced farm workers from Guthrie's beloved Oklahoma,
had been published the previous spring, and was still a major best-
seller. The film version of the novel, directed by John Ford, had pre-
miered in New York with great fanfare six weeks before. *The Daily
Worker*, a Communist newspaper, promoted Guthrie's appearance
with a picture of him strumming a guitar and with the caption
"'Woody'—that's the name, straight out of Steinbeck's 'Grapes of
Wrath'—sings People's Ballads."

It was a great night for Guthrie. Explaining that he was pleased
to perform in a "Rapes of Graft" show, he amused and moved the
audience, which included Alan Lomax, the budding ethnomusicol-
ogist who would go on to lasting fame by recording Guthrie's work
and that of other folk musicians. Shortly after the benefit, Lomax
persuaded Victor Records to produce an album of Guthrie's dust
bowl ballads. "The Victor people want me to write a song about
The Grapes of Wrath," Guthrie told his friend Pete Seeger, asking
him if he knew where he could find a typewriter. Seeger directed

him to the apartment of a friend, where, with a half gallon of wine, Guthrie sat down to work. The song that resulted, "Tom Joad," was a seventeen-verse ballad that tracked the plot of the book and the movie.

It should be noted that there are significant differences between the two. This is not only because a movie must necessarily condense a novel, but also because director Ford softened some of the novel's more radical edges. Steinbeck, for example, ends with the Joad family in very desperate straits, fleeing a rising flood and finding only temporary refuge in an abandoned barn (where, in a scene that underlines the importance of women, Rose Joad nurses a starving man). Ford, by contrast, ends with a battered-but-stabilized family on the road again, and Ma Joad commenting on the endurance of the people—not the necessity for change in the system.

Nevertheless, both book and movie share fundamental values. As historian Alan Brinkley noted in an essay comparing book and film, as far as both Steinbeck and Ford were concerned, "neither despair nor rage could adequately convey the real meaning of the Great Depression. Instead, the novel and film suggest, the true lesson of the time was the importance of community: not community defined in traditional, geographical terms; not in the community of a neighborhood or a town, or a region—but in a community of the human spirit."

CALIFORNIA DREAMER: John Steinbeck, circa 1939.

This point is made in Tom Joad's pivotal parting

words to his mother, which are similar in book and film (the following comes from the latter because it's shorter and uncluttered with reference to other characters in the story):

I'll be all around in the dark. I'll be everywhere. Wherever there's a fight so hungry people can eat, I'll be there. Wherever there's a cop beatin' a guy, I'll be there. I'll be in the way guys yell when they're mad; I'll be in the way kids laugh when they know supper's ready. And when the people are eatin' the stuff they raise, and livin' in the houses they build, I'll be there, too.

Woody Guthrie's version adapted the core of this passage for the climax of "Tom Joad":

Wherever little children are hungry and cry
Wherever people ain't free
Wherever men are fightin' for their rights
That's where I'm gonna be, ma
That's where I'm gonna be

These words lack the crisp clarity of book and film, but their musicality is apparent even on the page.

However urgent and moving the work of Steinbeck, Ford, and Guthrie, all were in some sense being outpaced by history. By the time Guthrie appeared at the Steinbeck benefit, many of the displaced Okies he sang about were finding jobs in California defense plants gearing up for World War II. That war, and the energies it unleashed, transformed the United States in the four years between the time Guthrie wrote the first draft of his response to "God Bless America" in February 1940 and his first recording of the song as "This Land Is Your Land" in the spring of 1944. Twenty years later, starving migrants were hosting backyard cookouts; the defining voice of California life (itself increasingly the defining voice of American life) was not Woody Guthrie, but the Beach Boys.

Of course, poverty did not disappear in California or anywhere else in America. And other struggles, most notably the Civil Rights movement, were only beginning. But with the exception of the early years of that movement, there was a steady ebbing of the egalitarian spirit—a spirit suffusing Whitman even as he wrote "Song of Myself"—that had animated the artists of the thirties.

Springsteen's discovery of Woody Guthrie in 1980 coincided with the advent of an era of accelerating inequality in the United States, a development he chronicled on *Nebraska* and subsequent records. But by the end of the decade even Springsteen had retreated somewhat from his concern with social injustice. Records like *Tunnel of Love, Human Touch*, and *Lucky Town*, while hardly rejecting the political stance of his earlier records, lacked the sense of active engagement that had characterized his music in the early eighties.

But during a sleepless night in early 1995 while trying to write new songs, Springsteen picked up *Journey to Nowhere*, a book on the new American underclass written by Dale Maharidge with photographs by Michael Williamson (they would go on to share a Pulitzer Prize in 1990 for *And Their Children After Them*, which traced the subsequent history of Alabama sharecropping families first chronicled in James Agee's classic 1940 study *Let Us Now Praise Famous Men*). *Journey to Nowhere* had originally been published in 1985, which is when Springsteen bought it, but only now was he actually reading the book. Maharidge and Williamson's depictions of the decaying industrial city of Youngstown, Ohio, and their portraits of contemporary boxcar hoboes were the direct inspiration for two new songs, "Youngstown" and "The New Timer." "What Springsteen is trying to do is something so incredible," said Maharidge in 1996, when *Journey to Nowhere* was reissued (with a new introduction by Springsteen). "He's a musical Steinbeck."

Springsteen made this political and artistic connection clear in his decision to title the ensuing album *The Ghost of Tom Joad*, and in the song of the same name that opens it. But his primary tie to Tom Joad, as he has made clear in interviews and in source notes that accompany the album, is the John Ford version. Whatever the lineage, though, it's apparent that Springsteen sought to make his own imprint on the material.

He does this in a number of ways. One is the use of contemporary details that anchor the songs in the present even as they resonate with the past. So, for example, "The Ghost of Tom Joad" opens with men walking along railroad tracks—and highway patrol choppers coming over a ridge. Steinbeck/Ford/Guthrie focus on poor white Southerners; Springsteen's locus is the Southwest, and many of his characters are nonwhite (this was true of some of Steinbeck's other fiction). While the original Tom Joad sought to navigate the shoals of the Great Depression, Springsteen's narrator, observing a line of people waiting for shelter, dryly welcomes "the new world order" proclaimed by George Bush. Indeed, there's a bitterness in "The Ghost of Tom Joad" that may even exceed that of Steinbeck. "The highway's alive tonight," begins the chorus on a hopeful note—only to end with an acerbic "But nobody's kiddin' nobody about where it goes." Thunder Road, it would seem, is a dead end.

Despite this apparent despair, however, Springsteen's Tom Joad casts his lot with the others, echoing the spirit—and even the letter—of the original:

Now Tom said, "Mom, wherever there's a cop beatin' a guy
Wherever a newborn baby cries
Where there's a fight against the blood and hatred in the air
Look for me, Mom, I'll be there
Wherever there's somebody fightin' for a place to stand
Or a decent job or a helpin' hand
Wherever there's somebody strugglin' for a place to be free
Look in their eyes, Mom, you'll see me"

But the obvious similarities between this Tom Joad and his predecessors may be less important than a more fundamental affinity. While this jaded narrator knows "nobody's kiddin' nobody," he keeps searching for—and at the end of the song claims to be "sittin' here in the campfire light with"—the ghost of Tom Joad.

"We're the people that live," Ma Joad says to her husband and son as they drive through California at the end of the film version of *The Grapes of Wrath.* "They can't wipe us out. They can't lick us. We'll go on forever, Pa, because we're the people that live." Almost a half century later, also in California, Springsteen introduced another song from *The Ghost of Tom Joad,* "Across the Border," by saying, "This song's about the mystery of human nature, human spirit. How people just keep going, keep going. . . . We've been beat up pretty bad, but we keep going." The ensuing song—think of it as "Thunder Road" with a female character named Maria—captures the essence not only of the Joads' ethos, but also their dream:

> *For what are we*
> *Without hope in our hearts*
> *That someday we'll drink from God's blessed waters*
> *And eat the fruit from the vine*
> *I know love and fortune will be mine*
> *Somewhere across the border*

Simplicity, mobility, hope: this is the art of republicanism.

THREE

Visions of Kings

SPRINGSTEEN AND THE AMERICAN DREAM

In the early morning hours of April 30, 1977, Bruce Springsteen finished a live show in Memphis, hailed a taxi, and asked the cab-driver to take him, his publicist, and band member Steve Van Zandt to a quiet restaurant. The driver, suspecting that these cus-tomers were out-of-town VIPs, suggested they drive by Elvis Presley's house. Springsteen enthusiastically agreed. He had never met Presley, but had just written a song, "Fire," expressly for him. Now he was headed for Graceland.

Springsteen and his entourage arrived at the gates of the man-sion at about 3 A.M. No one was visible, but the house lights were on. Acting on impulse, Springsteen scaled the gate and started up the long driveway. He had just about reached the front door when he was accosted by a security guard. Springsteen asked if Presley was home and was told he was not. "Well, now I'm pullin' out all the cheap shots I can think of—you know, I was on [the cover of] *Time,* I play guitar, Elvis is my hero, all the things I never say to anybody," he later recalled of his encounter with the guard. "Because I figure I gotta get a message through. But he just said, 'Yeah, sure. Why don't you let me walk you through the gate. You gotta get out of here.' He thought I was just another crazy fan—which I was."

Few would have regarded Springsteen as "just another crazy fan," except perhaps Presley himself, who since the time of the Beatles had been largely indifferent, if not outright hostile, to the rock artists of succeeding generations. On the other hand, there were many who thought Presley himself could only be taken seriously by, well, a crazy fan.

Yet even some of these people could not forget the young Presley, who had transformed age-old black and white musical traditions into a vehicle for expressing the excitement, even joy, of the American Century as it crested. As a child in the late fifties, that transformation had touched Springsteen, who first saw Presley on *The Ed Sullivan Show.* "Man, when I was nine, I couldn't imagine *not* wanting to be Elvis Presley," he later remembered. While later influences, notably Bob Dylan, were more obvious, to this day Presley remains a touchstone for Springsteen.

The reasons for Presley's appeal are musical, but also mythic. The simple outlines of Presley's life—of a poor, insecure boy who rose to fame and fortune through sheer force of will—represented a dazzling American Dream that Springsteen himself would live out. Springsteen saw himself as the inheritor of that Dream, and, one imagines, he fantasized about being recognized as the King's heir that night in Memphis.

Four months later Presley was dead, the victim of a drug overdose. By the end of his life, he was hardly a role model for anyone, a drug addict who in 1969 had successfully lobbied Richard Nixon to deputize him as a narcotics officer (the photo-op picture of the two men in the Oval Office has become a camp classic). Ever since, Elvis jokes have been a staple of popular culture, and a point of reference for others with larger-than-life appetites (like Bill Clinton, whose secret-service code name is Elvis).

But if Presley's life and death was the stuff of farce, it was also a tragedy. To commemorate it, Springsteen began performing a new song, "Johnny Bye Bye," in the early eighties. The style, lyrics, and even title of "Johnny Bye Bye" are patterned on the work of Chuck Berry, whose "Bye Bye Johnny" (1960) even shares the same opening lines: "Leaving Memphis with a guitar in his hand/with a one way ticket to the promised land." The references to "guitar" and "Memphis" immediately make one think of Presley. But while Berry's song is a paean to the joy and power of rock and roll, Springsteen's is ultimately a eulogy to lost hope:

> *They found him slumped up against the drain*
> *With a whole lot of nothin' runnin' in his veins*
> *Now bye bye Johnny, Johnny bye bye*
> *You didn't have to die, you didn't have to die*

"Johnny Bye Bye" is a relatively obscure song in the Springsteen canon (it was released in the winter of 1985 as the B side to the hit single "I'm on Fire"). But Presley remained an important figure for him, whether as a cautionary tale he would discuss in interviews, or as an inspiration for songs like "Fire," which became a hit for the Pointer Sisters in 1978–79 and for Springsteen himself in 1987.

Springsteen's most explicit form of homage, however, was his decision to begin singing Presley's "Follow That Dream" in his live shows of the eighties. The song from the 1962 film of the same name was released as Presley's cultural preeminence was beginning to ebb, and it is not one of his major hits. So Springsteen's decision to perform it represented something of a cultural statement. Its very title is emblematic of who Elvis Presley was to himself and the tens of millions of fans who adored him: a person who had indeed followed—and realized—a dream of success on an almost unimaginable scale.

Springsteen's admiration for Presley was not quite that simple, however, and his tribute did not take the form of mere imitation. Though he would pronounce with Presleyesque ardor that he would follow his dreams wherever those dreams might lead (among other places, to true love), Springsteen broadened the song's fairly generic meaning by adding an original verse:

> *Now every man has the right to live*
> *The right to the chance*
> *To give what he has to give*
> *The right to fight*
> *For the things he believes*
> *For the things that come to him in dreams*
> *Baby in dreams . . .*

In some respects, this passage is standard Presley rhetoric. But describing freedom as the right to give, or dreams as products of fights, is not exactly standard fare in Presley's corpus. By the mid-eighties, Springsteen's own dreams were becoming more complex, and more challenging, than living like a rock and roll king.

THE BARS OF GRACELAND

We [the E Street Band] wanted to play because we wanted to meet girls, we wanted to make a ton of dough, and we wanted to change the world a little bit, you know?
—BRUCE SPRINGSTEEN, 1984

In our day, the term "American Dream" has become a cliché most commonly invoked by real-estate agents and Hollywood screenwriters. The former use it in a tireless effort to sell home ownership, the most concrete version of the Dream. The latter use it to sell a vision of wealth, fame, and power all the more alluring for its seeming effortlessness.

It may be logical, then, that both these versions of the American Dream converge at Presley's baronial home. Here, he took care of his beloved mama, and here he fed his bottomless appetites (sustained via income from his movies). Its very name, Graceland, testifies to its almost totemic power as the supreme expression of the Dream, heavenly grace in earthly form.

But however potent a symbol, Graceland cannot wholly represent the American Dream in its many dimensions. It has gone by different names: "the American Creed," "the American Way of Life," or, simply, the "American Way." All are united by a common underlying faith that runs through the many versions of the Dream. This faith is rarely articulated explicitly, and it has never been formally codified. But it can be summed up in the following assertion:

Anything is possible if you want it badly enough.

Americans may invest in this Dream so heavily because America itself is a product of it. Its earliest formulation was perhaps best expressed by John Winthrop, the first governor of the Massachusetts Bay Colony, in a lay sermon he delivered to the Puritans in 1630 while still sailing the Atlantic. "We shall find that the God of Israel is among us, when ten of us shall be able to resist a thousand of our enemies; when he shall make us a praise and glory that men shall say of succeeding plantations, 'the Lord make it like that of New England,'" he reputedly said. "For we must consider that we shall be as a city upon a hill."

The heart of the Puritans' American Dream was what they called their "covenant," an implicit pact with God that he would provide for them spiritually if they formed a community to honor him according to his precepts as they understood them. This American

Dream was a religious dream, as were many subsequent versions of the Dream, including the massive evangelical revivals known as the "Great Awakenings" of the mid-eighteenth and early nineteenth centuries. As time passed, these versions of the Dream tended to become more individualistic, less focused on salvation through community than through personal redemption. But the original energy persisted, even as it diffused across the country at large, most obviously in the case of an increasingly secular work ethic.

By the end of the eighteenth century, another version of the Dream, this one more political, was articulated by the signers of the Declaration of Independence. Thomas Jefferson's assertions to the contrary, it was by no means "self-evident," then or now, that "all Men are created equal, that they are endowed by their Creator with certain inalienable rights," and that these rights can be summed up as "life, liberty, and the pursuit of happiness." But such was the will and good fortune of the Founders that they did achieve political autonomy from Britain, and bequeathed to us a vision of possibility that we have honored—if all too imperfectly realized—ever since.

There were a number of American Dreams in the nineteenth century. Some, like the Transcendentalists' quest for self-realization, were relatively modest in scope. "I have learned this, at least, from my experiment: that if one advances confidently in the direction of his dreams, and endeavors to live the life he has imagined, he will meet with a success unexpected in common hours," wrote Henry David Thoreau after his sojourn in the woods of Walden. Others, like the so-called "Manifest Destiny," were far more collective, though not especially communitarian. Coined by journalist John L. Sullivan, the term referred to the drive for a continental empire that stretched to the Pacific, the American Dream as imperial conquest.

In the decades following the Civil War, with capitalism ascendant and technology triumphant, the primary expression of the Dream was economic. In its most powerful and durable formulation, it was a hope that one's children would enjoy a higher standard of living than oneself. A variation on this Dream was expressed in the fictional characters of novelist Horatio Alger, whose poor boys made good *because* they were good (and lucky). Still others, like Andrew Carnegie, tried to couch this American Dream in terms of progress that allows those of modest means to achieve happiness no less than the millionaire. "Material prosperity is helping to make the national character more unselfish, more Christlike," Reverend William Wallace, Episcopal bishop of Massachusetts, wrote in 1901.

Whether or not this was really true, the maturation of American industrial capitalism in the early twentieth century led to yet another reorientation in the American Dream. Now it was less about religion, politics, empire, or money—though each continued to have its adherents—than about personal freedom and pleasure. Athletes like Babe Ruth and movie stars like Mary Pickford were enviable not simply because they were rich and powerful, but because they always seemed to be having a good time. This vision was expressed most perfectly not in real life, but in another fictional character: James Gatz, an ordinary boy from small-town Minnesota, who transformed himself into the fabulous Jay Gatsby to win the heart of the beautiful Daisy Buchanan in F. Scott Fitzgerald's *The Great Gatsby* (1925).

Fitzgerald had a sophisticated grasp of the American Dream. Gatsby, of course, fails to attain his; the woman to whom he pins his hopes is not really worthy of him. Not that Gatsby is so "great" either; in the end, he seems little more than a pathetic man who confuses appearances with reality. But even the clear-eyed narrator Nick Carraway cannot help but be moved by the intensity of the man's vision, a vision comparable to that of a European explorer who encountered a continent "commensurate with his capacity for wonder."

Ten years after the publication of *The Great Gatsby*, Elvis Aaron Presley was born in Tupelo, Mississippi. In an important sense, Presley was the opposite of Gatsby, because he really did achieve his Dream. That Dream has been vividly described by Greil Marcus in his now classic essay "Presliad," whose very title suggests the degree to which Presley's life evokes a myth of origin. Marcus's point of entry is country music, and the way in which Presley was nurtured by—and broke from—it. Marcus argues that while the Protestant work ethic in the North "set men free by making them strangers," Southerners, black and white, emphasized (segregated) community, one bound through rituals like music, which could provide solace for the heartbroken and consolation for rebels whose cause was lost. To be sure, there was plenty of hell-raising and good times to be had on Saturday night. But that's as far as it went. Come Sunday morning, there was a service to attend, and on Monday morning, everyone returned to work. What made Presley and his fellow rock and rollers special, Marcus says, was their attempt to make Saturday night last forever. "You had to be young and a bit insulated to pull it off," he conceded. But the promise of the idea was irresistible:

> Reality would catch up sooner or later—a pregnant girlfriend and a fast marriage, the farm you had to take over when your daddy died, a dull and pointless job that drained your desires until you could barely remember them—but why deal with reality before you had to? And what if there was a chance, just a chance, that you *didn't* have to deal with it?

Presley himself put it more succinctly: "When I was a boy, I was the hero in comic books and movies. I grew up believing in a dream. Now I've lived it out. That's all a man can ask for."

As Presley learned, however, the Dream itself turned out to be a "dull and pointless job." In this regard, he was just like Gatsby: his Dream was an unworthy one. Presley became a latter-day King Midas; by 1956, any song his voice touched went gold (a singer far more than a composer, by contractual arrangement he nevertheless received songwriting credit for many records), and simply appearing before the cameras guaranteed profits for any of his movies. Lacking an essential curiosity or even simple business acumen about his future, he left most of the crucial decisions shaping his career to the rapacious "Colonel" Tom Parker, who committed Presley to projects that were beneath him. Before long, his work was a profitable joke, and by the late sixties, it wasn't even so profitable anymore.

Presley's career was not simply a tale of perfect decline. All through this period, he showed flashes of commitment, and when it became unmistakably clear to him that he'd lost his touch, he turned Colonel Parker's plans for a 1968 Christmas special into an astonishing display of his resiliency and the springboard for his celebrated comeback. He recorded some of the best work of his life at this time, went back on the road for the first time in a decade, and conquered America all over again. But after the first few appear-

KING OF THE DESERT: A declining Elvis Presley in the mid-1970s, his years as a major Las Vegas attraction.

ances in Las Vegas, Presley acted like a man with "talent so vast it would be demeaning to apply it." In his words, becoming a hero onstage "was all a man could ask for," and after attaining this goal in the fifties, losing it in the sixties, and recapturing it in the seventies, he apparently had no idea what else to do except to take refuge in the dreamless sleep of narcotics. And so Presley's American Dream became his prison, and, ultimately, his tomb.

Reflecting on Presley's life and death in 1987, a decade after his death (and a decade after his own pilgrimage to Graceland), Springsteen called Presley's dream "a cult of personality" in which fame and wealth were the only objectives. He did so as a superstar in his own right, featured as the lead interview in the twentieth-anniversary issue of *Rolling Stone*. Once the voice (and even conscience) of the counterculture, the magazine was now itself devoted to cults of personality, attaining its commercial preeminence in the 1980s by stoking sleek, updated versions of Presleyesque fantasies.

But if Springsteen was in this world, he was not quite of it. "When I jumped over that wall to meet Elvis that night, I didn't know who I was gonna meet," he reflected. "And the guard who stopped me at the door did me the biggest favor of my life. I had misunderstood. It was innocent, and I was having a ball, but it wasn't right. In the end, you cannot live inside that dream."

THE (BLACK) REPUBLICAN DREAM

If you desire negro citizenship, if you desire to allow them to come into the state and settle with the white man, if you desire them to vote on an equality with yourselves, and to make them eligible to office, to serve on juries, and to adjudge your rights, then support Mr. Lincoln and the Black Republican party.

—Stephen A. Douglas, First Lincoln-Douglas Debate, Ottowa, Illinois, August 21, 1858

On March 20, 1956, the number one song in the United States was "Heartbreak Hotel," by twenty-one-year-old Elvis Presley. It sounded like nothing else on the airwaves. Haunting yet oddly assured, Presley tapped a wellspring of age-old vernacular musical traditions that surrounded him and gave them a new spin that sounded like the voice of modernity itself. It was the beginning of a great career.

That same day, the *New York Times* published one of its "Man in the News" profiles on a young preacher named Martin Luther King Jr., whose recent arrest in Montgomery, Alabama, had made national headlines. Blending philosophical principles that included those of Henry David Thoreau as well as Mohandas Gandhi, King represented a new generation of African Americans engaged in an epic struggle for freedom. Here, too, was the beginning of a great career.

Presley and King were two Southern men shaped by black religious traditions: Presley musical ones, King theological ones. Each in his way was an agent of integration—Presley on the cultural plane, King on the political. But the differences between them, in life and in death, are vast. Presley changed the nation's tune. King changed the nation.

King did it with a dream of his own, one he called "deeply rooted" in the American Dream. He described it most memorably at the Lincoln Memorial, in a melodious address that electrified the nation: a dream that his children would someday live in a country where they would be judged "not by the color of their skin but by the content of their character."

King wasn't alone in his quest to realize this redefined American Dream, of course. But more than any other figure, he articulated it in ways that most Americans could understand, and in logic they could follow, however reluctantly. At the core of that logic was a demand that the nation live up to the principles it had first enshrined in the Declaration of Independence, principles

POWERFUL VOICES: Arriving on the national scene virtually simultaneously in early 1956, Elvis Presley and Martin Luther King embodied different aspects of the struggle for racial equality. Springsteen, a child at the time, would later try to integrate their legacies.

which most Americans professed to honor and in which most Americans liked to believe. If you say you're for life, liberty, and the pursuit of happiness; if you say you believe in rule by law; if you say you believe that the Constitution really does guarantee everyone the same rights; well, then, you can't in good conscience discriminate, lynch, or, as a practical matter, segregate. And if you do—as television cameras repeatedly demonstrate that you do—then you have to change your words or change your actions. When push came to shove on King's watch, we chose, in terms of our laws, anyway, the latter.

King's more radical critics, like Malcolm X, accused him of conservatism, of having a misplaced confidence in the American legal system and its capacity for reform from within. Perhaps Malcolm X was right. In any case, he and other Black Power advocates like H. Rap Brown and Stokely Carmichael were certainly correct in considering King more conservative than they were. But it may be more useful to use a different term to understand King's words and actions: republican. Whatever else he may have been, King was an unusually acute and imaginative twentieth-century inheritor of the eighteenth-century tradition of the Founding Fathers.

In reading over his speeches and writings, one is struck by the degree to which King turned again and again to republican precepts to make his case. That case, of course, goes back to the very origins of the nation, whose creators, despite a nearly fatal compromise with slavery in the Constitution, knew that it was deeply problematic ("I tremble for my country when I reflect that God is just," Thomas Jefferson confessed of his fears about slavery). But the first major figure to invoke black freedom in republican terms was Frederick Douglass, one of the great integrationists in American history. Despite his deep and abiding hatred for slavery, which he knew firsthand, Douglass never rejected his claim on—or desire for—American nationality. "I am not indifferent, but profoundly solicitous for the character, growth and destiny of this American republic, which but for slavery would be the best governed country of the world," Douglass told a crowd in Rochester, New York, after the outbreak of the Civil War. "All that I have and am, are bound up in the destiny of this country." Despite numerous disappointments before and after the war, Douglass never surrendered his belief in republican precepts (and, more than coincidentally, was a steadfast advocate on another republican frontier—women's suffrage—throughout his life).

King is a direct inheritor of this durable strand of republican tradition, which repeatedly surfaces in his own work—and is often a justification for it. We have a duty, he said, to check the domination of a small but powerful minority that "cripples the economic and social institutions of our country and thereby degrades and impoverishes everyone," he explained in a characteristic magazine article of 1958.

He used the language and symbols of republicanism even more obviously three years later to explain the necessity for lunch counter sit-ins. The students were not fighting simply for themselves, he explained in an article for the *New York Times*. They were saving the soul of their country. "They are taking the whole nation back to those great wells of democracy which were dug deep by the Founding Fathers in the formulation of the Constitution and the Declaration of Independence. In sitting down at lunch counters, they are in reality standing up for the best of the American Dream." King would repeat similiar words throughout his life, most notably on the night before he died.

In the most fundamental sense, King's dream of being judged by the content of one's character represents the core of republicanism, the precept from which all else logically follows. In its earliest formulation, it was articulated as a bulwark against monarchical privilege; most recently it has been enlisted to counter discrimination in terms of sexual preference or gender. And while it can be a bit slippery at times (fixing one's criteria of what constitutes "character" has not been timeless or universal), it is the American creed that it never resides in terms of who one *is*, but rather in terms of what one *does*.

And if King's words (one form of action) established his republican credentials, his protests (another form of action) were at least as important. While his strategies of nonviolence were directly inspired by Gandhi, many of King's precepts were in keeping with the best aspects of early American life: of Christianity (specifically Protestantism) as the engine of social change; of small, tightly knit communities (like African Americans of Montgomery, Alabama) as his basic unit of political organization; of focusing on discrete means (like boycotts) to achieve discrete ends (the end of mandatory segregation). To these traditions he added another one we have not seen enough of in American life: what Christopher Lasch has called "the spiritual discipline against resentment," important less for the benefit of the oppressors than for the self-worth and dignity of the oppressed. Indeed, one can plausibly measure King's successes and failures in proportion to his fidelity to these precepts.

One final point. The dream of Martin Luther King was not simply about freedom, although it certainly was about that: the freedom to live, work, study, etc., where one wished. But it was also about *equality*, the idea that we really all are treated the same in our public lives. Freedom and equality do not always go hand in hand. Indeed, there are times when freedom is honored at the *expense* of equality, as when the rich seek "freedom" from paying taxes commensurate with their opportunities. A nation without substantial freedom is oppressive. What we've tended to forget in the years since King's death is that a nation without substantial equality can be even more so.

"We're reaping what's been sown, in a very sad fashion," Bruce Springsteen said around the time of the L.A. riots of 1992. "I mean, the legacy we're leaving our kids is a legacy of dread. That's a big part of what growing up in America is about right now: dread, fear, mistrust, blind hatred. We're being worn down to the point where who you are, what you think, what you believe, where you stand, what you feel in your soul means nothing on any given day. Instead, it's 'What do you look like?' 'Where are you from?' That's frightening." So frightening, in fact, that Springsteen began his first serious inquiry into race relations.

WHITE FLIGHT

Northern men, northern mothers, northern Christians, have something more to do than denounce their brethren in the South; they have to look at the evil among themselves.
    —HARRIET BEECHER STOWE, *Uncle Tom's Cabin*

Musically speaking, racial integration has always been important to Bruce Springsteen. This importance can be measured in terms of musicians in the E Street Band, among them David Sancious (a pianist who went on to have a distinguished jazz career), Ernest "Boom" Carter (a drummer who left to join Sancious), and Springsteen's longtime saxophonist Clarence Clemons. It can also be measured in terms of the artists whose work he has performed, among them Chuck Berry, Little Richard, and Gary U.S. Bonds. After encountering Bonds toiling as a lounge act in 1978, Springsteen wrote, played, sang, and produced songs on two albums for him, including his first hit single in almost twenty years ("This Little Girl" in 1981).

More decisively, African-American musical traditions are a cornerstone of Springsteen's own music. His first three albums in particular rely heavily on the percusive, rhythmic, and improvisatory traditions central to the African-American musical idiom. And while much (though not all) of his recent work has relied on folk and country music accents, even many of Springsteen's white influences—among them Woody Guthrie, Hank Williams, Bob Dylan, and The Band—themselves drew on black music to give their own work its uniquely expressive power (Dylan's notorious decision to play rock at the Newport Folk Festival in 1965 being a notable example).

All this said, race as an explicit *theme* in Springsteen's work is another matter. He has had almost nothing to say on the subject. Given Springsteen's acknowledged influences, it comes as something of a surprise to realize how little a role it plays in his lyrics. There's nothing specifically *discriminatory* about his songs, and the simple fact that a number of African Americans have recorded them (among them Donna Summer and the Pointer Sisters) suggests at least some racial elasticity. On the other hand, it's a little hard to picture a black protagonist bewailing his lack of personal autonomy in songs like "The Promised Land" or "Badlands." In some sense, these songs reflect the obsessions of a relatively naive white boy who is shocked to learn that the world is not his oyster.

One might say that Springsteen's songs are not overtly racial because he has cultivated a genuinely color-blind sensibility. There is some truth to that. A more likely explanation, though, is that like many white people in the 1970s and 80s, Springsteen avoided the topic of race because it seemed too incendiary. Many white audiences simply did not want to listen to stories about black people, and many blacks would find unconscious racism even in whites' best-intentioned gestures. Of course, it was impossible to sidestep the issue; since the nineteenth century, virtually all white popular musicians, even those who were avowed racists, have been too dependent on black culture to reject it completely. And silences can speak volumes. In the end, then, avoidance of racial matters does not represent an effective escape from them—or responsibility for them. This is true whether that avoidance is conscious, or, as may well be the case with Springsteen, unconscious.

In the years leading up to *Born in the U.S.A.* there is only one case in which Springsteen *does* directly discuss race: "My Hometown," a single from the album that became a top-ten hit in 1985. The song is sung from the point of view of a man who has lived his entire life in a small town, and is now witnessing its decline. His dismay takes on added poignance in that he is now a father, and is trying—but not completely able—to give his son the same sense of security his own father gave him. That security is symbolized by the two generations of sons who sit in their fathers' laps behind the steering wheels of their cars and navigate the local streets.

Characteristically, "My Hometown" deals with social issues—in this case economic deterioration, racial tension, and the connection between them—in a highly personal way.

> *In '65 tension was running high at my high school*
> *There was a lot of fights between the black and white*
> *There was nothing you could do*

Two cars at a light on a Saturday night
In the backseat there was a gun
Words were passed in a shotgun blast
Troubled times had come to my hometown . . .

Everything about "My Hometown"—the earnest voice of the singer; the gentle, melancholy lilt of the music; the familiar-yet-still-disheartening tenor of the story he tells—invites identification. "Yes," we're likely to think when we hear this song, "it's too bad these things happen. A real shame."

The situation this man describes does, in fact, have historical resonance. Unable to segregate themselves to the extent middle-class and upper-class whites did, working-class blacks and whites coexisted uneasily throughout the postwar period, and such eruptions were all too common—often followed by the white flight the protagonist of the song finally prepares to undertake. From this angle, the supposed victims of the song are perpetrators in their own right. Such a view may be too severe; economic forces like the closing of factories have as much to do with the narrator's motives for departure as racial ones.

But the real problem with this picture is that there's something airless, even antiseptic, about it. No one is actually creating or fomenting the racial tension; it's just there. So are the "words." And the "shotgun blast." A dismaying passivity characterizes the singer (and, arguably, Springsteen himself). Perhaps even more than overt hostility, *this* was the attitude that Martin Luther King gave his life to combat: the idea that racism was natural, even inevitable.

REDEEMING DREAMS

Maybe there's a reason to believe
We all will be received in Graceland
                    —Paul Simon, "Graceland," 1986

The Ghost of Tom Joad is an unusual record in the trajectory of Springsteen's career. Whether in praise or criticism, its shift in tone and content from its immediate predecessors was widely noted. But the most remarkable aspect of the album has drawn virtually no comment: that it represents Springsteen's most sustained exploration of race relations. In part, this silence may be because the very title of the record, alluding as it does to John Steinbeck's *The Grapes of Wrath*, has more to do with class than race (as does Springsteen's work as a whole). It may also be the result of thinking of race as a black-and-white proposition, when on the album, as in life, the picture is more complicated. But when viewed through the lens of color, *Tom Joad* represents a highly sophisticated and relevant document.

With *Tom Joad*, Springsteen broke—decisively—an implicit rule that had marked his career from the very beginning: only writing about situations he knew firsthand. For much of his career, this meant charting the psychic or external landscapes of the white working class to which he belonged. He was able to describe, and embody, a familiar American Dream of such people because he shared it.

Since the mid-eighties, however, Springsteen's experiences have been less those of a man chasing a runaway American Dream than those of one who has attained it—posing, at least theoretically, a problem for a man whose work was for so long premised on a form of psychological honesty. Whatever else may have impelled the songs from *Tunnel of Love*, *Human Touch*, and *Lucky Town*, one senses a kind of moral scruple about pretending to be something he is not. So, for example, the very first words out of Springsteen's mouth in *Tunnel of Love*, from "Ain't Got You," are "I got the fortunes of heaven in diamonds and gold." Springsteen begins his satire of television, "57 Channels (And Nothin' On)," with the line "I bought a bourgeois house in the Hollywood Hills." While most of his more recent songs are not so quick to issue these virtual apologias, and his music does not really focus on conspicuous consumption per se, Springsteen seems to have been careful not to overreach himself in the worlds he depicts in his work. And that goes for his depictions of race as well.

There is a kind of becoming modesty about such diffidence. This is especially true within the context of the late 1980s and early 1990s, which has been marked by a harder edge in race relations, typified by the cultural resurgence of Malcolm X on the one hand and the emergence of David Duke on the other. The era has been marked by a new emphasis on black nationalism, ranging from the increasing attention paid Louis Farrakhan (the most important leader of black Muslims after the apostasy and death of Malcolm X) to the popularity of rap artists like Public Enemy and Ice-T. The black nationalist position, with its stringency about racial identity and suspiciousness of the arrogance implicit in trying to represent the experiences of another racial group, has fostered a bracing awareness of the dangers in doing so. Ultimately, however, such self-imposed segregation is limiting, not only in an artistic sense, but in a moral one as well.

This cultural context is what makes *Tom Joad* such a surprising, risky record. The degree of Springsteen's narrative inventiveness is documented in the brief bibliography included in the album's CD booklet. These sources describe settings—the drug trade, Ku Klux Klan activity, and, of course, the Okie migration to California—a world apart from any he has ever known.

The geographic locus of *Tom Joad* is the American Southwest, especially Texas and California. But this is generally not the Texas of *Darkness on the Edge of Town* or the California of *Human Touch* or *Lucky Town*. Instead, it is that of an apparently irredeemable underclass, one even more impoverished than that of *Nebraska*. Once again, class is the crucial element informing these songs. But the specific reason for this impoverishment—and on this count the album as a whole is quite clear—is race. "Sinaloa Cowboys" illustrates the way in which illegal Mexican immigrants in central

California participate in the methamphetamine trade, and its disastrous results for two brothers who make as much in one day in the drug trade as they could in one year as migrant farmers. We know many other characters on the album are Latino, for example, because of their names (e.g., Bobby Ramirez of "The Line") or because of their settings and language (the boy prostitute of San Diego's "Balboa Park" grew up in "Zona Norte" and buys jeans "like the Gavachos wear").

Even as *Tom Joad* pays nuanced attention to the particulars of racial identity, however, it also points toward broader resonances, as the description of illegal methamphetamine manufacturing by Chicano immigrants in "Sinaloa Cowboys" suggests:

> *You could spend a year in the orchards*
> *Or make half as much in one ten-hour shift*
> *Working for the men in Sinaloa*
> *But if you slipped the hydriodic acid*
> *Would burn right through your skin*
> *They'd leave you spittin' up blood in the desert*
> *If you breathed those fumes in*

While "Sinaloa Cowboys" is explicitly situated in a Latino milieu, and gains credibility in its attention to localized detail, the underlying dynamics of the brothers' situation is basically the same as that driving the crack business among blacks in a northeastern city or an Asian drug cartel in the Pacific Northwest (the potential profits, and risks, are just as astronomical). Similarly, it would be very easy to imagine a black man as the edgy, ambivalent ex-con of "Straight Time" (he could be a character out of a Richard Wright story), the murdered boxcar mentor of "The New Timer," or even as the irritated spouse of "My Best Was Never Good Enough." None of these situations are *inherently* racial, but the burden of history—from the bonds of slavery to broken treaties—makes them disproportionately common in minority communities.

Most commonly, the racism that enmeshes the nonwhite characters of *Tom Joad* is not personal, but systemic. The border guard who narrates "The Line," for example, is not really a bad man; he's just doing his job in patrolling the border (and surrendering to a sexual pull he doesn't quite understand by letting Louisa through). The situation here is similar to "My Hometown" in that it depicts racism as an inescapable fog that cannot be fought and only sometimes escaped. But it also demonstrates Springsteen's increasingly sophisticated understanding of the ways in which oppression depends on silence, ignorance, and facelessness at least as much as it does on overt ill will.

Ill will, however, remains a big part of the equation, and is confronted directly on "Galveston Bay." This song, the last Springsteen wrote for the album, was inspired by a somewhat unlikely source: *A Season for Justice,* the memoir of Alabama Civil Rights activist Morris Dees, who founded the Southern Poverty Law Center in 1979 to combat hate crimes. Dees, who has since founded Klanwatch and become a nationally recognized expert on white separatist paramilitary organizations, achieved some of his greatest successes by winning huge financial judgments against groups like the Klan who trespass beyond free speech privileges to violate the civil rights of others.

In 1981, Dees became involved with a community of Vietnamese émigrés who had settled in Seabrook, Texas, and tried to make their livelihood through shrimp fishing. He agreed to represent the Vietnamese Fishermen's Association, a trade group led by Nguyen Van Nam, a former colonel in the South Vietnamese army who had led 10,000 troops until the fall of Saigon in 1975. It was then that he, like thousands of other refugees, made his way to the United States, where he settled near metropolitan Houston, whose Gulf climate approximated that of the delta country around Saigon. Colonel Van Nam and his compatriots then entered the shrimping industry, which was relatively accessible but extremely competitive. Racial tensions between white and Asian fishermen flared, and white groups sought the help of Louis Beam, the Great Dragon of the Texas Knights of the Ku Klux Klan. Through the courts, Dees succeeded in gaining an injunction against the Klan for violations of civil rights and antitrust statutes.

Springsteen took elements from this story as the raw material for "Galveston Bay." It is one of those songs on *Tom Joad* that barely functions as a piece of music. The melody and instrumentation are minimal, a mere hint of backdrop for the lyrics. Actually, "Galveston Bay" is less a song or even a poem than it is a sparse, vivid short story—one with a clearly etched setting, memorable characters, and an unpredictable plot that climaxes near the end of the song.

Springsteen reconfigures Colonel Van Nam as Le Bin Son, a (less distinguished) Vietnamese native who fought the Communists for fifteen years alongside U.S. forces until the fall of Saigon in 1975. Coming to the United States with his wife and daughter, he settles on the east coast of Texas and buys a shrimp boat with his cousin. Buffeted by history, Le nevertheless takes charge of his life and provides for his family. Grateful for what he has received as well as attained, he pauses to kiss his daughter before he heads off to work each day.

Meanwhile, the (apparently fictive) Billy Sutter also lives in Seabrook, Texas. Billy, a Vietnam veteran injured in combat, returned home in 1968 and entered the family's fishing business to support his own wife and son (whom, like Le with his daughter, Billy kisses before leaving for work each day). Like many of his friends who see Vietnamese refugees settling near Galveston Bay, Billy is uneasy and resentful. Although the narrator doesn't explicitly say so, he may be one of three Klan members who attempt to burn Le Bin Son's boat. When Le shoots and kills two of the men, and is cleared by a jury on the grounds of self-defense, Billy vows vengeance. "My friend, you're a dead man," he says with chilling irony.

Just as the hopeful Mary of "Thunder Road" reappears as the hopeless wife and mother of "The River," Billy Sutter can be viewed as a later incarnation of the Vietnam vet protagonist of "Born in the U.S.A.," his passion and defiance curdled into cynicism and hatred. By this point in his career, Springsteen had shown an almost frightening familiarity with evil, a familiarity that surfaces, for example, in *Tom Joad*'s murderous bank robber of "Highway 29" and in the seductive temptations of "Straight Time." At the climax of "Galveston Bay," Billy Sutter reaches out for a dark, bloodthirsty American Dream, one as old as John Winthrop's city on a hill:

> *One late summer night Le stood watch along the waterside*
> *Billy stood in the shadows*
> *His K-bar knife in his hand*
> *And the moon slipped behind the clouds*
> *Le lit a cigarette, the bay was still as glass*
> *As he walked by Billy stuck his knife in his pocket*
> *Took a breath and let him pass*

Our final view of Billy has him drinking a glass of water, kissing his sleeping wife, and heading back to cast his net into Galveston Bay. From such actions, we can infer that his decision not to murder Le is rooted in his unexpected recognition of a shared humanity, and a glimpse of a different, better American Dream. Rather than remain in a spiritual wilderness, the prodigal son goes home, and chooses to become an unlikely disciple of a very great King.

COMMON SENSE

As Americans, we are all descendants of George Washington—
and his slaves.
        —MICHAEL LIND, *The Next American Nation*

"I would not be understood as advocating intermarriage between the races," Frederick Douglass once wrote, addressing the deepest fear of many whites in the late nineteenth century, and one many Southerners in particular swore through most of this century that they would never allow to happen. But Douglass's remark was not meant to reassure such people. "I do not say that what I say *should* come to pass, but what I think is likely to come to pass, and what is inevitable," he explained.

This was not intended to be an incendiary statement. "I am not a propagandist but a prophet," Douglass asserted. Unlike many of his fellow Americans, however, he was not at all troubled by his prediction. It was part of a patient, hopeful expectation that his country was in a transitional stage to a truly transnational America in which the contributions of all would be recognized.

Sadly, those of Douglass himself have gone largely unrecognized outside the academic community. And while miscegenation—a term invented during the Civil War by Democrats seeking to tar Republicans by alleging that they were for it—no longer generates quite the reflexive loathing it once did, entrenched attitudes of fear and hatred across racial lines remain a powerful reality, as the O. J. Simpson trial vividly documented.

Attitudes, of course, are very difficult to change—so difficult, in fact, that many are skeptical of even trying. "You can't legislate morality," went one of the truisms of the 1950s, usually spoken by whites resistant to ending segregation. To such people, Martin Luther King had an answer: "It may be true that morality cannot be legislated, but behavior can be regulated. The law may not change the heart, but it can restrain the heartless." It was precisely because attitudes were so difficult to change that laws became a necessary first step—a prelude, not a solution, to articulating a new notion of common sense that really would give heart to the heartless.

In King's most famous address, he envisioned a world in which the sons of slaves and former slave owners broke bread together at a table of brotherhood. But the core of King's dream was not simply that this would happen, but that it would be an ordinary event, an *unremarkable* occurrence. This greatest American Dream, appropriately enough, continues to challenge us in its very simplicity.

Bruce Springsteen, of course, has had neither the experiences nor the vision of people like Frederick Douglass and Martin Luther King. Relative to them, his achievements may seem small, even ordinary. But it is a measure of *their* achievements that he has so thoroughly assimilated their common-sense dream, and that its significance for him has only grown. In an important sense, he is their son, a product of the same cultural intermarriage that produced Elvis Presley, and one who instinctively makes room for other outsiders at the national table.

FOUR

Borne in the U.S.A.

SPRINGSTEEN AND THE BURDEN OF VIETNAM

"Brooooooce!"

The concert hall was full—like virtually every concert hall where Bruce Springsteen has played for the last twenty years—with chanting fans. (To the untrained ear, it sounded like "Boo!") But this audience, which filled New York's Beacon Theater in December 1995, was small, nothing like the stadiums Springsteen filled during his heyday in the eighties. Given the loyalty of his fan base and his legendary reputation for live performance, he could still have sold out any size venue he wished even in the 1990s, but Springsteen had always liked more intimate spaces, and he considered them especially appropriate for his tour to support *The Ghost of Tom Joad.*

Like the settings of this tour, the songs seemed modest.

UNPLUGGED: Springsteen in Asbury Park, November 1996.

Springsteen performed without the backing of the fabled E Street Band, playing many of his best-known songs accompanied only by his own acoustic guitar. Even when he had toured with the band, this was something he did periodically. On *Live 1975–85*, "No Surrender" went from an upbeat rock song to an elegiac ballad; during the *Tunnel of Love* tour, an acoustic version of "Born to Run" replaced a full rock arrangement. Such reworkings kept these songs fresh for both Springsteen and his audience, allowing them to be heard in a new light.

On this tour, "Born in the U.S.A.," Springsteen's song about a ravaged Vietnam veteran, underwent a similar transformation. When the hit single was released in 1984, it was an up-tempo rock and roll anthem whose raw power belied the despair of the character who sang it. On this night, however, it was stripped down to its core as a *cri de coeur* for a betrayed American Dream.

> *Down in the shadow of the penitentiary*
> *Out by the gas fires of the refinery*
> *Ten years burnin' down the road*
> *Nowhere to run, ain't got nowhere to go*

Springsteen played slide guitar, and sang the song with a raspier voice than his usual full-bodied tenor. It ended not with the stirring chorus of the record, but with an earlier line: "Nowhere to run, nowhere to go." In the words of a *New York Times* reviewer, "Born in the U.S.A." had become "a holler of impotent desperation."

Hearing the song performed this way, it was hard to believe that a decade before, Chrysler chairman Lee Iacocca had reputedly offered Springsteen $12 million to sing it and show his face in a commercial for Chrysler cars. Iacocca, whose self-titled 1983 autobiography promoted a vision of the business executive as folk hero, had been called "the Bruce Springsteen of business" by *Rolling Stone,* and was anxious to convert his image as well as Springsteen's into financial currency. But Springsteen refused this and all other offers.

Instead, Chrysler commissioned a new jingle with the slogan "The Pride Is Back/Born in America" (though the minivans promoted in the ads were assembled in Canada). Sung by Kenny Rogers and Sandy Farina, the jingle won a 1986 *Advertising Age* award for "best original music." Yet even the producer of the jingle, Joan Neary, was clear about what inspired the piece. "There's a certain bell sound in there that's definitely Springsteen," she explained. "And of course, the hook line—'the pride is back, born in America'—is pretty similar. But the commercial didn't really copy his song. It's just got the *spirit* of his music."

A number of other commercial enterprises aimed to capture

the "spirit" of Springsteen in the eighties. Burger King's "This Is a Burger King Town" evoked "My Hometown"; the 1986 B movie *No Surrender*, among others, used Springsteenesque imagery like variations of the *Born in the U.S.A.* album cover in its advertising. Of course, Springsteen was not the sole inspiration for the wave of uplifting, patriotic iconography in the Reagan-dominated mid-eighties. But his work did have elements that could be appropriated for such purposes.

That appropriation had to be selective, however, sidestepping the social critique that marks much of Springsteen's music generally, but "Born in the U.S.A." in particular. Neary, the jingle writer, was aware of this. "Even though what came across most in 'Born in the U.S.A.' was the chorus, we do realize that the lyrics of that song were more critical of America—all that Vietnam veteran stuff and all," she said. "But I do think 'Pride' makes a statement the way that 'Born in the U.S.A.' did. It's, like, the pride in our country was gone for a long time and now it's back, you know?"

It was precisely such glib manipulations that led Springsteen to reconfigure "Born in the U.S.A." a decade later in an effort to restore its critical edge. "I read how many times this song was misinterpreted," Springsteen told a Los Angeles audience in 1995. ". . . But one thing I do know is that more people bought the record than bought any of my other records. [He held up his hands, balancing imaginary scales.] I was misinterpreted; I sold a lot of records. [A bigger grin.] . . . But the songwriter always gets another chance to get it right."

It's often exciting to hear an old song played in a new way. That notwithstanding, people like Lee Iacocca and the jingle writer of "The Pride Is Back" really did grasp something fundamentally true about "Born in the U.S.A.": it *is* about "pride." Even a casual, first-time listener to the song usually grasps this—in fact, the grit and determination the song exudes is far more obvious than the lament at its core.

The *kind* of pride at stake, though, is complex, if also visceral. It is a kind of pride born of failure, a pride that comes from an acceptance of the burden of history. Our traditional American mythology—of effortless success, of moral certainty, of the American way as the best way for all—resists both failure as well as burdens of history. (In the words of another advertising slogan of the eighties, "Who says you can't have it all?") More than any other event in the twentieth century, the Vietnam War challenged that mythology. What "Born in the U.S.A." did was help open up a space where both failure and history could be confronted and integrated into a vision of who we are as a people, and it did so in a form that has lasting value no matter what Lee Iacocca, thoughtless listeners—or even Bruce Springsteen himself—might do or say.

MOURNING IN AMERICA

Don't fret too much over this Vietnam thing, Sam. You shouldn't feel bad about any of it. It had nothing to do with you.
—IRENE HUGHES, MOTHER OF SAMANTHA HUGHES, THE PROTAGONIST OF BOBBIE ANN MASON's *In Country*

In the official ideology of the United States—in that mythic place where all people are equal before the law, where big dreams and hard work pay off, and where right makes might—there is relatively little room for defeat. Of course we know that American history is not a string of effortless victories. The triumph of Yorktown was preceded by the bitter ordeal of Valley Forge; MacArthur had to lose the Philippines in order to take them back. And the Alamo is still remembered, albeit somewhat selectively, as a martyrs' grave rather than as the site of an opportunistic land grab. Moreover, generations of grieving wives and mothers know all too well the price of victory, a price that seldom leads to jubilation on the part of those who pay it.

To some extent, the lack of space for defeat is historical: almost always the victors, we have no legends of invasions weathered, as in Mexico and Russia; millennial dynasties laid low, as in Egypt and China; or vanquished nationhood awaiting resurrection, as in Israel and Poland. To a great extent, our knowledge of what it means to lose a national struggle comes from the Native Americans we have defeated. That's something we have, or have allowed ourselves, only a limited ability to understand at all, and something we've tried to grasp only to a limited extent, notably in a strain of the western film tradition that includes *Cheyenne Autumn* (1964), *Little Big Man* (1970), and *Dances With Wolves* (1990).

Prior to Vietnam, the most notable exception to this tradition of victory was the experience of the seceded Southern states in the Civil War. Here was a struggle that was an unambiguous failure, at least in military terms, but a struggle that would capture even the imagination, North and South, for the next century as "the Lost Cause." The precise parameters of the term are rarely articulated; it's usually a vague slogan that encompasses narrow interpretations of states' rights, a broad sense of the honor of fighting for family and home, and virtually never a confrontation with the institution of chattel slavery, which Confederate vice-president Alexander Stephens (before the war, anyway) called the "cornerstone" of the Southern way of life.

"The Cause" was promulgated in popular fiction, music, and eventually film, and some of the best-known works of American culture, notably *The Birth of a Nation* (1915) and *Gone With the Wind* (1939), condensed and codified the mythology of a bucolic social order destroyed by hotheaded rebels or brutish Yankees. In any case, almost from the moment of Robert E. Lee's surrender, sober contemplation of Southern defeat shaded, almost imperceptibly, into celebration that did little to examine the underlying causes of that defeat by anything other than overwhelming numbers. So, for example, the Charlie Daniels Band told us that "The

South's Gonna Do It Again," in his signature tune of the early 1970s, or Hank Williams Jr. asserted that "If the South Would Have Won (We'da Had It Made) in the late 1980s. Just *what* the South's gonna do—or just *who* "we" are—is never explained. Doing so would undoubtedly prove difficult, sticky, or repellent. Nevertheless, the Confederate flag remains a potent icon in college dorms, pickup trucks, and Southern state capitals.

There is no sense of celebration surrounding the American memory of Vietnam, however. Whether it's those on the left who argue that we should never have gotten involved, or those on the right who argue that the left lost the war, all agree that our Vietnam experience was a nightmare whose effects linger. It's an ironic consensus, compounded by the fact that this sense of disaster is unaccompanied by the literal devastation that blanketed Vietnam. Moreover, the almost obsessive sense of self-congratulation that has accompanied subsequent American involvement in places like Grenada and Kuwait (the Gulf War in particular precipitated countless parades) suggests ongoing uncertainty about national self-confidence and will.

Comparisons with collective memory of other wars makes the Vietnam case all the more striking. One gets a vivid sense of the basic national stance toward World War II, for instance, by looking to the culture of war movies during and after it: in the twenty-year period between *Casablanca* (1942) and *The Longest Day* (1962), the conflict is almost always portrayed as an essential—and triumphant—struggle of good over evil. Humphrey Bogart may be a little more reluctant than John Wayne, but there was never any doubt as to who the good guys and bad guys were. Wayne himself virtually defined the subgenre of heroic World War II movies, with appearances in *The Fighting Seabees* (1944), *Sands of Iwo Jima* (1949), *In Harm's Way* (1965), and many others.

While roughly 450 World War II movies were released during the war, only one Vietnam film came out during that conflict. This was *The Green Berets*, a 1968 release starring, of course, John Wayne. Made at the height of the war, it can be considered a kind of booster film of the type made during World War II. By the time of the Tet Offensive, however, doubts about the war made it difficult to sell an unalloyed celebration of the American effort—or, for that matter, anything at all about the war. For the next decade, Hollywood and pop culture generally avoided Vietnam altogether.

When the subject was taken up again in the late seventies, treatments of the war exhibited a pattern that would be common for over a decade: the depiction of Vietnam as a surreal, incomprehensible world in which all normal rules and expectations were ignored or inverted. This tendency was first manifest in writing on the war, notably Michael Herr's *Dispatches* (1977), widely considered the finest reportage to come out of the conflict. It was not, however, reportage in the conventional sense of the word. Avowedly subjective, profane, and iconoclastic, Herr went to great lengths to describe the war in perceptual terms at least as much as factual ones. So, for example, the Tet Offensive was "a huge collective nervous breakdown," conducted in a country that was "a dark room full of deadly objects." The cinematic equivalent of such prose was director Francis Ford Coppola's epic *Apocalypse Now* (1979). Coppola and co-screenwriter John Milius made the film an Americanized version of Joseph Conrad's *Heart of Darkness*, with Martin Sheen's search for the ominously elusive Marlon Brando as a parable of latent American savagery.

This approach to the Vietnam War, while compelling and incisive, is also somewhat problematic. First, however real such depictions might seem, they take American failure in the war—a failure that could plausibly be attributed to poor strategy, faulty intelligence, the hard-won resilience of the enemy, or moral weakness on our own part—and project it into the realm of the irrational, inscrutable, irredeemable. There's more than a little racism in this approach, too: instead of being portrayed as determined, tragic, and fallible people, the Vietnamese become an unknowable other—contemptible or terrifying, but rarely anything in between. In this line of thinking, we lost in Vietnam because we had to: the deck was stacked in a deadly game in which we didn't have a clue as to how to play.

While a number of other movies would draw on a Coppolaesque sense of "The Horror" (notably Stanley Kubrick's 1987 film *Full Metal Jacket*), a somewhat different, less ironic strategy was more common, especially among those movies that fall under the category of what film scholar Pat Aufderheide has called the "noble-grunt film." Its essence can be grasped in the most basic plot description of the 1978 film *The Deer Hunter*: three basically decent guys from the heartland leave their mill town, experience The Horror, and return with wrecked lives. There's no mention of strategic objectives, national goals, or even brotherhood within any military unit, even when the three are prisoners with other Americans. It's as if the only way to salvage the Vietnam movie as a credible form is to marginalize the big picture and project a small one.

This may be why so many movies about Vietnam—from *Coming Home* (1978) to *Born on the Fourth of July* (1989)—focus much of their action on the domestic scene, whether during the war or after it, and on the scars of the Vietnam vet and his loved ones. For the regular moviegoer in these years, a veteran who was not taciturn, self-pitying, and potentially violent seemed like an aberration. What makes these people sympathetic characters is not the cause that sent them overseas (they were lied to), or even having seen combat (the enemy was invisible), but simply their returning home. Mere survival is heroism, and cynicism the final ideal. By the end of the decade, Aufderheide suggests, the noble-grunt movies may have helped Americans recover "not for anything U.S. forces did in Vietnam, but simply for having felt so bad for so long."

It was one thing to feel less bad; it was another to feel good. A number of American films in the 1980s attempted to portray military involvement in a more sympathetic light, only to reveal the limitations and contradictions involved in such an attempt. The most commercially successful version was *Top Gun* (1986), essentially a 110-minute recruiting commercial for the U.S. Navy. There's a hollowness at the core of the movie, though, because there's no real adversary. "If I can't shoot this sonofabitch, let's see if we can have some fun with him," says Tom Cruise during an incident with a Soviet-made MIG fighter early in the film. By the time he finally gets his chance for some real action, a rescue mission on a disabled communications ship that "wandered" into foreign territory, one wonders if any of these characters—or any of the filmgoers who flocked to the movie in droves—had ever heard of the Gulf of Tonkin.

MANIFEST DESTINY: Sylvester Stallone returns to Vietnam in *Rambo: First Blood Part II* (1985).

But perhaps the pivotal figure in this quest for post-Vietnam heroism is a movie character who throughout the eighties was often cited as Bruce Springsteen's foil: Sylvester Stallone's Rambo. There are some important similarities between Springsteen's "Born in the U.S.A." persona and Stallone's alter ego. Both characters are emotionally scarred veterans. Both are prime specimens of masculinity. And both have a laconic vernacular style that seems to be a repository of deep-seated moral certainty.

Actually, such qualities were hardly unique to Springsteen's and Stallone's personas; they represent sturdy American archetypes. From James Fenimore Cooper's Leatherstocking to the characters of John Wayne, such traits were considered emblematic of an ideal American male shaped by native soil. Indeed, Rambo himself has Indian blood, a symbolic explanation for his resilience and ingenuity, as well as his tragic view of life. A cursory look at the *Rambo* movies suggests, however, that his character is less a means for attaining mature masculine wisdom than it is for expressing macho resentment in the cowboy rhetoric of Ronald Reagan, himself often—and more plausibly—compared with Rambo.

The initial film in the series, *First Blood* (1982), introduces John Rambo. A misunderstanding between Stallone and a policeman leads to car crashes, the arrival of the National Guard, the incineration of much of a town before Rambo's superior officer, Richard Crenna, finally confronts him in an empty police station. "It's over, Johnny," Crenna advises, giving Stallone the chance to put his rage into words: "It wasn't my war. You asked me, I didn't ask you. And I did what I had to do to win. Then I come back to the world, and I see all those maggots at the airport protesting me, spitting, calling me baby killer and all kinds of crap. Who are they to protest me? Unless they've been me and been there?"

Rambo has a point, and it's one that no doubt represents the rage of many veterans, as well as noncombatant war supporters at home. Yet his actions—and the depictions of those who oppose him— have something of a paranoid, even homicidal quality that competes with the viewer's sense of Rambo as a hapless victim ("They drew first blood" is his justification). These tendencies are even more pronounced in *Rambo: First Blood Part II* (1985), which implies that the U.S. government conspiratorially avoids retrieving its POWs and MIAs from Vietnam. *Rambo II* is one of a number of eighties movies, like *Missing in Action* (1984), that involve returning to Vietnam to set right some individual wrongs. When Crenna proposes an undercover mission to find American prisoners, Stallone asks, "Do we get to win this time?" (A third Rambo film, *Rambo III* (1988), set amid the Russian war in Afghanistan, was a box office flop, probably ending the saga.)

This is a brief, and necessarily simplistic, gloss of Vietnam in popular culture that overlooks important countercurrents. For example, Oliver Stone's Vietnam movies include *Heaven & Earth* (1993), a notable exploration of a (female) Vietnamese perspective. Brian De Palma's *Casualties of War* (1989) depicts grunts who are not noble at all. Nor can all the grief depicted in noble-grunt movies be reduced to by-products of aggrievement. Robin Williams injects humor and humanity into Barry Levinson's *Good Morning, Vietnam* (1987). Moreover, film was only one medium to engage with the topic in these years. Novelists like Bobbie Ann Mason and Tim O'Brien wrote nuanced works that wrestled with Vietnam's ambiguous, ambivalent legacy to the United States.

But the most immediate cultural backdrop for "Born in the U.S.A." was not the *inter*cultural dialogue across journalism, film, and fiction media, but rather the *intra*cultural dialogue in rock and roll music in the years preceding Springsteen's song. In the sixties, of course, rock's tendencies were overwhelmingly antiwar. Perhaps the defining song of the Vietnam era was Country Joe and the Fish's "Feel-Like-I'm-Fixin'-to-Die-Rag." Released in 1967, it encapsulated the Summer of Love: sarcastic, profane, and from San Francisco. Country Joe and the Fish were on the roster at Woodstock two years later, and "Fixin'-to-Die" was prominently featured in the 1970 film documenting the event. There were a number of other important antiwar songs in the era, among them Buffalo Springfield's "For What It's Worth" (1967), Jimi Hendrix's "Hey Joe" (1967), and the Jefferson Airplane's "Volunteers" (1969). But few were as memorable—or as polarizing—as "Fixin'-to-Die."

Like Hollywood, the counterculture was relatively silent about Vietnam for most of the seventies. To some extent, this was surely a matter of the war being viewed as a bad trip most would rather forget. But like Lyndon Johnson and Richard Nixon, rock and rollers suffered from a credibility gap. Ignorant of and hostile toward the war experience, representing it may have seemed insuperably difficult or pointless.

There were a handful of performers, however, who took the challenge of representing war in the late seventies. Part of what makes the Talking Heads's "Life During Wartime" (1979) striking is precisely its modern-day protagonist's assertion that what he was going through was radically different from anything he had ever known ("this ain't no party/this ain't no disco," he explains). In "Powderfinger," a song from his now classic *Rust Never Sleeps* (1979), Neil Young posits an imaginary landscape in which an inarticulate young man instinctively responds to an invasion by grabbing a gun—subsequently speaking from beyond the grave. Young sings the song with heartbreaking effect, and his backing band, Crazy Horse, provides a gnarled, dissonant backdrop. In its harrowing depiction of a life destroyed by a reflexive embrace of armed conflict, "Powderfinger" is one of the great antiwar songs in the history of popular music.

It was only in the early eighties, however, that Vietnam itself would be explicitly discussed in popular music. Billy Joel weighed in with "Goodnight Saigon" from *The Nylon Curtain* (1982), an album with thematic similarities to Springsteen's own *Nebraska*. "Goodnight Saigon" is a seven-minute epic, complete with the sound effects of crickets and helicopters—a kind of musical equivalent of *Apocalypse Now.* In its invocation that "we would all go down together," however, its fatalistic tone was much closer to the noble-grunt aesthetic of *The Deer Hunter* and subsequent Vietnam movies.

Somewhat simpler—and perhaps more affecting—is the Charlie Daniels Band's "Still in Saigon" (1982). The dominant mood of "Still in Saigon," however, is one of sheer confusion on the part of a veteran who does not understand himself or others upon his return. For him and for millions of others, Vietnam was less a foreign conflict than an inner civil war.

GENERATIONAL DESTRUCTION

I know one of the worst effects of this whole thing is the way it's ravaged my own image of myself, taken my mind off higher things, restricted my ability to become involved in causes or people—I honestly feel so screwed up tight that I am incapable, I think, of giving myself, of really loving.
—BILL CLINTON, WRITING TO A FRIEND ABOUT THE
DRAFT, AUGUST 20, 1969

Even before Vietnam was a lost cause, it was an ambivalent one at best for millions of those who were chosen to fight it. Living in a post-draft era, it's easy to forget that the Selective Service played a major role in shaping the lives of young men for twenty-five years following World War II, and that its reach was especially dramatic during the Vietnam War. For men like Bill Clinton and Dan Quayle, the draft was an especially unwelcome presence, not simply because they did not wish to go to war, but also because that strong desire to evade or resist it was coupled with gnawing feelings that they really *should* go. Through combinations of principle, luck, opportunism, or evasion, many people escaped the draft. But they could not escape being haunted by it, whether in terms of their subsequent career paths or by the simple knowledge that others were not so lucky.

Springsteen had no doubts about the Vietnam War or his participation in it: he was opposed to both. This was not a matter of careful consideration of the pros and cons, however. "There wasn't any kind of political consciousness down in Freehold in the late sixties," he explained later. "It was just a small town, and the war seemed very distant. I mean I was aware of it through some friends that went." One such friend was Bart Hanes, the drummer in Springsteen's first band. "'Well, I enlisted,'" Springsteen recalls Hanes telling him. "I remember he didn't even know where Vietnam *was*. And that was it. He left and he didn't come back. And the guys who did come back were not the same."

Right around the time Bill Clinton was drafted (he went ahead with his Rhodes Scholarship to Oxford), so was Bruce Springsteen (he had dropped out of Ocean County Community College, forfeiting any hope for deferment). Unlike Clinton, who wrung his hands and dragged his feet, Springsteen knew his course of action:

> . . . when I got on the bus to take my physical, I thought one thing: *I ain't goin'*. I had tried to go to college, and I didn't really fit in. I went to a real narrow-minded school where people just gave me a lot of trouble and I was hounded off the campus—I just looked different and acted different, so I left school. And I remember bein' on that bus, me and a couple of guys in my band, and the rest of the bus was probably sixty, seventy percent black guys from Asbury Park. And I remember thinkin' like, what makes my life, or my friends' lives, more expendable than that of somebody who's goin' to school? It just didn't seem right.

But the U.S. government was only one of the forces with which Springsteen had to contend. Another was family pressure—specifically that of Springsteen's father, Douglas, a World War II veteran who, like many fathers of the era, bitterly resented the attitudes of the younger generation, which they considered self-absorbed and unpatriotic. Springsteen was not a hippie in the classic mold. But he did, however passively, oppose the war—and exhibit the signal characteristic of the counterculture for men: long hair.

Hair—the title and subject of a hit musical in 1968—became a powerful symbol of the distance between Springsteen and his father that year, and it figures at the center of a monologue that would later be the staple of Springsteen's live shows. "When I was growing up, me and my dad used to go at it all the time over almost anything," he would begin. "I used to have really long hair, all the way down past my shoulders." For the elder Springsteen, long hair was symptomatic of his son's shortcomings, but there was nothing wrong with him a tour of duty in a place like Vietnam couldn't fix. As Springsteen would go on to explain (this particular version comes from the live version of "The River" included on *Live 1975–85*):

> The first thing he would always ask me [when the younger Springsteen came home after the two had a fight] was what did I think I was doing with myself. And the worst part about it was that I could never explain it to him. I remember I got into a motorcycle accident once and I was laid up in bed, and he had a barber come in and cut my hair. And man, I could remember telling him that I hated him and that I would never, ever forget it. And he used to tell me, "Man, I can't wait 'til the army gets you. When the army gets you they're gonna make a man outta you. They're gonna cut all that hair off of you and they're gonna make a man outta you."

According to the elder Springsteen, a "man" had short hair. And would stand up for a fight. This might not be masculinity in its entirety but it was a start, one his son had not even made.

As it turned out, the cause of Springsteen's haircut, his motorcycle accident, saved him from the draft. Because of it—and because he stayed up all night before the exam, and answered his questioners as erratically as he could—he was classified 4-F, effectively ending the possibility of his entering the army. By that point, of course, the Tet Offensive had demonstrated that the Viet Cong's will to fight was greater than the U.S. Army had calculated. Realizing that public trust in him and the war effort had been permanently damaged, Lyndon

Johnson decided not to run for reelection. His successor, Richard Nixon, would soon enough be bogged down in the Vietnam quagmire—and a Watergate affair that suggested not only bad judgment on the part of the American government, but corruption as well.

And Douglas Springsteen? His son related what happened upon his return from his examination.

> My dad said, "Where you been?"
> I said, "I went to take my physical."
> He said, "What happened?"
> I said, "They didn't take me."
> And he said, "That's good."

At this point, the crowd roars, as it did when Springsteen revealed earlier that he failed his physical ("ain't nothing to applaud about," he told them). The moral of the story is clear: Vietnam was a bad war, and in the end, even people like Douglas Springsteen could see that and allow the generation gap to close. The worst thing was that the son could never explain; the best was that he didn't have to. In a specific, limited, but important sense, this constitutes a happy ending.

And that may be fine as far as it goes. The crowd can even feel complacent that the villain of the story is converted. But as Springsteen knew, it was not really the end of the story, and his subsequent career has become a sustained exploration of his recognition of the limits of his own vision as a boy on the bus.

A turning point came in 1981, when he read Ron Kovic's Vietnam memoir *Born on the Fourth of July,* which chronicled a naive young patriot's descent into Vietnam and his later opposition to the war as an act of patriotism. With the memory of Bart Hanes in mind, Springsteen asked manager Jon Landau to help him find a way to help Vietnam veterans. Landau, in turn, contacted Woody Guthrie biographer (and *Primary Colors* author) Joe Klein, who put Springsteen in touch with Bob Muller, a former U.S. Marine Corps lieutenant who headed an organization called Vietnam Veterans of America. Springsteen went on to give a number of benefit performances for VVA that virtually single-handedly saved the organization from financial collapse. Muller himself went so far as to say that, "Without Bruce Springsteen, there would be no Vietnam veterans movement."

This is surely an exaggeration, but it is fair to say that Springsteen was among the first to build bridges between veterans and rock and rollers—or, more important, between those who served and those who didn't. In so doing, he made a powerful statement about the responsibility we have to those who acted in good faith on behalf of their government, even when others profoundly disagreed with its policies or suspected that it was corrupt.

Other champions of veterans—like Ronald Reagan—would eschew this approach by instead insisting on the winnability of the war or its moral legitimacy. "I think that what's happening now is that people want to forget," Springsteen said around the time of Reagan's reelection. "There was Vietnam, there was Watergate, there was Iran—we were beaten, we were hustled, and then we were humiliated. And I think people got a need to feel good about the country again. But what's happening, I think, is that that need—which is a good thing—is gettin' manipulated and exploited."

In any case, Springsteen's engagement with veterans had at least two other salutary consequences. The first is that it established a pattern he would later replicate in other kinds of philanthropic work. Throughout the *Born in the U.S.A.* tour, for example, he would devote one night's show to a particular charity—a food bank, for example—to which he would make a contribution and invite the audience to do so as well as part of a broader sense of republican citizenship. "I think people on their own can do a lot," he said. "I guess that's what I'm tryin' to figure out now: where do the aesthetic issues that you write about intersect with some sort of concrete action, some direct involvement, in the communities where your audiences come from?" Such an approach suggested one answer.

The other consequence was in the artistic realm. Springsteen's VVA benefit took place at the end of his long tour to support *The River*. After the tour ended in 1981, he returned to New Jersey for his first sustained break from recording and performing in three years. Springsteen's subsequent reflections took his music in a new direction.

NATIONAL ANTHEM

And always, they would ask you with an emotion whose intensity to shock you to please tell it, because they really did have the feeling that it wasn't all being told for them, that they were going through all of this and that somehow no one back in the world knew about it. They may have been a bunch of dumb, brutal, killer kids (a lot of correspondents privately felt that), but they were smart enough to know that much.

—MICHAEL HERR, *Dispatches*

On January 3, 1982, Springsteen made a tape with demo versions of a number of songs for his next album (which he seriously considered naming *January 3, 1982*). He had recorded them in his living room, accompanied only on an acoustic guitar, with little intention of having them function as any more than a kind of note-keeping for further reference. Eventually, these demos would form the core of *Nebraska*.

One of the songs from this very first group was called "Born in the U.S.A." This particular version had a faster pace than what came later, and it had a different melody. But the lyrics were the same. "It was a real odd thing, and it was not like anything else on the *Nebraska* album," Jon Landau later recalled. "And it was not like any other thing I've ever heard from Bruce—it sounded alien. It just didn't sound like it fit." Springsteen put the song aside.

Springsteen's next step was to present the new material to the E Street Band. The group endured two weeks of frustration while Springsteen tried to shoehorn *Nebraska* songs into band arrangements that he and Landau felt distorted them (he would ultimately release the album with the songs just as he had recorded them on that demo tape). Concluding that they were getting nowhere, and with valuable studio time already booked, Springsteen—to the surprise of Landau and others—turned to "Born in the U.S.A." "To me, it was a dead song," Landau said. But Springsteen thought the very thing that was hampering the *Nebraska* material would help "Born in the U.S.A."—what Landau called "that turbulence and that scale" of a full-fledged rock song.

So Springsteen ran through it, and taught keyboardist Roy Bittan the riff that would become its dominant motif. He told drummer Max Weinberg to keep going after he finished the verses and then asked the band as a whole to play it in its entirety. Landau recalls that it was the second complete take that ended up on *Born in the U.S.A.*, an album dominated by live (as opposed to studio-constructed) tracks. The producer-manager described the recording of "Born in the U.S.A." as "the most exciting thing that ever happened in a recording studio."

The excitement one hears in this recording is palpable, but difficult to describe. It opens with Bittan's synthesizer and Weinberg's snare drum, both of which seem as if they're being played in a cavernous space. Bittan's phrase has a vaguely martial air to it; Weinberg's snare sounds like a shotgun. Without anything that actually resembles one, the song evokes a march: energetic yet precise.

Born down in a dead man's town
First kick I took was when I hit the ground
End up like a dog that's been beat too much
Till you spend half your life just coverin' up
Born in the U.S.A. . . . .

Considered alone, these words sound like they could be sung by a mournful Mississippi Delta bluesman. But—and this is crucial to the power of the song—Springsteen does not sing them that way. His voice is raspy yet focused; he sounds positively ferocious. Weinberg punctuates the words "hit the ground" with his bass drum. This underlines what's being described, but it also adds even more energy to the song—as if an engine is being jump-started. Indeed, before Springsteen begins the next verse, a prominent rhythm guitar enters the mix, churning the song forward:

> *Got in a little hometown jam*
> *So they put a rifle in my hand*
> *Sent me off to a foreign land*
> *To go and kill the yellow man*

In their terse, assonant style ("jam," "hand," "land," "man"), these lyrics establish a somewhat different argument than that of much popular culture about the Vietnam War. In works like *Born on the Fourth of July,* a sense of betrayal is so powerful because the victims of the war had held the nation's ideals in such high esteem. Here, however, betrayal has taken place as soon as this man "hit the ground," long before he was ever sent abroad.

In fact, while he's hardly blameless—as this not-so-noble-grunt admits, he got *himself* in a "hometown jam"—the very fact that he's sent abroad is a by-product of misguided, if not cynical, social policy. In many communities in the postwar years, judges dealing with youthful delinquents offered the armed forces as a substitute for jail time in the hope that both the army and the youth would benefit from the experience. Very often, neither did. "We tried to persuade ourselves that all we needed was better leadership to bring the delinquents around," General Colin Powell recalled of such soldiers he encountered in the 1950s and 60s. "Meanwhile, good troops saw the bad ones get away with murder, a situation destructive of morale overall."

If the army was not a happy experience, neither was returning home, where the veteran of "Born in the U.S.A." finds little in the way of endlessly invoked American opportunity.

> *Come back home to the refinery*
> *Hiring man says, "Son, if it was up to me . . ."*
> *Went down to see my VA man*
> *He said, "Son, don't you understand now . . ."*

The folks back home mean well, but they lack the power to even finish their sentences in credible ways; in a metaphorical sense, they can't finish what they start. The protagonist, by contrast, represents himself and others in concrete, vivid language, even when describing an absence:

> *Had a brother at Khe Sahn*
> *Fighting off the Viet Cong*
> *They're still there, he's all gone*

This sense of clarity extends not only to himself and loved ones, but other war victims as well.

> *He had a woman he loved in Saigon*
> *I got a picture of him in her arms now*

The image of an American and a Vietnamese in an embrace serves as an ironic counterpoint to everything the Vietnam War was about. There are limits to Springsteen's vision here: like most American artists, he has relatively little to say about the horrible costs of U.S. intervention on the Vietnamese, and his representation of Asia as a woman is part of a long, dishonorable tradition of "orientalism" in Western depictions of the East—one obvious example being the hit musical *Miss Saigon*. Nevertheless, the singer's remembrance of a lost, shattered world goes to the very heart of what "Born in the U.S.A." is about: making us know, and care, about losers. In that regard, it's crucial that the narrator does unto others what he implicitly asks that we do unto him.

But he never asks for our pity, and that's also crucial to the power of the song. In the last verse, the one Springsteen finally turned into a dirge a decade later, he stands in the shadows of the penitentiary and refinery with nowhere to run. But his chant of "Born in the U.S.A." is less a lament than it is an assertion of exactly what the Chrysler jingle writer said it was: pride. Pride not in the hope for, or fulfillment of, American Dreams, but pride in the will to survive them. That's why this man makes the improbable declaration, "I'm a cool rocking daddy in the U.S.A." at the end of the song: he's recasting the very definition of what it means to be a success in America.

A will to survive does not necessarily mean one *will* survive, however. The flip side of "Born in the U.S.A."—both literally and figuratively—is "Shut Out the Light," which was released as the B side to the "Born in the U.S.A." single (and has never since resurfaced). "Shut Out the Light" is sung from the point of view of an exhausted vet for whom darkness invites horrifying flashbacks. Springsteen took the core of that song and incorporated it into "Born in the U.S.A." by having the narrator quietly say, "No, no, no" or "Oh my God, no" between the verses. Here, then, is one more countercurrent in the song, and powerful evidence that for this man, the war is not, and will never be, over.

The music of "Born in the U.S.A." is also suggestively ambiguous. At the end of the song, Weinberg goes into an extended drum solo while the rest of the band seems strained simply to remain in the established chord progression. Eventually, it pulls together again—only to fade out. If there really is triumph here, it is only one part of our national story.

Perhaps no one knew that better than Abraham Lincoln. More than any other American politician, he expressed the view that tragedy and failure were as much a part of the drama in which he lived as the Union's ultimate success in arms. At the very moment of victory, when he had been reelected and Confederate surrender was a month away, he devoted his second inaugural address to focusing on loss. "Neither party expected for the war, the magnitude, or the duration, which it has already attained," he said in words that apply to Vietnam as well. "Each looked for an easier triumph, and a result less fundamental and astounding." Attributing blame not only to a slave-holding South, but also to a complacent and sinful North, he argued that God "gives to both North and South this terrible war, as the woe due to those by whom the offence came." And he ended his address with an invocation concurrent with that of "Born in the U.S.A.":

> With malice toward none; with charity for all; with firmness in the right, as God gives us to see the right, let us strive on to finish the work we are in; to bind up the nation's wounds; to care for him who shall have borne the battle, and for his widow, and his orphan—to do all which may achieve and cherish a just, and a lasting peace, among ourselves, and with all nations.

FIVE

The Good Life

SPRINGSTEEN'S PLAY ETHIC

Like the American Dream, the work ethic is a concept central to who we like to think we are as a people. In recent decades, however, the work ethic has become a particular source of unease. Celebrating Labor Day in 1971, for example, then-president Richard Nixon saluted "the dignity of work," but felt compelled to add, "Let us also recognize that the work ethic is undergoing some changes." That Nixon regarded such changes as not for the better could be safely taken for granted. On the other hand, people have been lamenting the ebbing of the work ethic for a long time. "God sent you not into this world as a Play-house, but as a Work-house," read one Puritan maxim. Even in the era most observers consider the heyday of the work ethic, the very necessity for such an admonition suggests that countertendencies abounded.

The American Dream has always been an elastic term whose definition has not been fixed. The definition of the work ethic, by contrast, has. It received its best-known elaboration in sociologist Max Weber's classic book *The Protestant Ethic and the Spirit of Capitalism*, first published in a German scholarly journal in 1904–1905 and translated into a U.S. edition in 1930. Rooted in the "ascetic Protestantism" of the Reformation, Weber described the emergence of a conception of work not as a brutal necessity, but rather as a calling.

Far more than most academic theories, Weber's work has proved remarkably durable not only in the academy, but also in the popular discourse of journalists, businessmen, and even ordinary working people. Nowadays, the common lament is that the old focus on work has degenerated into an obsession with leisure; a society once focused on making things now seems hell-bent on consuming them. So while complaints about the decline of the work ethic are nothing new, they take on a special intensity as the United States loses its economic preeminence in the world.

Yet even when it was at its height, for a number of reasons, the work ethic was never the only model for thought and behavior in the United States. First, a large segment of the population was not Protestant, and while it would be fair to suggest that the work ethic affected ethnic Catholics or Jews in the nineteenth and twentieth cen-

GOODS SCHOLAR: Max Weber, author of *The Protestant Ethic and the Spirit of Capitalism*, in 1918.

turies, they never shed their social identities altogether, even when their behavior corresponded to WASP norms. Second, a large segment that *was* largely Protestant, African Americans, was largely enslaved for 250 years, and could not share the hope for the upward mobility at the core of the work ethic. Nor, for that matter, could many white Protestants, who for any number of reasons (fractured family life, a lack of will or talent, repeated failure in the marketplace) found the work ethic an impractical strategy for making their way in the world.

For these and other people, an alternative model was available, one which could be called a *play* ethic. The play ethic is not a simple negation of the work ethic that celebrates idleness. Nor is it a more philosophical sensibility that prizes sedentary contemplation. Rather, it involves a focused, energetic commitment to play not for a livelihood, personal advancement, or social obligation, but as an end in itself.

Having said that, there is a paradox at the heart of the play ethic. Just as the worldly work ethic had otherworldly implications (i.e., it could provide clues as to whether one would be among the saved), so, too, the play ethic connotes much more than mere play. It's not so much an *escape* from everyday life as a means to enrich, even redeem it and in the process become part of a broader community. It is in this way that one can really speak of a play *ethic*.

It's not always easy to take play seriously. Nowhere is this more true than in popular music. "It's only rock & roll," the Rolling Stones told their listeners in their song and album of 1974. Most rock and rollers before and since, from garage band guitarists to superstar vocalists, define what they do *in opposition to* the workaday world.

Bruce Springsteen does not. The great irony of his career is that a man who makes a living through play plies his trade with exhausting intensity. In a way, that makes sense; anyone who gets paid as handsomely as he does to do what he wants can be expected to put in long hours. But perhaps the most revealing aspect of Springsteen's "vocation" (a word that points to the almost religious nature of the way in which he practices his profession) is not what it reveals about him. Rather, it's the possibilities of both work and play for the rest of us in a country where the value of both has long been eroding.

WORKING SOLUTIONS

I think that all the great records and great songs say, "Hey, take this and find your place in the world. Do something with it, do anything with it. Find some place to make your stand, no matter how big or small it is." That's a pretty wonderful thing for a record to do.
                                           —BRUCE SPRINGSTEEN, 1981

If some people have been lamenting the decline of the work ethic from almost the moment of its inception, others have experienced the decline of work itself for about as long. Whatever the real defects of Puritan society, it was possible there to believe that the work one did could be personal, communal, and sacred all at the same time. The fruits of one's labors were not instantly siphoned off to a landlord—or, if they were, one could reasonably hope to be a landlord oneself one day. And *all* work was seen as part of a vast project to build a city on a hill.

In fact, far from being limited to New England, a number of observers have noted the extraordinary social fluidity throughout early Anglo-American society, fluidity that scared some but was positively liberating to others. A mix of pilgrims, entrepreneurs, journeymen, and indentured servants jostled in colonial society, the lines between them often blurred. Even the great evil of slavery was less rigid than it became in the late eighteenth and early nineteenth centuries; major urban slave revolts in New York City in 1741 and Richmond in 1800—the mere fact of which indicated at least some resistance to labor subordination—included white participants.

The advent of industrialization in the nineteenth century decisively segmented American life in a number of ways. First, workers themselves were segmented from each other as work was increasingly split into smaller, more repetitive, and less satisfying tasks characteristic of the assembly line. Second, American families became increasingly segmented; the origins of the perception stay-at-home mother and laboring father as the dominant social model had its roots in industrial capitalism (although generally only well-to-do mothers could actually afford to stay at home, and many of those who did worked out of their homes). Finally, work itself was now segmented from the rest of the workers' lives. Now work was less a calling, however necessary, than a matter of brute survival.

In the twentieth century, however, there is a widespread sense that work has become less oppressive. In part, this is because the advent of the labor movement has given some workers a measure of leverage over their bosses (though that has begun to ebb). In part, too, the government has stepped in and arrested the worst abuses of private power—from child labor to cartels—that have typified unchecked corporate growth. Another reason, and one that should not be underestimated, is the obvious benefit industrial capitalism has conferred in providing safety, convenience, and pleasure to those able to afford them. From air-conditioning to microwave ovens, the fruits of mass labor have made even the most difficult lives more comfortable.

But perhaps the most valuable coin in the realm of modern work—to many, its sole justification—is leisure. Leisure is a somewhat different thing than play. Its connotations are not so much the kind of emotional and physical engagement required of play, but freedom from any kind of engagement at all. For the most thoroughly drained workers, the freedom to do nothing at all is especially prized. For more privileged ones, leisure represents the opposite of production: consumption.

Indeed, consumption—or the buying of things—is the favored form of leisure in contemporary American society and one that helps sustain the economy as a whole. Obviously, a good deal of consumption in daily life, such as of food, clothing, and shelter, is essential and is done by everyone. But much of it is conducted solely as a form of leisure. Shopping (or, more specifically, spending) has become *the* national pastime. There's nothing inherently wrong with that. For some, shopping is, in fact, a form of play.

But long before the advent of the shopping mall, older traditions of play offered relief from new forms of work. The principal repository of these traditions is popular culture. Essentially, popular culture is a modern offshoot of preindustrial folk culture. Like folk culture—which continues to exist to this day in the rich traditions of handicrafts and communal rituals that range from ethnic cuisines to parades—popular culture relies on readily available materials and common techniques. The difference is that popular culture is refracted (and magnified) through the prism of mass production. One historian has elegantly defined popular culture as "the folklore of industrial society."

Popular culture, of course, has itself become a highly elaborate form of consumption—in the narrowest sense, paperback novels, videocassettes, compact discs, and other cultural documents are savored precisely because they're perfectly useless things. But it's no accident that many of the most cherished forms of pop culture have been produced by people—women novelists (from Fanny Fern to Willa Cather), black musicians (from Bessie Smith to Louis Armstrong), ethnic stage and screen actors (from Sophie Tucker to Abbott and Costello)—of modest backgrounds with few illusions about the laboring life. Though they had distinguished and often satisfying *careers,* most of their audiences simply had *jobs,* which had important implications for the tenor of their art. While the popular culture they and others produced was a part of the world of consumption, it offered critiques of work and leisure from within.

Bruce Springsteen is very much an artist in this tradition. For all the commentary on Springsteen's earnestness, his embodiment of durable American values, his wholesomeness, it's striking to realize that nowhere do his characters celebrate the dignity of work, declaim it as a source of strength or self-worth, or prescribe it as a cure for personal or social ills. Their real interests lie elsewhere.

No one really works on Springsteen's early records. The only song that even hints at wage-earning is "Does This Bus Stop at 82nd Street," in which an insouciant narrator wanders an urban landscape "where dock worker's dreams mix with panther's schemes to someday own the rodeo." (Even here, the clear implication is that work, like the radical politics of black nationalism, is something of a game.)

Beginning with *Born to Run,* however, Springsteen characters increasingly became aware of the way in which working-class adult life is tethered to labor. Without exception, they speak about it in negative terms. So, for example, the passionate motorcyclist of "Night" begins by saying, "You get up every morning at the sound of the bell/You get to work late and the boss man's giving you hell." Even in songs where work isn't discussed directly, like "Born to Run," one nevertheless senses its oppressive reach as the very thing that "rips the bones from your back," *the* reason why the narrator and his erstwhile lover "gotta get out while we're young."

This stance toward what Karl Marx called "alienated labor" intensifies on subsequent albums, as even the briefest survey suggests. "Daddy worked his whole life for nothing but the pain," observes the singer of "Adam Raised a Cain," seeking to escape a similar fate. The son of "Independence Day" declares his freedom from a similarly alienated father by asserting, "They ain't gonna do to me what I watched them do to you." On *Born in the U.S.A.,* the protagonists of two successive songs, "Working on the Highway" and "Downbound Train," work on chain gangs, their bondage literal as well as figurative. Work is only one part of the lives depicted on these records, and there is some real happiness. But it doesn't come from a job.

This is not to say that these people don't recognize the necessity for work, or acknowledge its stabilizing role in their lives. Unemployment destroys the lives of characters in songs like "The River" and "Johnny 99." Occasionally, some joy can even be wrested out of work, as when the driver of "Open All Night" enjoys some fried chicken from Bob's Big Boy with his favorite waitress while out on the road (of course, he's taking a break when he does so). But work is never an end in itself.

Nor is consumption much in the way of compensation. Springsteen is not a doctrinaire critic of consumerism—"People never sold out by buying something," he has said—but he has an acute eye for its sheer ruthlessness. In "You Can Look (But You Better Not Touch)," a man goes shopping at a mall, and when he almost knocks over a lamp is sternly warned that if it breaks, he will pay the cost. In some sense, however, the mere fact of commerce itself exacts a price, as is suggested in what seems to be a description of a television advertisement:

Well I came home from work and I switched on channel five
There was a pretty little girly lookin' straight into my eyes
Well I watched as she wiggled back and forth across the screen
She didn't get me excited, she just made me feel mean
You can look, but you better not touch . . .

Part of the insidious quality of consumer capitalism is the way in which it objectifies everything in sight—leisure, sexuality, even customers (or, in industry parlance, "markets")—into commodities that can be bought and sold. In this regard, the word "mean," which suggests not only frustration, but cheapness, even impoverishment, is especially appropriate.

Play is a very different matter. To a striking degree, it is a source of epiphany. Nightclubs, boardwalks, even fishing expeditions—these are sites where Springsteen's characters find true romance, demonstrate heroism, come to understand themselves. Sometimes simply *not* working *is* an end in itself, so valuable that characters *do* declaim such freedom as a source of strength and self-worth: "When I'm out in the street, I walk the way I wanna walk," says the dockworker of "Out in the Street" at the end of the working day. And people find—as well as make—beauty from the flotsam of consumer culture: Roy Orbison records ("Thunder Road"), photographs on walls ("Candy's Room"), even gas station signs ("Jungleland").

This depiction of play as a source of insight is especially apparent in one of Springsteen's favorite settings, amusement parks. One good example is "4th of July, Asbury Park (Sandy)." Like many of his early songs, "Sandy," a love song about two boardwalk drifters, is characterized by affectionate descriptions of beach bums. But there's a sense of irony directed at "those boys from the casino who dance with their shirts half open like Latin lovers on the shore," one that suggests a new level of sophistication about the world beyond the boardwalk. Then the singer turns that irony on himself:

And me I just got tired of hangin' in them dusty arcades
Banging them pleasure machines
Chasin' them factory girls under the boardwalk
Where they promise to unsnap their jeans
And do you know that Tilt-a-Whirl down on the South Beach
  drag?
Well I got on it last night and my shirt got caught
Man, they kept me spinning there
Didn't think I'd ever get off

Being trapped on an amusement park ride—on the "drag," no less—becomes a symbol for this man's restlessness with mechanical forms of leisure and his yearning for more satisfying forms of play. Moreover, there's a suggestion that the superficiality of the singer's relationships are being mirrored by those "pleasure machines." He confesses that his affair with a waitress is now over and asks his friend Sandy to be his companion in a quest for something better: "For me this boardwalk life's through/You oughta quit this scene too."

Amusement parks are only one example of the prominent role of play in Springsteen's art; there are, of course, a number of others. One of the most important, not surprisingly, is playing music. "We learned more from a three-minute record than we ever learned in school," asserts the singer of "No Surrender," who later speculates to a friend that "maybe we could cut someplace of our own with these drums and these guitars." In "Rosalita (Come Out Tonight)," this aspiration becomes a reality, as the protagonist (reputedly Springsteen himself, for obvious reasons) joyfully reveals to Rosie that he has received a record contract and should now be able to gain her parents' blessing. Songs such as these suggest the centrality of play in these peoples' lives, and the intensity of their hope that it can become a material blessing as well as a psychological one.

ONLY ROCK & ROLL

When Bruce Springsteen sings on his new album, that's not about "fun." That's fucking triumph, man.
—Pete Townshend of The Who on *Born to Run*, 1975

Charles Cross attended his first Bruce Springsteen concert in the summer of 1974, when he was sixteen, using a fake ID to gain admittance to New York's fabled Bottom Line nightclub. Cross was unfamiliar with the emerging artist's work. But as Springsteen played a guitar solo on a tabletop, his sweat dripping on Cross, the future founder of a Springsteen fan magazine imagined that he had been "baptized in some alien way." Over the next four years Cross roamed venues from coast to coast to catch Springsteen shows.

Cross's true conversion experience, however, took place on December 20, 1978, when he saw a Springsteen show at the 5,000-seat Seattle Center Arena. When it was over, he felt exhilarating exhaustion. "I'd been on twenty-mile runs that had left me with more energy," he recalled. "My knuckles were bleeding, my ears were ringing like an errant auto alarm, and I was so hoarse from shouting that I sounded like Sally Kellerman with a head cold." Wandering up to the stage, he saw the set list Springsteen had used to plan the concert and realized that he had run through it hours before, making much of the show wholly uncharted. Dazed, he watched roadies dismantle the sound system.

Suddenly, Springsteen ran on stage with a towel around his neck, stood in front of a band member's microphone with an unamplified guitar, and launched into a version of Buddy Holly's "Rave On." The crew managed to get the sound system working in the middle of this, his fourth encore, and fans began streaming back into the hall. When Springsteen left the stage again, security guards tried to move the crowd out of the building, but fans resisted leaving until the lights went out, leaving them to find their way in the dark. Cross finally returned home in the snow sometime after four A.M. the next morning. "It had never felt more like Christmas," he wrote.

There have been many live performers in the last fifty years who have attracted passionate followings comparable to that of Bruce Springsteen. The Grateful Dead sold relatively few records over the course of its thirty-year career, but the band's concerts were always a cause for celebration. A Rolling Stones tour is usually an international media event. And James Brown has been known to generations of concertgoers as "the hardest-working man in show business."

But Springsteen may well be unique in the degree to which he has sought to make playing—in the general and specifically musical sense of the term—a form of joyful work. This intensity is obvious during his shows, but it's discernible offstage, too. "At every date he goes out and sits in every section of the hall to listen to the sound," technician Bruce Jackson observed in 1978. "And if it isn't right, even in the last row, I hear about it and we make changes. I mean every date, too." The photograph accompanying Springsteen's liner notes to *Live 1975–85* shows him with a guitar roaming the aisles of an arena as part of a sound check, suggesting attention to detail as well as a sense of deliberation to accompany his spontaneous actions on stage.

Indeed, for Springsteen at least, a concert seems to have less in common with a frat party than a barn raising; while there's an undeniable sense of pleasure in the proceedings, one senses a desire for exertion as well. "An evening with Springsteen—an evening tends to wash over into the a.m., the concerts lasting four hours— is vivid proof that the work ethic is alive and well," conservative columnist George Will wrote after attending a show in 1984.

Yet as satisfying as Springsteen's concerts may be for him and his fans, a pressing question remains: What utility or relevance does this play-as-work ethic have for those of us who are not well-paid rock stars (or newspaper columnists)? What are we supposed to do? Is there any way we can recapture the spiritual sustenance and vitality that the work ethic once conferred? Springsteen answered this question by way of the most celebrated industrial engine and consumer appliance of all: the automobile.

VEHICLES OF MEANING

I think that cars today are almost the exact equivalent of the great Gothic cathedrals: I mean the supreme creation of an era, conceived with passion by unknown artists, and consumed in image if not in usage by a whole population which appropriates them as a purely magical object.
—ROLAND BARTHES, *Mythologies*, 1957

Play, we began by saying, lies outside morals. In itself it is neither good nor bad. But if we have to decide whether an action to which our will impels us is a serious duty or is licit as play, our moral conscience will at once provide the touchstone. As soon as truth and justice, compassion and forgiveness have part in our resolve to act, our anxious question loses all meaning. One drop of pity is enough to lift our doing beyond intellectual distinctions.

—JOHAN HUIZINGA,
Homo Ludens [MAN THE PLAYER], 1938

I love those Beach Boy songs. I love "Don't Worry Baby." If I hear that thing in the right mood, forget it. I go over the edge, you know? . . . So I write "Racing in the Street" and that felt good.

—BRUCE SPRINGSTEEN, 1985

In the twentieth century, the most important means used for Americans to go to work—or to go play, or to go do just about anything else—has been the automobile. The story of the development and proliferation of cars is one that intersects with many others: the evolution of technology, the advent of mass production, the growth of organized labor, the acceleration of consumerism, etc. And surrounding these broad, impersonal processes a number of myths and symbols (e.g., cars = freedom) have developed that have been woven into the fabric of everyday life.

Cars were emblems of modernity when they emerged a hundred years ago—supplanting railroads, the emblem of modernity in the nineteenth century—because they resonated with long-standing American obsessions. Neither cars nor railroads (nor movies, another symbol of modernity) can truly be said to have been *invented* here, as they have important European antecedents or origins. But they have been uniquely embraced by, and identified with, the

United States because of specific historical conditions that made them flourish here: the nation's huge size, its infatuation with technological innovation, and the relative affluence of its middle class, among other factors. These conditions crystallized most clearly in Henry Ford's assembly-line production of the Model T, a car he unveiled with great success in 1907, in part because he paid his workers enough money so that they could think about buying one themselves.

Ever since the advent of the Model T, cars have been a kind of fulcrum between work and play. Usually paid for with wages, they have been both a means and a goal of labor. No one, however, has ever written a great book or made a great movie about driving to work. For most Americans, the *real* value in owning a car is what you can do with it when you're *not* working.

The car has a venerable history in all the popular arts, but its appeal has nowhere been greater than in rock and roll music. Perhaps this is because both cars and rock and roll were emblems of U.S. economic and cultural supremacy at mid-century, when unprecedented levels of disposable income fueled their growth. It is surely more than coincidental that a song many popular music historians consider the first rock and roll record, Jackie Brenston's 1951 hit "Rocket 88," is about a car. Elvis Presley ratified his transformation from poor white trash to nouveau riche white trash by purchasing cars compulsively, and the model he sang about most often and most lustily (in, for example, "Baby, Let's Play House") is a pink Cadillac—a car largely inappropriate for anything *but* play in socially unsanctioned ways.

The consummate rock poet of the automobile, however, was Chuck Berry. Long underrecognized as one of the greatest American popular songwriters of the twentieth century, Berry wrote a series of deceptively complex songs with automotive themes throughout his career. The most famous was his 1955 hit "Maybelline," in which the narrator, driving a plebeian Ford, tries

POETRY IN MOTION: Chuck Berry fused interracial rhythms and vivid images in a number of songs that explored the nuances of automotive culture.

to overtake the Cadillac that carries his girlfriend away. (For Berry, play, no less than work, is a site of class struggle; his song "No Money Down," a loving description of a new car, is haunted by the specter of the finance company that will take it away.) Deploying a guitar sound that evoked a running engine—Berry did win lasting renown as a guitarist, perhaps because of his flamboyant performance style—"Maybelline" is one of the canonical works of early rock and roll. Berry went to jail in 1962 on a trumped-up charge of transporting a Mexican prostitute across state lines, suggesting the potency of race, sex, rock, and cars for those who sought to police behavior.

In the early sixties, the major poets of the automobile were the Beach Boys, who in songs like "Little Deuce Coupe," "Fun Fun Fun" (both 1963), and "I Get Around" (1964) offered an even more shimmering vision of play than Presley had. The power of the Beach Boys' music lay less in lyrics or their public image than in the sheer soaring beauty of their harmonies, which evoke the happiest moments of the American Century. Their voices conjured up a world that existed largely as (white) fantasy, though even its sternest critics would concede its charm.

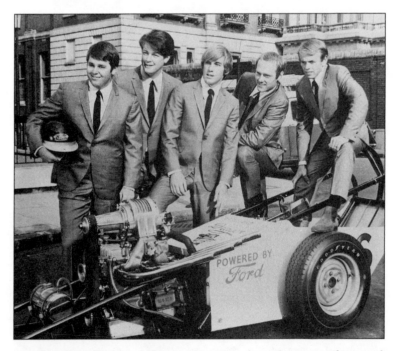

FUN FUN FUN: The Beach Boys in the 1960s. An undercurrent of pain and struggle animated many of the group's seemingly playful songs.

Given their centrality in American life in these years, it is not surprising that cars would be included as part of the indictment against "the system" made by the radicals of the late sixties. As the Civil Rights movement crested and protest over the Vietnam War rose, cars were regarded by the counterculture as just another symbol of a corrupt technocratic order that was materialistic, wasteful, and bad for the environment. Rather than lovingly describing a car the way Berry did, the hippies of the late sixties preferred Volkswagen Beetles (a pointedly foreign car) or beat-up vans as the automotive statement of choice. Psychedelic indulgence, not loving craftsmanship, was celebrated in The Who's "Magic Bus" (1967). For Carole King the road became a tired cliché in "So Far Away" (1971).

Meanwhile, American mastery of the automotive market, itself an index of American mastery of the global economy, was slipping. The energy crisis of the seventies revealed the degree to which the freedom a car supposedly offered was now dependent on Arab oil. Functional, inexpensive Japanese cars began beating the heirs of Henry Ford at their own game. The so-called "malaise" of American society in the era could be seen on any parking lot or in any gas station.

It was within this context of skepticism and even decline in which, automotively speaking, Bruce Springsteen came of age. But as anyone with even a passing familiarity with his music knows, cars are absolutely central to Springsteen's music in a Presley/Berry kind of way, his favored subject, setting, and symbol. "Everybody is saying that cars and girls are all I sing about!" he observed in 1987. "Then I realized, 'Hey! that's what Chuck Berry wrote about!' So it wasn't my idea. It was a genre thing, like detective movies."

Like a gifted genre artist, Springsteen has used cars in all kinds of ways. Sometimes, they are the explicit subjects of celebration. "There she sits, buddy, just lyin' in the sun/There to greet the working man when his day is done," says the singer of "Cadillac Ranch," in which cars connote the opposite of work. Yet even such seemingly straight-

ON THE ROAD (AGAIN): Next to playing a guitar, no activity is more central to Springsteen's life and work than driving.

forward songs can have ambiguous overtones. Springsteen has called "Ramrod," another paean to cars and girls from *The River*, as "one of the saddest songs I've ever written." This is not only because of the powerful sense of anachronism that characterizes it ("Hey little dolly with the blue jeans on," goes the opening line), but also because of the grim realities that are always a backdrop for fun ("I've been working all week, I'm up to my neck in hock/Come Saturday night I let my ramrod rock"). Springsteen also uses cars to chart psychological stress, and even collapse. One of the most poignant examples is "Used Cars," one of a number of songs from *Nebraska* where cars and driving play pivotal roles. The novel concept here is that of a *used* car, with its implications of limited means and shopworn aspirations. "Mister the day the lotttery I win I ain't never gonna ride no used car again," its boy protagonist declares, his very determination a form of pathos.

On no album, however, are automobiles more important than *Darkness on the Edge of Town*. With one (significant) exception, every song at least mentions cars and/or driving. And more than on any other album, cars are intimately bound up in questions of work and play.

Tellingly, those who have given up—the men of "Factory"—walk. Sung from the point of view of a son sadly observing his father, "Factory" describes men who have lost the will to make a break:

> *End of the day factory whistle cries*
> *Men walk through these gates with death in their eyes*
> *And you just better believe, boy, somebody's gonna get hurt*
> *   tonight*
> *The work, the working, just the working life*

Lacking anywhere to go after work, these men project their aggressions onto themselves and others. In the words of another son, that of "Adam Raised a Cain," "Daddy worked his whole life for nothing but the pain/Now he walks these empty rooms looking for someone to blame." A lack of play is not simply unfortunate, but dangerous.

"Racing in the Street," by contrast, is essentially Springsteen's manifesto on the value of play. But the song is also a commentary on rock history, making subtle connections—and subtle departures—from his rock and roll forebears and their visions of play.

One can begin seeing what Springsteen is up to in "Racing in the Street" by looking at the first verse of the song.

> *I got a '69 Chevy with a 396*
> *Fulie heads and a hurst on the floor*
> *She's waiting for me down at the parking lot*
> *Outside the Seven-Eleven store*
> *Me and my partner Sonny built her straight out of scratch*

And he rides with me from town to town
We only run for the money, got no strings attached
We shut 'em up and then we shut 'em down . . .

If one had never actually heard this song, one might imagine it having a raucous, playful beat. It seems like something the Beach Boys or a like-minded inheritor such as Van Halen might perform—a chronicle of cars, girls, and good times rooted in working-class life (the auto parts, the 7-Eleven, the adolescent braggadocio).

But "Racing in the Street" lacks any such buoyancy. In fact, the song is a ballad. It begins with an almost dirgelike piano, and Springsteen sings the lines slowly, even reverently, with no further accompaniment. Insofar as a specific time is evoked, it is the turbulent Vietnam era. That Springsteen would do so is not accidental. This becomes clear in the next lines of the song, which suggest an acute consciousness of popular musical history:

Tonight, tonight the strip's just right
I wanna blow 'em all out of their seats
Summer's here and the time is right
For racin' in the street

The crucial line is the third one, which occupies a strategic place in the rock canon. In the summer of 1964, Martha and the Vandellas had a huge smash for Motown Records with "Dancing in the Street." The song, while not overtly political, nevertheless became a black anthem during the urban riots of the sixties. Four years later, wryly inverting any innocuous overtones in "Dancing in the Street," the Rolling Stones released "Street Fightin' Man," a song in which summer provided the perfect opportunity for *fighting* in the streets. Best known for its famous rhetorical question about what can a poor boy do but play in a rock band, the song has been a favorite of Springsteen's live performances for many years now.

Again, however, the important issue here is mood. Whether in joy or anger, both "Dancing in the Street" and "Street Fightin' Man" are marked by an ebullience notably absent in "Racing in the Street." But if Springsteen's song lacks the spontaneity of the others, one does sense the quiet confidence that competence brings:

> *We take all the action we can meet*
> *And we cover all the northeast state*
> *When the strip shuts down we run 'em in the street*
> *From the fire roads to the interstate*

There is a perceptible quickening of the song's pace by this point, attributable in large part to drummer Max Weinberg's measured rim taps and subtle use of the hi-hat. It's as if the narrator of the song is warming up like one of his engines.

The entry of Danny Federici's organ at the end of the first verse signals the arrival of the song's key assertion:

> *Some guys they just give up living*
> *And start dying little by little, piece by piece*
> *Some guys come home and wash up*
> *And go racin' in the street*

These lines encapsulate Springsteen's vision of work and play. In one sense, it's a fairly straightforward matter: work destroys, play preserves; work pollutes, play purifies. But in this description, grace is not simply conferred to all. Rather, the elect are those who have the strength to play. As in the case of Puritan religion, however, there is no straightforward equation as to who is saved and who is not; we're not told *which* guys start dying, or *why* some come home and wash up, only that some do. For those who do, such salvation—however fleeting or even misleading—is a palpable experience. Springsteen sings the chorus more expressively (his "*Tonight,* tonight the strip's just right" has bite), and the entrance of the whole band arrangement suggests that the song has opened up full-throttle, so to speak. In this sense, the serene musical bridge that follows is figurative as well as literal: we're hearing the sound of a man who has made it to the other side.

And then something surprising happens. As the bridge comes to a close, the music tapers off, leaving just a piano and a singer again. It's as if he's crossed back into darkness. But he has a reason:

I met her on the strip three years ago
In a Camaro with this dude from L.A.
I blew that Camaro off my back
And drove that little girl away . . .

Here we seem to be back in the realm of the Beach Boys, though again the tone is somber (and L.A. has become a land of glitzy excess). Perhaps a better analogy would be with Berry's "Maybelline" in its sense of class conflict and a struggle for the heart of a woman. Unlike Berry's protagonist, however, this one is a winner. But the woman in question is not:

. . . there's wrinkles around my baby's eyes
And she cries herself to sleep at night
When I come home the house is dark
She sighs, 'Baby did you make it alright'
She sits on the porch of her daddy's house
But all her pretty dreams are torn
She stares off alone into the night
With the eyes of one who hates for just being born . . .

For Berry, the Beach Boys, and in the songs of countless other rock artists, women are trophies won and lost in contests, and "Racing in the Street" would appear to be no exception. What's different here, though, is an unusual sense of compassion and clarity of description. Moreover, Berry's Maybelline, however compelling she may be, is mute. This woman is not: she speaks listlessly, but clearly, in body language as well as speech. Never mind the guys—*she's* dying little by little, piece by piece. The protagonist notices this, and responds:

For all the shut down strangers and hot rod angels
Rumbling through this promised land
Tonight my baby and me, we're gonna ride to the sea
And wash these sins off our hands
Tonight, tonight, the highway's bright
Out of our way, mister you best keep
'Cause summer's here and the time is right
To go racin' in the street . . .

In earlier versions of the chorus, Springsteen follows the line beginning "Tonight, tonight" with a singular pronoun: "*I* wanna blow 'em off in my first heat"; "*I* wanna blow 'em out of their seats." In the final chorus, the pronoun becomes plural: "Out of *our* way." Play becomes communitarian, something one does not only to save oneself, but also something one does for (or at least in honor of) others. Again, one could argue that this woman is only coming along for the ride, but previous evidence (that Camaro) suggests that the road has some romance for her, too. And like a true sportsman, this victor expresses magnanimity for the "shut down strangers" who have lost not out of condescension, but, rather, identification. Far from mindless amusement, this is deeply engaged play that takes on a moral dimension.

GOOD WORK

We refer to the exceptionally talented artist as gifted, conceive her work as a gift to the world, and focus on the spontaneous self-forgetfulness that is often said to characterize play and the creative process. Only our reduction of work to labor has led us to stigmatize play as frivolous.
—JACKSON LEARS, *Fables of Abundance*, 1994

Hannah Arendt was perplexed. The noted philosopher and critic of fascism (she had come to the United States as a refugee from Hitler's Germany) had been deeply impressed by the launching of the Soviet *Sputnik* satellite in 1957, which she considered the most momentous development in human history, greater even than nuclear fission. Like splitting the atom, however, human mastery of the heavens was not being celebrated as an occasion of joy, but rather of mounting anxiety. A space race—one more front in a tense Cold War—was underway, fueling a current of unease in the most prosperous society the world had ever known. Insofar as there was any shared feeling of optimism, Arendt noted, it took the form of hope that it was now finally possible to escape the earth.

In her 1958 book *The Human Condition,* Arendt tried to understand how the world had reached this state of affairs. She believed a good deal of the problem derived from modern conceptions of work and leisure. To explore the matter, she defined three key terms: "labor," which is done to maintain everyday life; "work," which involves making durable things; and "action," or memorable behavior in the public sphere. In ancient society, action was considered the greatest activity, usually performed in the realm of politics. In Periclean Greece, action was predicated on freedom from labor, and in some sense, then, was dependent on having others (wives and/or slaves) to do an actor's labor for him.

The advent of industrialization gave labor new importance in capitalist societies. Ironically, however, the growing wealth and leisure of such societies had not resulted in a diminution of labor, but its near overthrow of work and action, as "making a living" had become our paramount preoccupation. As Arendt explained, leisure was "never spent in anything but consumption, and the more time left to [a laborer], the greedier and more craving his appetites." In such an environment, work was increasingly a matter of producing disposable commodities, and action (which, in an age of labor-saving devices, no longer depended on slavery) was viewed as an irrelevant or unnecessary distraction. The essential symbol of modern life, then, had become an ever more elaborate treadmill.

There are alternatives, however, to this set of arrangements, alternatives that may ultimately mean the difference between life and death (spiritual and literal, individual and collective). At the core of those alternatives is a sense of play, i.e., a willingness to think and act independently of the vicissitudes of labor. In such an enterprise, Bruce Springsteen provides a worthy example. It may seem ridiculous to consider him a latter-day Pericles—or, for that matter, a Hannah Arendt. But if we are willing to suspend our disbelief, it becomes possible to see his music as work, and his concerts as action. All it takes is a willingness to play along.

SIX

Model Man

Springsteen's Masculinity

On June 29, 1984, Bruce Springsteen made "Dancing in the Dark," his first video, during the opening night of the *Born in the U.S.A.* tour in St. Paul, Minnesota. Technically, this was actually the second Springsteen video; "Atlantic City," released in late 1982, was comprised of spare black-and-white footage of that city shot from a car. But "Dancing in the Dark"—the single had been released a month earlier, and was moving up the pop charts—was the first in which Springsteen decided he would actually appear, and as such marked his inauguration into the MTV era.

The video was directed by Brian De Palma, an accomplished Hollywood director best known then for his hit films *Carrie, Dressed to Kill,* and *Scarface* (he later directed *The Untouchables* and *Mission Impossible*). Originally, "Dancing in the Dark" was to have a storyline, but Springsteen and De Palma decided ultimately to make it a simple performance video that reenacted a common scene at Springsteen concerts: his extending a hand to a woman in the audience to come on stage and dance with him. For this role, De Palma cast Courteney Cox (future star of the hit television series *Friends*).

The Bruce Springsteen who appears in "Dancing in the Dark"—the camera begins at his feet and moves upward, pausing with a tight shot of his crotch—is noticeably different from the blurred, but unmistakably slight, figure pictured on the album sleeve of *Nebraska* less than two years before. Springsteen has always been an attractive person. But prior to the release of *Born in the U.S.A.*, he was not a prime specimen of masculinity. Never a big man (Clarence Clemons quite literally played that part), Springsteen's early seventies image was that of a Beat street poet: skinny, bearded, unkempt. He changed his look slightly in the late seventies by shaving his beard and donning an occasional sports jacket, though his scruffiness never entirely disappeared.

The Springsteen of "Dancing in the Dark," by contrast, sports perceptibly larger biceps and a much broader chest. The man who refused to have his picture retouched for album covers was now a plausible subject of teen fantasy. "His jeans were as tight as rubber gloves, and he danced like a revved-up sports car about to take off," thinks Sam Hughes, the adolescent female protagonist of Bobbie Ann Mason's novel *In Country*, as she watches the video in her Kentucky home. Later, Sam daydreams about hitting the road and finding a Springsteen concert. "And he would pull her out of the front row and dance with her in the dark," she imagines.

In the months that followed, the handsome, youthfully thirty-something Springsteen came to represent a vibrant, working-class, white male heterosexuality in pop music. At a time when Michael Jackson's sexual identity was unclear, Prince's eroticism boldly crossed gender boundaries, and Madonna turned femininity into a series of disposable images, Springsteen represented the vital center: short hair, blue jeans, work shirt, and an occasional bandanna or baseball cap to absorb the sweat of his brow. "What do I like about him? He's a fox!" explained one fifteen-year-old when queried about Springsteen's appeal in 1985. "He's down to earth. He's so cool, he's not like any other rock star. He acts normal. Prince overdresses; he don't dress like a normal person. Bruce'll wear jeans; he don't care."

Springsteen may have been down to earth, but his appearance in the *Born in the U.S.A.* era was not exactly unselfconscious. As British sociologist Simon Frith wrote at the time, Springsteen was dressed up as a worker even when he wasn't working; "he's never even seen flashily attired for a night out," the way a real working-class person would be. (Undoubtedly recognizing the contradictions involved in his life, Springsteen began dressing up in the late eighties and nineties, though he still seems most comfortable in casual clothes.) To use the language of academics, sex roles are "socially constructed," and that goes for heterosexuals like Springsteen as much as his transvestite contemporary, Boy George of Culture Club.

People like Boy George have long attracted attention among such scholars because their extravagant, iconoclastic personae serve as an inverted mirror to society at large: by adopting an "abnormal" appearance, they help clarify just what we consider "normal" to be. Because "normal" can be boring or even oppressive, those who reject it are often discussed in a positive, even celebratory fashion. Conversely, those who choose to represent gender traditions most aggressively—like Springsteen's foil, Rambo—are analyzed as icons of dangerous, even murderous impulses that lie just beneath the surface of the population at large.

Less, it seems, has been said about what healthy, mainstream masculinity looks (or sounds) like in contemporary American life. In part, this is because people rarely choose to live their lives according to abstract social labels. In part, too, it's because a middle ground is harder to chart than obvious extremes. But perhaps the most important reason "healthy" is difficult to grasp is because its parameters keep changing.

Despite—or perhaps because of—these complexities, Springsteen offers observers an unusually vivid picture of manhood. One reason is that in a very real sense he has grown up in public; since the release of his first album in 1973, he has revealed himself as a carefree youth, an angry young man, a troubled husband, and a mature father. These roles would be discernible even without hearing his records; while the character of one's politics or religion may be a private matter, one's gender is something that can literally be gauged at face value on an album cover or music video (if not a tabloid magazine).

Moreover, there is a very self-conscious, even autobiographical, dimension to Springsteen's stance toward masculinity, one that makes this chapter somewhat different than the preceding ones in this book. Springsteen may be an innovative commentator on republicanism or the work ethic, but his responses to such subjects are often unwitting and in any case are not necessarily central to what he thinks his work is about. The same cannot be said of this topic. "A lot of [my] music is focused around what defines my manhood to me, what are my commitments—how to try to stick by them as best as possible," he said in 1992. Far more than elsewhere, then, tracking Springsteen's own personal development is crucial to understanding that music. Such an understanding hinges not on any one song in particular (the way, say, "Born in the U.S.A." is a compressed history of the Vietnam War), but rather in the *story* that can be told through a *series* of songs over a quarter of a century. Actually, it would be more accurate to speak of *stories;* manhood is an inevitably plural term, encompassing a variety of roles and realms in everyday life. These stories, in turn, are a part of a much larger, older, and ongoing national drama about manhood in America.

BROTHERHOOD

> *. . . The one I love lay sleeping by me under the same cover*
> *in the cool night,*
> *In the stillness in the autumn moonbeams his face was*
> *inclined toward me,*
> *And his arm lay lightly around my breast—and that night I*
> *was happy.*

> —Walt Whitman, "When I Heard
> at the Close of Day"

The boys of Clary's gang had heard that Abe Lincoln was not a bad fellow. Bill Clary, who ran a saloon in the growing frontier settlement of New Salem, had heard the nineteen-year-old newcomer described at length by his friend Denton Offutt, who had teamed up with Lincoln in 1831 and started a general store. There were stories about Lincoln's honesty, like the one in which he had walked six miles to pay back a woman a few cents he had accidentally overcharged her. But what really interested Clary was Offutt's claim that Lincoln was an excellent wrestler. He bet Offutt the princely sum of ten dollars that Lincoln could not defeat Jack Armstrong, the reigning Clary's Grove champion. At Offutt's urging, Lincoln reluctantly accepted the challenge.

Spectators came from miles around to witness the event, wagering knives, trinkets, drinks, and cash. Armstrong, short and powerful, sought to close in on Lincoln and exploit his own superior strength. The gangly Lincoln literally sought to keep Armstrong at arm's length and wear him down. There are conflicting accounts of what happened next; a number of historians think Lincoln may have beaten Armstrong, only to be threatened en masse by the gang. In any case, all accounts agree that Armstrong stepped forward and offered Lincoln his hand. From then on, the new arrival had the permanent respect and affection of the boys of Clary's Grove.

This is an old, perhaps apocryphal story, from a world very different than ours. And yet the fundamental dynamics of the situation are very familiar. In fact, they elucidate the values of what historian E. Anthony Rotundo describes as the "boy culture" of the nineteenth century, values that remain a part of the boy culture of our time: courage (in this case, a physical challenge and a willingness to take on all comers); loyalty (for Lincoln, in honoring Offutt's commitment; for the Clary's Grove boys, in defending Armstrong—and befriending Lincoln); mastery (wrestling talent on Armstrong's part, and probably Lincoln's as well); and, above all, independence (Lincoln's willingness to enter an unfamiliar social milieu). Certainly, these are not values limited to boys, who in this story were probably what we would call adolescents or even young adults, nor are they without appeal to women. But it is also clear that boy culture values have distinctive accents, such as an emphasis on physical prowess, or a tendency to resist adult authority.

Contemporary popular culture is a vast repository for depictions of boy culture. Hollywood is a particular storehouse; *Diner, Glory,* and *Dead Poets Society,* to cite three very different movies from the 1980s, all depict groups of young males trying to maintain a code of boy culture values even as they navigate the shoals of the larger society. But perhaps the preeminent home for boy culture is popular music—from the relative innocuousness of the Beatles to the deadly stakes of Tupac Shakur, it has been an often obsessive focus in art and life.

Few artists have premised their careers on male bonding to the extent Bruce Springsteen has. That in itself is less important, however, than the high degree of self-consciousness that has accompanied Springsteen's depiction of same-sex friendship, and its evolution over time. While for most men such relationships are often (literally) outgrown, for him they have been a matter of lifelong concern.

Springsteen's early albums depict an adolescent milieu of street brawling, car racing, and constant partying, one usually dominated by boys. With a cast of characters having names like Hazy Davy, Wild Billy, and Killer Joe, "Spirit in the Night" typifies this world:

Now the night was bright and the stars threw light
On Billy and Davy dancin' in the moonlight
They were down near the water in a stone mud fight
Killer Joe gone passed out on the lawn

Killer Joe notwithstanding, this is a vividly animated world; even the darkness is "bright." Stars don't simply shine light; they *throw* it. In fact, Springsteen elsewhere describes these characters as *built* like light, and their dance reflects a kind of boundless energy. Such images are common on Springsteen's first two albums. "The kids down there are either dancin' or hooked up in a scuffle," observes the narrator of "The E Street Shuffle" of a typical street scene of stylized mayhem.

The narrators of these songs note such activities with amusement, but they're never wholly detached from this adolescent world, even when they've presumably outgrown it. "Well, my feet finally took root in the earth," says the narrator of "Growin' Up" in one of the rare uses of the past tense on either *Greetings from Asbury Park* or *The Wild, the Innocent, and the E Street Shuffle*. "But I got me a nice little place in the stars." And with that he's off again, resuming a catalog of further adventures with a zeal that seems very much present tense.

Women (or perhaps more accurately, girls) are present on these albums, not only as romantic interests that have been part of Springsteen's music from the very beginning, but also in accounts of boyish adventure. So girls really are allowed in the clubhouse. Yet for all their sexuality, women like Crazy Janey of "Spirit in the Night," who join Hazy Davy and company at Greasy Lake, are virtually one of the guys—or at any rate, are women in what is clearly a man's world. Otherwise, they are the "little pretties" who attend the rock shows described in "Tenth Avenue Freeze-Out" and who are appreciated but viewed largely from a distance.

Perhaps the most striking characteristic of Springsteen's first three albums is the intensely social quality of his settings: his characters are almost always in groups, a kind of pack mentality characteristic of young males. "The midnight gang's assembled, and picked a rendevous for the night," explains the narrator on "Jungleland." Later, he notes, there will be an "opera" on the turnpike, and a "ballet" in the alley, metaphors for street fights that emphasize their collective—and romantic—qualities.

Indeed, there's an almost erotic subtext animating many of these encounters. Here again, there is little that is new. When Lincoln left New Salem for the growing city of Springfield in 1837, he kept his lodging costs low by sharing a bed with his friend Joshua Speed. It seems unlikely that they ever did more than just that. As a number of historians have argued, the concept of homosexuality is a largely twentieth-century invention. Ironically, the fact that same-sex relations were so thoroughly beyond the pale legitimated a much wider range of contact than was common later; as Rotundo explains in his book *American Manhood*, "a man who kissed or embraced an intimate male friend in bed did not worry about homosexual impulses because he did not assume he had them." Only after anxieties about race and gender intensified at the turn of the century—typified by Theodore Roosevelt's insistence on "the strenuous life"—did the line between what we now call gay and straight sharpen.

Yet even in a century with pronounced sexual anxiety over homosexuality, boy culture has always allowed a measure of what Walt Whitman called "adhesiveness" between men. Nowhere has this continuity with older forms of male bonding been more obvious than in the archetypal rock and roll band. For all the connotations of modernity and rebellion we commonly associate with rock, it has in this context been positively Victorian. The reasons are obvious enough: until recently, rock and roll has been a largely male enclave; it has celebrated the rootlessness and antiauthoritarianism characteristic of boy culture; and it has made male bonding a virtual fetish, from the coy dancing inmates of "Jailhouse Rock" (1957) to Thin Lizzy's "The Boys Are Back in Town" (1976). Indeed, rock has allowed presumably heterosexual men so much homoerotic license—consider all that makeup Mick Jagger wore in the sixties and seventies—that it provided more than adequate cover for secretly gay men, like Elton John and Freddie Mercury of Queen, to do likewise without the fear of reprisals from rock fans whose hatred of disco in the seventies was rooted in no small amount of homophobia.

Like other classic rock groups, Bruce Springsteen's E Street Band was celebrated as a male fraternity by members and fans alike (at least until the mid-eighties, when Patti Scialfa joined it). Springsteen has never exhibited the kind of sexual flamboyance of the Rolling Stones or David Bowie—indeed, his work may be viewed as an oblique rejection of their European decadence—but his performances are marked by a surprising amount of sexual subversion. It is most apparent in the case of his relationship with Clarence Clemons, with whom his contact ranged from their affectionate pose on the cover of *Born to Run* to the exuberant kisses they routinely exchanged during live shows. Springsteen showed similiar intimacy with guitarist Steve Van Zandt in the way they gazed into each other's eyes while sharing a microphone throughout any given evening.

Such intimacy, sexual or otherwise, diminishes markedly with the release of *Darkness on the Edge of Town* in 1978. It's not altogether clear why this happens. Perhaps Springsteen's legal problems with manager Mike Appel, problems that put his career in hiatus for months (and delayed his next album for years), played a role in distancing him from a boy culture still very much present on *Born to Run*. More generally, simple aging may have played a role. In any case, the men of *Darkness* are largely isolated. Although many of these songs do feature men in groups, a feeling of solidarity is largely missing, unless it is that of a passively shared oppression. In a sense, *Darkness* is an album about the transition to adulthood— "Mister, I ain't a boy, no I'm a man," declares the protagonist of "The Promised Land"—and the end of the often nurturing relationships of adolescence. To become a man, apparently, means going off on one's own. So, for example, the narrator of "Darkness on the Edge of Town" stands alone on a hill, cut off not only from his wife but also the car racing that used to be a big part of his life. Never again would Springsteen *write* about brotherhood with quite the same insouciance of his early career, even if he continued to *perform* rituals of brotherhood on stage.

BLOOD BROTHERS: Springsteen with longtime friend and saxophone player Clarence Clemons in a characteristic pose. Springsteen's depiction of male relationships crosses boundaries of race, age, and sexual preference.

This is not to say that Springsteen lost sincere feelings of fraternity with his fellow men. Quite the contrary. But his records of the 1980s and '90s are marked by a more bittersweet quality, a consciousness of loss that always seems at least implicit and is sometimes a good deal more than that.

This sense of love and loss is especially powerful in one of Springsteen's few songs that explicitly deals with brotherhood in a literal sense: "Highway Patrolman," from *Nebraska*. "Highway Patrolman" tells the story of Joe Roberts and his wayward sibling, Frankie. The two men are bound by a lifetime of shared experiences, which extends to both of them dancing with Joe's wife, Maria. From such past pleasures a tie of loyalty is formed. This sense of loyalty has a dark side—Joe is, after all, abetting the escape of a likely felon—but as he explains, "when it's your brother sometimes you look the other way." The brother here is literal, of course, but the implications are broader.

By the time of *Born in the U.S.A.*, the valedictory strain in Springsteen's vision of brotherhood became the central theme of a number of tracks, notably "Bobby Jean." A song of farewell to a cherished friend (reputedly Steve Van Zandt, who left the E Street Band in 1984), "Bobby Jean" describes two sixteen-year-olds who were inseparable companions. "There ain't nobody, nowhere, nohow/who could ever understand me the way you did," explains the singer. The language here might be that used by a lover; indeed, the name Bobby Jean is ambiguous enough to refer to a female as well as a male. Only the typically male wanderlust and rock band solidarity the song describes lead one to conclude that it is an ode to friendship rather than romance. But in contrast to "Growin' Up," the pastness of these experiences is emphatic, so much so that for characters like the aging baseball player of "Glory Days," they become oppressive, almost pathetic.

At their best, however, memories of a shared past are not a burden but a valuable resource that enriches the present. "No

Surrender," which precedes "Bobby Jean" on the second side of *Born in the U.S.A.*, includes accounts of happy childhood memories—cutting classes, listening to music, and swearing blood oaths. But harsh realities also intrude:

> *Now young faces grow sad and old*
> *And hearts of fire grow cold*
> *We swore blood brothers against the wind*
> *Now I'm ready to grow young again*
> *And hear your sister's voice calling us home*
> *Across the open yards*
> *Well maybe we could cut someplace of our own*
> *With these drums and these guitars*

As with "Bobby Jean," it's easy to read an autobiographical subtext here, for Springsteen did indeed "cut someplace" of his own. But what does it mean to grow young again? Springsteen offers his answer in the final verse:

> *I want to sleep beneath peaceful skies*
> *In my lover's bed*
> *With a wide open country in my eyes*
> *And these romantic dreams in my head*

What seems to happen is that a boy's aspirations for male friendship get transferred to another person (usually a woman) with whom such possibilities may yet be realized. In other words, this character grows—but not gives—up. There is loss in this development, but hope, too, and in this version of the song, buoyed by its garage-rock arrangement, that hopeful quality is stronger than the elegiac one.

In the decade following *Born in the U.S.A.*, however, Springsteen showed distinctly less interest in male friendship. *Tunnel of Love, Human Touch,* and *Lucky Town* all focus on other aspects of masculinity. (When Springsteen included "No Surrender" on *Live*

1975–85, he chose a slow, acoustic version that underlined the song's melancholy elements.) In these years, marriage and children were his primary interest.

The release of *Greatest Hits* in 1995 spurred Springsteen to make, in the words of Walt Whitman's 1889 edition of *Leaves of Grass,* "a backward glance o'er travel'd roads." In the case of male relationships, the primary evidence for this reassessment are two previously unreleased songs included at the end of the album, "Blood Brothers" and "This Hard Land." "We played king of the mountain/out on the end/The world came chargin' up the hill/ and we were women and men," begins this narrator, neatly encapsulating many of the elements of boy culture discussed here. Yet it's the burdens of adulthood that dominate the song, from the mundane struggles of everyday life to the memories of those who have "fallen in their tracks." Unlike the singer of "No Surrender," the key issue for this man is not to grow young again, but rather to find a way to age gracefully. "I'll keep movin' through the dark with you in my heart," he concludes, offering a vision of dignified adulthood that rejects stasis even as it honors the past.

Somewhat more romantic in outlook is "This Hard Land," which dates back to 1982. A song about frustrated dreams, "This Hard Land" does not really focus on brotherhood until its conclusion, but does so there in an unusually vivid way. Springsteen himself had described it in the liner notes of the album as "one of my favorite last verses":

> *Hey Frank won't ya pack your bags*
> *And meet me tonight at Liberty Hall*
> *Just one kiss from you my brother*
> *And we'll ride until we fall*
> *We'll sleep in the fields*
> *We'll sleep by the rivers*
> *And in the morning we'll make a plan*

Well if you can't make it
Stay hard, stay hungry, stay alive
And meet me in a dream of this hard land

By the end of the verse the singer almost seems to assume that Frank won't make it—a sense of fatalism pervades the song, as its very title suggests. But even unrealized dreams seem to strengthen, rather than weaken, those that embrace them. To Springsteen, it would seem that this combination of memory and hope, expressed in a boyish idiom, forms the essence of brotherhood.

If this was the end of the story, one might conclude that Springsteen had a positive—but limited—view of the role men play in each other's lives. Essentially, his work tells a tale of bonds formed in childhood that get lost in adulthood but that cast a rosy afterglow. There's little sense of men having *ongoing* relationships as adults in Springsteen's records of the seventies and eighties. In the nineties, however, a richer picture of brotherhood comes into view.

The most notable example of this development is "Streets of Philadelphia," which moves brotherhood into new realms—not simply that of a bond of blood, sex, or friendship, but love in its most physical and metaphysical dimensions. Like "Highway Patrolman," Springsteen's only other song that deals with men's relationships in an explicitly adult context, "Streets of Philadelphia" is, on the surface at least, about loss: a dying man addresses a companion. "Oh brother are you gonna leave me wastin' away?" he asks in a weary voice, seeking connection on the eve of his departure from the world. That connection is all the more important because his isolation is so great; as he explains to his partner, "Ain't no angel gonna greet me/It's just you and I my friend." Rightly or wrongly, this man feels his companion is the only soul mate he has.

There are many dimensions to this song, but one of the most

important is largely implicit: that these are two people deeply involved with each other, in a relationship that has little to do with childish antics or otherwise pressing rituals of domesticity. Indeed, their very unselfconsciousness is indicative of Springsteen's maturity; only a grown man comfortable with himself could sing these words—not simply as an act of sympathetic imagination, but as a matter of earned wisdom.

This broadening and deepening of brotherhood is reinforced throughout *The Ghost of Tom Joad.* "Sinaloa Cowboys," a more stark version of "Highway Patrolman," also deals with two siblings on the edge of the law. This time, however, both (Mexican) brothers are on the wrong side of it. Even before they entered the drug trade, their father had warned them that El Norte would extract a price from them, and it does when one is killed (blood brothers indeed). And while their tie will sustain the surviving brother—during the burial he extracts the ten thousand dollars they had hidden in the ground—so, too, will it cast an undying shadow of sorrow.

Ultimately, however, *Tom Joad's* importance as a statement about brotherhood has less to do with a particular story or lyrics than the way the album as a whole invites us to think of the term as extending beyond the realm of family or friends. In "Youngstown," a downsized steel worker tells a former employer "rich enough to forget [his] name" that he has a social obligation to the community in which he gained his wealth. The uncle of the narrator in "Straight Time" urges his nephew to resume a life of crime by saying "Charlie, remember who your friends are"—a statement which, however misguided, suggests that some ties are more important than blood. In a much more positive vein, the resolution of the racial conflict at the heart of "Galveston Bay" makes an argument for all men—even enemies—as brothers. Here is the ultimate definition of brotherhood: love that transcends boundaries.

HUSBANDRY

hus·ban·dry (noun) 1: the care of a household 2: the control or judicious use of resources: CONSERVATION
— *Webster's Seventh New Collegiate Dictionary*

Bruce Springsteen emerged as a songwriter in the 1970s at a crucial juncture in the history of love and marriage, when the advent of the women's movement actively questioned—and altered—the social rules governing relations between the sexes. There is little indication that he took any formal interest in the movement either in his public statements or in his songs. Nonetheless, in tracing the trajectory of his music in the quarter century since he began making records, one can discern a clear pattern of accommodation to the social changes wrought by feminism without an enervating compromise of male sexual identity.

Like many boys who grew up where and when he did, Springsteen was no paragon of feminist enlightenment. The 1950s are widely considered a time of traditional sex roles, the age of *Father Knows Best*, when men labored in the workforce, women stayed at home to raise children, and gender inequality (like the sexual double standard) was a fact of life. While this perception is something of a distortion—Springsteen's mother, Adele, like many working-class women of the time, continued to work for wages— its power was greater in the early postwar era than it was before or after the Cold War.

There is little indication that Springsteen ever aspired to be a traditional family man. But even as a self-styled rebel against the deadening conventions of working-class life, he appears to have unconsciously absorbed very traditional ideas about women and sex. In many of his most famous songs—"Thunder Road," "Born to Run," and "Racing in the Street"—it is the man who is unambiguously (and uncritically) placed in the driver's seat.

There is, however, another side to this story: a strain of sexual egalitarianism, one that corresponds to other forms of egalitarianism in Springsteen's work, that has been apparent from the very beginning. As noted, Springsteen casually integrated women like Crazy Janey of "Spirit in the Night" into predominately male settings throughout his early career. Moreover, when one moves away from such group settings into those of intimacy, women come into their own more decisively.

There is no finer example of this egalitarianism at work than "For You," from *Greetings*. This is an insouciant song with prolix lyrics so characteristic of Springsteen's early work. But it is more focused than most, and despite its breezy tone, more serious. Its narrator addresses a woman who has apparently attempted suicide. But he refuses to let her illness excuse her behavior:

> *Honey get your carpetbaggers off my back*
> *You wouldn't even give me time to cover my tracks*
> *You say, "Here's your mirror and your ball of jacks,"*
> *But they're not what I came for*
> *And I'm sure you see that's true*
> *I came for you . . .*

For all his obvious affection, he's mad at her, and it's a measure of his respect that he refuses to let her illness (or the "carpetbaggers" around her) excuse her behavior. Ensuing verses describe a relationship between outsiders, outsiders who have generally interacted as equals but who have periodically exchanged the upper hand: "Remember how I kept you waiting/when it was my turn to be the God?" It's not clear exactly why this woman is in such trouble, but the sheer energy of the song makes it hard not to believe the kids are all right. In any case, "For You" showcases a recurrent Springsteen vision of love as partnership.

"Fourth of July, Asbury Park (Sandy)" also illuminates Springsteen's vision of romance as partnership. Like many songs in his early work, "Sandy" is characterized by affectionate descriptions of boy culture. But now there's an almost imperceptible irony directed at the adolescent narcissism of "the boys from the casino who dance with their shirts half open." The narrator admits that such immaturity has also characterized his own life. His relationship with a waitress, marked by a similar gaudiness, is now over ("she won't set herself on fire for me anymore"), and he asks Sandy to be his companion on a quest for something more meaningful: "For me this boardwalk life's through/You oughta quit this scene too." Here again, friend becomes lover while remaining an equal.

Such an approach to romance has its risks, of course. "Backstreets," from *Born to Run*, shows what happens when the foundations of an egalitarian relationship are shattered. "One soft infested summer me and Terry became friends," this narrator begins (note the description of their relationship as a friendship, and Terry's androgynous name, both of which reinforce a feeling of underlying kinship). They're romantic rebels who dance in the dark, huddle together in cars, and roam the backstreets of the title until Terry leaves him for another man. Terry ultimately returns, but this cannot erase the narrator's bitterness:

Laying here in the dark
You're just an angel on my chest
Just another tramp of hearts
Crying tears of faithlessness
Remember all the movies, Terry
We'd go see
Trying to learn to walk like the heroes
We thought we had to be
And to find out after all this time
We're just like all the rest
Stranded in the park
And forced to confess to
Hiding on the backstreets . . .

One could say that this man, who sings these lines in agony, is being a little histrionic here, perhaps even vindictive. He's less mature, still invested in fantasies that the protagonist of "Sandy," for example, has begun to question. As a character in a story, however, he's quite compelling, and it's clear that in this moment of disillusionment what he mourns is not simply one person's unfaithfulness but a sense of shared hope between equals. "'Backstreets' establishes a situation in which a man and a woman are not just lovers, but best friends," Springsteen biographer Dave Marsh has written. "If she seems a dream, that's only because she is an equal—something people rarely are in life."

The women of Springsteen's best songs are also girls who want to have fun, gaining rights of uncensored sexual expression generally denied women in pop music until the 1980s. "Fire," the song he wrote for Elvis Presley but which became a top-ten hit for the Pointer Sisters in 1978 (it is included on *Live 1975–85)* is all about sex, and the ambiguous reality that no really does sometimes mean yes. The *Nebraska* couple of "Open All Night" experience so much pleasure from eating that it takes on sensual overtones:

> I met Wanda when she was employed behind
> the counter at the Route 60 Bob's Big Boy
> fried chicken on the front seat, she's sittin' in my lap
> wipin' her fingers on a Texaco road map
> I remember Wanda on Scrap Metal Hill
> with the big brown eyes that make your heart stand still

At the same time, neither sex in particular or a man in general can always be an adequate source of satisfaction. As literary critic Martha Nell Smith notes in her insightful essay on sexuality in Springsteen's music, in "Candy's Room," there is "no man," not even the one who loves her, who "can keep Candy safe." This is a point Springsteen would go on to make repeatedly, as in *The River's* "Point Blank," whose female character waits not on Romeos but on welfare checks; *Nebraska's* "Used Cars," in which a mother nervously fingers her wedding band while her husband impotently negotiates with a car salesman; and in *Tunnel of Love's* "Spare Parts," in which a mother discards her hope of romance in order to become a more focused and effective parent.

What's really striking about Springsteen's vision of women, though, is the way neither sexual aggression nor economic independence need compromise a femininity valued by men and women alike. Ever since the seventies, Americans have wrestled with whether the feminist quest for social equality required a surrender of customs (like men holding doors for women) and protections (such as sexual harrassment laws), which, however limited, are nevertheless of real value to women in traditional relationships or other situations. Are such customs, protections, and differences— often labeled "chivalry"—practical, or even permissible, in a world where men and women are truly equal?

Springsteen has offered an oblique answer to this question in his decision to perform and record the Tom Waits song "Jersey Girl," which closes *Live 1975–85*. In the song, a man's efforts on his lover's behalf are rooted in a deep understanding of her (ongoing) struggles, as well as her desire to express herself through heterosexual romance.

> *I see you on the street and you look so tired*
> *I know that job you got leaves you uninspired*
> *When I come by to take you out to eat*
> *You're lyin' on the bed fast asleep*
> *Go in the bathroom and put your makeup on*
> *We're gonna take that little brat of yours*
> *And drop her off at your mom's*
> *I know a place where the dancin's free*
> *Now baby won't you come with me*

The issue here is less a matter of equality or chivalry than simple consideration. Without ever explicitly saying so, this is a man who sees a worker, a (single) parent, and a woman who needs romance in her life to sustain all these roles. A philosophically consistent answer on the issue of sexual difference and social equality is less compelling than a pragmatic stance of generosity—a value which neither is nor should be gendered.

This sense of imaginative projection, of empathy, also animates Springsteen's more traditionally male stances. By the 1980s, even his odes to lust implicitly acknowledge other perspectives. "Darlington County" is sung from the point of view of a guy trying to pick up women, but his charm stems from his sense of irony, even absurdity: "Our pa's each own one of the World Trade Centers/For a kiss and a smile I'll give mine all to you." The narrator of "Dancing in the Dark" makes a John Wayne–esque declaration that "This gun's for hire," but does so acknowledging his personal frustrations (the very title of the song is a metaphor for making the most of a life constrained by limitations).

Even "I'm on Fire," arguably Springsteen's most machismo song, is marked by such countercurrents. "Hey little girl is your daddy home/did he go and leave you all alone," this man begins, blurring the line between lover and parent (the understated, even smoldering mood of the music greatly contributes to the power of the song). Either way, however, the narrator's characterization of his rival is plain: he's inadequate—and absent. But then he makes a stark confession:

> Sometimes it's like somebody took a knife baby edgy and dull
> And cut a six-inch valley in the middle of my skull
> At night I wake up with the sheets soaking wet
> And a freight train running through the middle of my head
> Only you can cool my desire
> I'm on fire

He's telling her that she needs him—but also that he needs her. Far from playing hard to get, he's conveying that need with frightening intensity.

The complexities of "I'm on Fire" to some degree reflect Springsteen's own personal development and evolving preoccupations. By the time he was writing this material, he was well into his thirties, a time when a man is often making, or consolidating, lifetime commitments. "Everyone seems to hunger for THAT relationship and you never seem happy without it. I think you do tend to think about that particular thing around thirty," he said in 1981, when he was thirty-one and still years away from marriage himself but apparently considering it. "But even up until then, when I was writing all the earlier songs, 'Born to Run' and stuff, they just never seemed right without the girl. It was just part of whatever that person was doing. It wasn't gonna be any good without her."

Still, however important love is to the men who populate Springsteen albums from *Greetings* to *Born in the U.S.A.*, it's always to some degree secondary. To invoke Springsteen's formulation, "Born to Run" wouldn't quite sound right without the girl, but the girl somehow wasn't the core issue. How a man might *sustain* a relationship; whether a life *centered* on romantic partnership might be worth pursuing; what it actually *means* to be a man: these are questions that went largely unexplored from the early seventies through the mid-eighties.

Then, during his tour to support *Born in the U.S.A.*, Springsteen met actress/model Julianne Phillips, whom he married in 1985. To the casual observer, this seemed like an understandable, even typical move in an age of postfeminist celebrity. Rock star/model-actress marriages were particularly common: in the mid-eighties, Billy Joel and Christie Brinkley, Mötley Crüe drummer Tommy Lee and Heather Locklear, and Whitesnake vocalist David Coverdale and Tawny Kitaen were all celebrated as two-career couples who also happened to be sex symbols—sex symbols whose beauty and flaunted sexuality nevertheless embodied very conventional, even rigid, notions of manhood and womanhood. (All of these marriages, perhaps not incidentally, ended in divorce.)

But while Springsteen shared space in *People* with all these figures, it became clear relatively quickly that for him marriage was not simply a good public relations move. Upon completing his tour, he established a new life rooted in heterosexual domesticity, and with the release of *Tunnel of Love* in 1987, inaugurated a new phase in his life and work. Unlike any record he had made before, *Tunnel of Love* was a virtual concept album about love and marriage, with romance as the explicit theme of every song. While this is not especially surprising—the same could conceivably be said of albums by Mötley Crüe and Whitesnake—the degree of complexity and turbulence that marked the record far exceeded that of any of his counterparts, including the often reflective Joel.

But *Tunnel of Love* is more than a document of Springsteen's marital difficulties. It also charts the difficulties at the end of the twentieth century for men and women grappling with changing expectations, as women increasingly took on roles that had once been the sole province of men, and men were expected to show a new awareness of, and willingness to adjust to, the wishes of women. Springsteen's strategy in navigating these currents has involved retaining traditionally gendered words and concepts but endowing them with a broader, more flexible meaning.

Take, for example, "toughness," a long-standing masculine ideal. On the surface, at least, the song "Tougher Than the Rest" sounds like an old-fashioned assertion of a man's value. "Well it's Saturday night/You're all dressed up in blue," Springsteen drawls to a slow, chugging rhythm, sounding, in fact, very much like a tough guy. (It's worth noting parenthetically, however, that the girl wears blue, stereotypically a "boy" color, and that the video for the song features gay couples fleetingly interspersed with straight ones.) But what exactly does toughness mean? Physical strength? A hard-boiled style? This character elaborates an answer in the final verse:

> *Well it ain't no secret*
> *I've been around a time or two*
> *Well I don't know, maybe you've been around too*
> *Well there's another dance*
> *All you gotta do is say yes*
> *And if you're rough and ready for love*
> *Honey I'm tougher than the rest*

For all his laconic, competitive assertions, it's clear that for this man, toughness means a willingness to work at romance and to endure its disappointments. By this standard, women have to be tough, too, i.e., "rough and ready for love." Although rooted in a male lexicon, Springsteen intends the term to have non-gendered applications.

Although never invoked so directly, toughness is upheld as a necessary quality throughout *Tunnel of Love* because, far from offering refuge or release, even the most successful relationships are depicted as often dogged struggles. If amusement park rides in "Sandy" were an *unwanted* diversion from the real world, and those of "Jersey Girl" a *welcome* diversion from the real world, the roller coaster of "Tunnel of Love" is inextricably *part of* the real world, a place where hopes and fears surrounding romance are as present as anywhere else. Nevertheless, while love may be a struggle, it still beats the alternative, as the abandoned, but more experienced, lover of "When You're Alone" tells his partner. "There's things that'll knock you down that you don't even see coming," he tells her. While he can sympathize with and even forgive her need to light out on her own, he won't be able to simply forget about it if she does. "Now it ain't hard feelings or nothin', sugar," he says. "It's just nobody knows, honey, where love goes/But when it's goes it's gone, gone." Here, too, is a kind of toughness: a sober-minded realism about the rules of love, and an acceptance of that which is beyond one's control.

But the great paradox of *Tunnel of Love* is that a man does have some control over his feelings, and the most successful of them master the most potentially destructive impulse of all: a man's thirst for control over the terms of his relationships. This thirst, and the struggle to contain it, is one of the most important themes of the album, conveyed in a number of songs that unfold like parables.

A case in point is "Cautious Man." The third-person narrator of this story/song describes a protagonist named Bill Horton, who, "when something caught his eye, he'd measure his need/And then very carefully he'd proceed." Horton's fear of commitment makes him seem like an old man and an immature boy simultaneously. Nevertheless, not even he can resist the appeal of love as he meets, and marries, a young woman. But in the fright of a bad dream, he prepares to flee the fears love seems to have unleashed. Then, in a moment of clarity, he realizes when he gets to the highway that "he didn't see nothin' but road." Exchanging an unproductive superstition for a promising reality, he heads back home, brave enough to face the ongoing risks domestication offers.

Other men are not so fortunate. "You play the loving woman/I'll play the faithful man," says the suspicious husband of "Brilliant Disguise," locked in a struggle for control with his wife in a war of perceptions. The barfly husband of "One Step Up," by contrast, honestly professes his love for his wife, but can't quite change "the same old act" that leads him to flee home (again). And Bobby, the deadbeat lover and father of "Spare Parts," leaves home for good rather than accept responsibility for his actions. None of these men are able to trust, accept, or sacrifice in ways that would allow them to achieve a fuller sense of manhood.

Taken as a whole, *Tunnel of Love* articulates what might be called a "Springsteenian" definition of manhood as a form of emotional investment and risk-taking, a willingness to participate in the building of something larger than oneself. This is not a radical departure from boy culture, which also prizes courage and teamwork. But the ends toward which Springsteen applies these values are at once broader, deeper, and more inclusive than the often parochial goals (like wrestling matches) of boys.

Human Touch and *Lucky Town*, released in the aftermath of Springsteen's divorce from Phillips and subsequent marriage to E Street vocalist Patti Scialfa, builds on this new model of manhood. In the case of *Human Touch*, this includes a rejection of traditional machismo. Back on *The River*, one of Springsteen's characters boasted of having the sexual powers of James Dean or a secret agent man in "I'm a Rocker." But the protagonist of "Real Man" doesn't "need no gun in my fist" to prove his masculinity. The love of a good woman matters far more to him than the superficial heroism of a Rambo or a James Bond.

A similar skepticism about the accepted conventions of romance marks "Real World." "Ain't no church bells ringing/Ain't no flags unfurled," he says in the chorus. "Just you and me and the love we're bringing/Into the real world." Conversely, the reluctant but decisive break that is the subject of "The Long Goodbye" stems from a realization that a man has lived under false pretenses. "Sure did like that admirin' touch/Guess I liked it a little too much," he explains.

Springsteen's penchant for taking accepted ideas and terminology for manhood and reconfiguring them receives its supreme expression in "Man's Job." Other songs in the Springsteen canon may be emotionally richer or more artistically satisfying, but "Man's Job" is notable for the way in which it sums up his masculine ethos. For that reason, it is worth exploring in some detail.

"Man's Job" has a venerable musical pedigree. Although its production is crisper and cleaner (some might say whiter) than its forebears, it has a traditional R & B groove characteristic of the soul music of the late sixties produced by artists like Sam & Dave, whose hit singles "Soul Man," "Hold On! I'm Comin'," and "When Something Is Wrong with My Baby" (all 1967) articulate a male ethos similar to Springsteen's. In fact, Sam Moore himself appears on "Man's Job," sharing vocals with Springsteen there and elsewhere on *Human Touch*. His presence is indicative of Springsteen's acute sense of musical tradition and acknowledgment of the sources for his own vision of manhood.

"Man's Job" is a monologue song in which a man in a romantic triangle argues for his worthiness for the heart of a woman.

> *Well you can go out with him*
> *Play with all of his toys*
> *But takin' care of you darlin'*
> *Ain't for one of the boys*

The key words here are "toys" and "boys," both of which imply immaturity, and, thus, unfitness for a successful relationship. Yet this character is not content simply to dismiss her choice of a competitor as child's play; he asserts that she's involved in a dangerously reckless game.

> *Oh there's something in your soul*
> *That he's gonna rob*
> *And loving you baby, lovin' you darlin'*
> *Loving you woman is a man's man's job*

The progression from "baby" to "darlin'" to "woman" charts a spectrum from dependency to maturity that accentuates the power and appeal of "woman." Simultaneously, Springsteen reorients the phrase "man's job," which traditionally refers to hard physical labor, toward the arduous task of maintaining and building a relationship. This "man's man's job" is in contrast to a "ladies' man" job—i.e., a con job marked by stealth and weakness.

> *Well now his kisses may thrill*
> *Those other girls that he likes*
> *But when it comes to treatin'*
> *A real woman right*

Well all of his tricks
They won't be enough
'Cause lovin' you baby, lovin' you woman
Is a man's man's job . . .

"Boys" rely on mere sexual appeal. "Men" focus their energy on "women" (as opposed to "girls") and true consideration of what they want or need.

Thus far, the tone here has been one of certitude. But then, in a move that gives the song much of its drama, the cool, collected veneer of the narrator is shattered at the bridge:

You're dancing with him, he's holding you tight
I'm standin' here waiting to catch your eye
Your hand's on his neck as the music sways
All my illusions slip away

As in any good story, there is a moment of doubt. This man may have worked out a clear argument, but it doesn't mean he's persuaded her—or himself. Having taken a risk in pressing his claim, he now pays the price of humiliation. In fact, we never finally learn whether he wins this woman's hand, but he ultimately persists in his pursuit, in the process further amplifying his sense of manhood:

Well if you're looking for a hero
Someone to save the day
Well darlin' my feet
They're made of clay
But I've got something in my soul
And I wanna give it up
But gettin' up the nerve, gettin' up the nerve
Gettin' up the nerve is a man's man's job

In short, real strength means acknowledging weakness. Real mastery of one's self allows one to become vulnerable to another. Real freedom lies in the power to make lasting commitments.

The songs of *Lucky Town*, which evinces a masculine ideal close to the ethos of "Man's Job," are more intimate, less focused on common social situations than on deeply personal, even autobiographical ones. This intimacy is obvious, for example, in "If I Should Fall Behind," where a man describes his relationship with his fiancée as a partnership, one in which he is as likely as she is to need help:

Now everyone dreams of a love lasting and true
But you and I know what this world can do
So let's make our steps clear so the other may see
And I'll wait for you
If I should fall behind
Wait for me

What might otherwise be a fairly conventional expression of lifelong commitment is textured by its allusions to hard-earned experience ("you and I know what this world can do"), and the way in which a frank recognition of personal limitations is linked with—even a condition for—marital success. If these are not actually convictions acquired in the aftermath of a failed marriage, they are clearly those of a man who hopes that the lessons of past missteps can help him overcome future ones.

With "Book of Dreams," however, Springsteen brings the accumulated experience that accompanies mature visions of manhood full circle. The first verse is paradigmatic of the song as a whole:

I'm standin' in the backyard
Listenin' to the party inside
Tonight I'm drinkin' in the forgiveness
This life provides
The scars we carry remain
But the pain slips away it seems
Oh won't you, baby, be in my book of dreams

"Book of Dreams" is a joyful song, but quietly, meditatively so. The happiness has a dappled quality, mixed with sorrows that remain but somehow leaven the proceedings. "We dance 'neath the stars' ancient light into the darkening trees," the groom explains, in characteristically chiaroscuro language, enumerating a series of wedding rituals (the bride showing off her wedding dress to her friends, toasts being offered, and the couple meeting under a wedding garland) with a savored, self-conscious quality. At the same time, however, that chorus—"Oh won't you, baby, be in my book of dreams"—has an adolescent, even innocent quality. It sounds like a line a girl group like the Ronettes might have sung in the early sixties. A wise man, Springsteen seems to be saying, always retains the wonder of a child.

FATHERHOOD

Some people get a chance to change the world, and other people, they get a chance to make sure the world don't fall apart.
—BRUCE SPRINGSTEEN ON HIS FATHER, 1980

Bruce Springsteen has been more open about his relationship with his father than any other aspect of his life. He's done so not through his songs per se—Springsteen tends to relate experience in figurative or emotional terms rather than literal ones—but rather in his live performances, especially the monologues he uses to introduce songs. His father frequently surfaces as a character in these and other stories—as a hectoring critic, as an enraged authority figure, and as an innocent victim of social forces beyond his control.

Commenting on an early postwar photograph of his father in his soldier's uniform, Springsteen once said, "He looked like John Garfield in this great suit, like he was going to eat the photographer's head off. I couldn't ever remember him looking that defiant or proud when I was growing up. I used to wonder what happened to all that pride, how it turned into so much bitterness." What happened, it would seem, is what had already happened to generations of working-class men before Douglas Springsteen. For a century now, middle- and upper-class American fathers have wrestled with their responsibilities to their children, navigating between their own aspirations, the findings of social scientists, and challenges to their prerogatives by feminists. For many working-class fathers, however, such issues were (and remain) largely beside the point. Tethered to tedious jobs with long hours and little pay, such men were often remote from their children, literally as well as emotionally.

Based on Springsteen's own recollections, Douglas Springsteen was very much a father in this tradition—loving but taciturn, frustrated and frustrating. "My father, he worked in a lot of places, worked in a rug mill for a while, drove a cab for a while, and he was a guard at the jail for a while. I can remember when he used to work down there, he used to always come home real pissed off, drunk, sit in the kitchen," Springsteen related as a means of introducing a cover version of the Animals song "It's My Life." "At night, at about nine o'clock, he used to shut off all the lights, every light in the house. And he used to get real pissed if me or my sister turned any of 'em on. And he'd sit in the kitchen with a six-pack and a cigarette."

The point of this and similar stories was to show how the frustrations of the father would eventually be vented on the son—in some cases quite literally, as in this story, included as part of a 1978 version of "Growin' Up" on *Live 1975–85:*

> When I was growing up, there were two things that were unpopular in my house. One was me, and the other was my guitar. We had this grate, like the heat was supposed to come through, except it wasn't hooked up to any of the

heating ducts; it was just open straight down to the kitchen, and there was a gas stove right underneath it. When I used to start playing, my pop used to turn on the gas jet and try to smoke me out of the room. And I had to go hide on the roof or something.

This is meant to be an amusing story, and Springsteen chuckles as he relates it. But a sense of resentment is also quite apparent, resentment that is finally the most salient aspect of this anecdote. But Springsteen's songs themselves are rarely quite this simple, which is one reason why his recordings are finally more complex and interesting artistic productions than his live performances are. What a monologue like this does do, however, is provide a kind of key for listening to a song (in this case, a sense of conflict that textures the generally ebullient spirit of "Growin' Up").

Indeed, monologues notwithstanding, parents are generally absent on Springsteen's first three albums. Given the adolescent settings of much of his early music—these are records of boys, not men—it's not surprising that both mothers and fathers are largely absent. Those parents who do appear, like the overbearing father of "Rosalita (Come Out Tonight)" are killjoys who in their protectiveness deprive their daughter—and the boyfriend who narrates the song—of happiness. Of the two, Rosalita's father is the more imposing figure; he's one who "lower[s] the boom" and whose knowledge of her boyfriend's penury prompts his refusal to sanction their romance. With the help of a recording contract, however, true love conquers all, including ineffectual (and largely two-dimensional) parents.

This man is *somebody else's* father. When Springsteen characters began discussing *their own* fathers, the picture changes dramatically. Gone is the relative detachment that marks a song like "Rosalita," replaced by much more active emotional involvement. Still, the terms of this new sense of engagement remain largely negative;

THE REBEL: James Dean.

loved or hated, fathers are almost always a problem to be confronted, if not solved.

Springsteen began writing a string of father-son songs in the late seventies, a time in his life when he was finally able to gain some perspective on his own troubled relationship with his father. But he also drew on pop culture sources to tell his stories. "Adam Raised a Cain," for example, was inspired by the film version of John Steinbeck's *East of Eden* (1955), in which the troubled son Cal Trask, played by James Dean, struggles to deal with the misplaced rectitude of his father, Adam, played by Raymond Massey. Douglas Springsteen lacked the wealth and standing of Adam Trask, and Springsteen himself, while something of a James Dean figure, avoided the fatalism that suffused Dean's characters. But the resulting song captured the stunted strivings that often characterize relationships between fathers and sons:

> *In the Bible Cain slew Abel*
> *And East of Eden he was cast*
> *You're born into this life payin'*
> *For the sins of somebody else's past*

The character singing these lines does so in a voice of barely restrained fury. But having an explanation for his father's bitterness tempers his own. Moreover, this son recognizes a temperamental kinship with his father: "He was standin' in the door/I was standin' in the rain/With the same hot blood burnin' in our veins."

Indeed, even at their most severe, Springsteen's sons never lose the ability to view their fathers with empathy. "Through the mansions of fear/through the mansions of pain/I see my daddy walk through those factory gates in the rain," observes the child narrator of "Factory." He may plausibly worry that he will someday face the same fate, or, more directly, that he'll be one of those people who's "gonna get hurt tonight" when the men return home from work. But even more than "Adam Raised a Cain," "Factory" suggests the increasing sophistication with which Springsteen portrays the frustrations of fathers on their own terms.

Expressing sympathy for fathers is one thing; wanting to become one is another, something no Springsteen character of the seventies wants to do. "Then I got Mary pregnant/And, man, that was all she wrote," relates the narrator of the title track of *The River.*

THE BAD BOY: Robert Mitchum.

REEL MAN: John Wayne in *Red River* (1948). Springsteen would wear similar clothes in his *Born in the U.S.A.* heyday.

Pregnancy is strictly a trip wire to disaster: prospective fatherhood precipitates a shotgun wedding, a dead-end job, crushing financial burdens, and destroys the love between two people.

If becoming a father is a drag, so, too, is remaining a son. But on "Independence Day," this no longer seems inevitable. Gentle but firm, the protagonist of this song makes a break, and does so in a way that suggests a new maturity in Springsteen's sons:

> *Well Papa go to bed now it's getting late*
> *Nothing we can say is gonna change anything now*
> *I'll be leaving in the morning from St. Mary's Gate*
> *We wouldn't change this thing even if we could somehow*

Ironically, the son here sounds positively parental, telling his father to go to bed and fatalistically concluding that things couldn't have been any different. He's thoughful, even solicitous, and he recognizes that they have a good deal in common. But he refuses to travel down the same path: "They ain't gonna do to me what I watched them do to you." In the end, independence means leaving town.

This is, of course, a standard masculine formulation, one that runs from classic westerns like *Shane* (1953) to rock songs like the Allman Brothers' "Ramblin' Man" (1973). "All men must make their way come Independence Day," intones the singer, the very title of the song comparing his break with that of the very origins of the nation. But by the early eighties, Springsteen characters are discovering that independence is not always attained by mere physical separation. In fact, it may not even really be altogether possible.

Nebraska documents a new sense of skepticism about such autonomy, especially in regard to parent-child relations. The album is haunted by sons who cannot shake off the specter of their fathers. The most obvious example is "My Father's House," in which a son wakes up to awful regret over breaking with his father, only to find that his bid for reconciliation comes too late. The child narrator of

"Used Cars" feels the sting of the petty humiliations his father endures, and makes his own declaration of (future) independence: "Now mister the day the lottery comes in/I ain't ever gonna ride no used car again." The likelihood of such an event ever coming to pass is remote, however, while that of more humiliation is not. Once a vision of contempt and anger, Springsteen's view of fathers was now one of guilt and shame.

This pall of despair began to lift in the mid-eighties, but slowly. In "My Hometown," a Springsteen character describes his experiences with his father as well as those with his son, and both relationships appear reasonably healthy. "I'd sit on his lap in that big old Buick and steer as we drove through town," the narrator relates, repeating the ritual with his own boy. But the overall thrust of the song is one of declension, as the vibrant community of the child becomes the decaying downtown of the father. However interesting the relationship between father and son may be, Springsteen's purpose is less to chart male relationships than it is to use them as a vehicle for socioeconomic commentary.

A similar investment in parenting is evident in "Seeds," from *Live 1975–85*. This father, a displaced oil worker, certainly cares for his children, but his harrowing financial straits deprive him of the ability to do so properly. "Parked in the lumberyard freezin' our asses off/My kids in the backseat with a graveyard cough," he explains. It's not this man's fault that he's living in a family in crisis—that's the point of the song, and Springsteen makes it compellingly—but it's a dysfunctional family nonetheless.

Not until *Tunnel of Love* did a fuller vision of what fatherhood could mean emerge in Springsteen's work. Perhaps his first marriage in 1985 was the catalyst, for it is in "Walk Like a Man," where a son addresses his father on his wedding day, that unambiguously positive images of paternal interaction are first described. "All I can think of is being five years old following behind you at the beach/tracing your footprints in the sand," he tells him. The son's memories are not without their shadows ("Well I was young and I didn't know what to do/When I saw your best steps stolen away from you"), and the father's experiences were of limited direct utility ("I didn't know there'd be so many steps/I'd have to learn on my own"). But father has communicated something intangibly valuable to son, something that enlivens his sense of himself as a man.

On *Tunnel of Love*, Springsteen also gives his first positive expression to what becoming a father might mean in "Valentine's Day":

> *This friend of mine became a father last night*
> *When we spoke in his voice I could hear the light*
> *Of the skies and the rivers, the timberwolf and the pines*
> *And that great jukebox out on Route 39*
> *They say who travels fastest travels alone*
> *But tonight I miss my girl mister, tonight I miss my home*

Vicariously, this man zeroes in on the heart of parenthood: a sense of connection. This can take the form of seeing unity in nature, as well as the man-made. But most important of all, it takes the form of recognizing ties to others, ties that may finally count more than a boy's dream of autonomous freedom.

When Springsteen wrote "Valentine's Day" in 1987, he had not yet become a father; the first of his three children was born in 1990. Judging from his subsequent music, fatherhood was a watershed experience. When a child is born to a subsequent Springsteen character—in *Lucky Town*'s "Living Proof"—the experience is so overwhelming that it takes on religious dimensions.

> *In his mother's arms it was all the beauty I could take*
> *Like the missing words to some prayer that I could never make*
> *In a world so hard and dirty, so fouled and confused*
> *Searching for a little bit of God's mercy, I found living proof*

Like the child of "The River," this one has transformative effects, but while that one destroys, this one resurrects. "Living

Proof" is all the more significant within the context of fifteen years of recorded indifference or anger about fatherhood on Springsteen's part. Perhaps more than any other song, it showcases a man who has finally grown up.

Ironically, one important manifestation of Springsteen's maturity is a new willingness to deal with fatherhood in ways that do not always reach epiphanal intensity. *Human Touch* closes with Springsteen's version of "Pony Boy," a playful folk song. In a very different vein, the father of "Souls of the Departed" considers murdered children in East Compton, and confronts not-altogether-honorable impulses to insulate his own:

> *Tonight as I tuck my own son in bed*
> *All I can think of is what if it would've been him instead*
> *I want to build me a wall so high nothing can burn it down*
> *Right here on my own piece of dirty ground*

In some sense, such sentiments bring us back to the issue of class and the ways in which economics shape fatherhood. The fathers of Springsteen's more recent songs, like Springsteen himself, have options that the ravaged fathers of "Seeds"—or fathers like Douglas Springsteen—did not. For these men, the issue is how they will *use* their opportunities to build strong families, not whether they'll *have* such opportunities in the first place. Perhaps a desire *for* those opportunities, whether realized or not, is one measure of mature masculinity.

Fathering, then, is not a matter of biology, and a child is not simply a matter of blood kinship. In "The New Timer," a song from *The Ghost of Tom Joad,* fatherhood is a kind of mentoring, as an old railroad hobo teaches a young man the ropes. When this father figure is senselessly murdered, the younger man thirsts for revenge. But he also thinks about the son he abandoned for a life on the road. It does not appear that he will return any time soon; although he prays to Jesus for mercy, his heart still lusts for vengeance against the old-timer's murderer. But he seems to know, if not quite feel, what being a man should really be about.

This particular Springsteen manhood story—of hostility and indifference toward fatherhood, followed by increasing engagement with and transformation into it—can be read in a number of ways. The songs discussed here, for example, chart a classic Oedipal sequence of rage, anxiety, and acceptance. But they are also redolent of a much more specific historical development: a new emphasis placed on fathering in the late twentieth century, one that can be glimpsed in phenomena ranging from childbirth classes to the furor over the fictional television character Murphy Brown's decision to raise a fatherless child. Here, as in so much else, the women's movement has played an important role. For if feminism has helped women make the psychological (if not economic) shift into the workplace, it may also be helping men make a similar shift into the home.

THE EDUCATED MAN

It is not enough, anymore, to ask that men become more like women; we should ask instead that they become instead more like what both men and women might *be.*
—BARBARA EHRENREICH, 1984

"We are living at an important and fruitful moment now, for it is clear to men that the images of adult manhood given by the popular culture are worn out," Robert Bly wrote in *Iron John*, a book that many credit with the rise of the so-called "men's movement" of the 1990s. "By the time a man is thirty-five he knows that the images of the right man, the tough man, the true man which he received in high school do not work in life. Such a man is open to new visions of what a man is or could be."

For Bly, the source of such new visions was, in fact, a very old one: folk tales. But he may have been too quick to dismiss popular culture. One can certainly see why he was tempted to do so; whether in the glamorized violence of much heavy metal or in the reductive sexuality of television shows like MTV's *Singled Out,* popular culture often panders to what is worst in us.

But that isn't all it does. Fred Astaire is as much a part of the cultural history of manhood as Rambo; the I've-been-there critique of Coolio's 1995 hit "Gangsta's Paradise" is as much a part of rap music's exploration of masculinity as Ice-T's widely denounced 1992 song "Cop Killer." Part of the responsibility—and joy—of growing up in a democratic republic lies in sorting out the various messages we receive and trying to figure out what works. As with a good woman, the most important thing one can do to become a good man is to learn how to listen.

SEVEN

Inherited Imagination
SPRINGSTEEN AND AMERICAN CATHOLICISM

In December 1969, *Playboy* magazine published an essay by literary critic and historian Leslie Fiedler, who made an arresting, if somewhat offhand, remark in the middle of the piece: "To be an American (unlike being English or French or whatever) is precisely to imagine a destiny rather than inherit one; since we have always been, insofar as we are Americans at all, inhabitants of myth rather than history." This assertion seemed to come out of nowhere, simply dropped into the text without any effort to explain or justify it. If Fiedler's remark was not quite obvious, it was nevertheless assumed to be clear—and true.

To some extent, the remark is both clear and true. "To imagine a destiny rather than inherit one" is a rather apt way of describing the American Dream. And the American Dream is precisely the kind of "myth" Fiedler was talking about: a widely shared belief that survives independently of factual verification (which, in this context, is another name for "history"). Much of this book has been written under explicitly "Fiedlerian" premises, attempting to show in any number of ways—whether in terms of upward mobility, a search for community, even sexual attitudes—that Bruce Springsteen has sought, and even succeeded, in rejecting inherited destinies in favor of imagined ones.

But there is another tradition in American life—a deep, broad, and varied tradition—that has always been skeptical of imagined destinies supplanting inherited ones. The heir of slaves who feels a bond with Africa; the child of Ellis Island immigrants who holds fast to folkways or ethnic cuisine; the woman who knows in her bones that biology is the final form of destiny: these are people who cannot (or, even believing that they have free will, *do* not) believe that inheritances can be tossed aside.

But the most powerful, long-standing source of inherited identity in American life is religion. This has been true from the very beginning. For all the energy and confidence the Puritans invested in their New World, their faith nevertheless rested on a bedrock of predestination, i.e., that a person's spiritual fate was sealed from the time of birth. It was a faith that specifically rejected the practices of a corrupt Catholicism in which heavenly grace had become a commodity bought and sold by priests and politicians in a wayward Europe.

Yet even as these Calvinists clutched their fiercely independent faith, a belief in the possibility of true believers holding fate in their own hands seeped into New England. It's not hard to understand why. Given the immensity of the hardships they faced—the fierce cold and storms, the blight of disease, the hostility of other colonial powers and heathen Indians (a hostility, it should be added, for which they bear a good deal of responsibility)—it's hard to blame them for thinking that if not actually a matter of their own will, their survival might at least be a sign that they were doing *something* right. By the mid-eighteenth century, increasing numbers of English colonials were flirting with the Dutch doctrine of Arminianism, which held that an individual was empowered to affect his or her own salvation.

By the early nineteenth century, American Protestantism was dominated by the doctrine of perfectionism, which, in marked contrast to an older Puritan theology, posited the ability of people to effect their own redemption. Perfectionism was one of the signal characteristics of the religious revivals that swept the nation in the early nineteenth century, and it soon had secular consequences, notably in the struggle to abolish slavery, which began as a religious movement and ended as a political one. Ever since, the perfectionist strain of American Protestantism has, in widely diffused or altered form, influenced a wide variety of movements, ranging from the agrarian Populism of the 1890s to the utopian counterculture of the 1960s. In this regard, the hippies of the sixties and the Christian fundamentalists of the nineties have a lot in common: both regarded the transformation of the world as possible, even inevitable. In this regard, too, one can say that the American Dream is essentially a Protestant dream, one whose origins, by however byzantine a path, can be traced to Martin Luther's decision to decide for himself—leading many other Protestant sects (and individuals) to do the same.

However, there have long been other communities in American society who could not take imagined destinies for granted, among the most prominent of whom are Catholics. Of course, at some level the Catholic tradition (and within this context, the Jewish tradition as well) emphasizes personal responsibility; the ability to discern—and choose—good or evil is at the heart of what it means to be a Christian. But unlike Protestants, whose varied theologies rest on the assertion of an individual conscience in the forging of a closer relationship to God, official Catholicism has always insisted on the primacy of the church hierarchy in shaping the entire structure of life on earth. Such a stance was one reason American Protestants were suspicious of Catholic fitness for participation in democratic society, and it was not until the election of John F. Kennedy in 1960 that the issue was apparently resolved.

For Protestants, anyway. In the years since, the story of American Catholic relations with Rome has been one of dissonance—over a strictly male clergy, over contraception, abortion, and premarital sex, over homosexuality, and, most recently, over clerical sexual conduct with the laity. Actively or passively, millions of American Catholics have resisted many church teachings, some by leaving the church altogether.

Like Judaism, however, Catholicism is a kind of ethnicity that is not shed lightly. Many Catholics uncomfortable with aspects of the catechism have chosen to become "cafeteria" Catholics, picking and choosing among church teachings while retaining a loyalty to basic rituals like weekly Mass or the seven sacraments. For such people, the church offers an important avenue for community too important to sacrifice on the altar of doctrine. Others have renounced Catholicism with a vehemence that belies an ongoing emotional involvement. It was for such people that the phrase "Once a Catholic, always a Catholic" was coined.

Wherever they situate themselves, American Catholics are confronted by a powerful tension between worldly aspiration and otherworldly obligation. It may be no coincidence, then, that some of the most highly charged commentary on the American Dream of worldly success has come from Catholics. It may seem foolish to suggest that the careers of Kate Chopin (born Katherine O'Flaherty), F. Scott Fitzgerald, Margaret Mitchell, Billie Holiday, Eugene O'Neill, Jack Kerouac, Martin Scorsese, Robert Mapplethorpe, and Madonna—to name just a handful of prominent Catholic artists—would have anything in common. But they and many others have all circled, often obsessively, around the tension between transcending the limits into which they were born and honoring the obligations, moral and otherwise, of their origins.

Bruce Springsteen is an interesting case in this regard. He has achieved a secularized Protestant dream of grace without the severe trauma that marked the careers of Fitzgerald, Holiday, Mapplethorpe, and others. And yet a strong vein of skepticism, even doubt, about that dream has long been a part of his musical vision. For a man who has experienced an unusual degree of success, he has persistently explored failure in a variety of forms. He's too much of a republican—a political tradition built on Protestant theology—to surrender hope for a better world. But often unwittingly, he's too much of a Catholic to forget the costs of even *articulating* an American Dream, never mind pursuing one.

At the core of Springsteen's Catholicism is an "analogical imagination," a term coined by theologian David Tracy to describe a distinctively Catholic way of understanding the world. Analyzing the work of Thomas Aquinas, Martin Luther, and John Calvin, Tracy posits a Protestant "dialectical" imagination that tends to divide spirit and matter, in contrast to a Catholic vision of fundamental unity, or analog. The former is an individualistic sensibility that emphasizes the distance between God and man, while the latter is more communal, emphasizing God's presence in the world.

Catholic sociologist Father Andrew Greeley has vividly described the difference between the analogic imagination of Protestants and the dialogical imagination of Catholics in pop music terms. "The church in the Madonna video 'Like a Prayer,' with its stained glass and candles, stands for the Catholic tradition in a way that a church that looks much like a Quaker meetinghouse cannot." Her symbolic vocabulary—one that draws heavily on darkness, rain, and other metaphors some might consider clichés— is conditioned on a specifically (though not uniquely) Catholic penchant for drawing on collective iconography. Springsteen's similarly obvious affinity for such metaphors, from cars to darkness, has similar ethnic, class, and religious roots—all of which, it should be added, are interrelated.

Such metaphors, and the analogic imagination that animates them, are not simply a curious quirk in Springsteen's musical personality. As with manhood, his attitudes toward Catholicism can be traced over time, with similarly illuminating results. Doing so vividly illustrates how religion functions not so much as a set of doctrines or rituals, but as a way of thinking, feeling, and living in the world—even when we are unaware of (or specifically reject) church doctrine.

Perhaps the most important and striking thing about Springsteen's subtle but powerful Catholic imagination, however, is the way it parallels his politics, aesthetics, and other topics explored in this book. His religious sensibility is the supreme expression of Springsteen's signal contribution to American culture, religious and otherwise, as a whole: his capacity for exploring old ideas and themes, adapting and reinvigorating them through the medium of popular culture, and giving them a new power and relevance in our lives.

RISING SON

Some people pray, some people play music.
—BRUCE SPRINGSTEEN, CA. 1976

On July 8, 1978, Bruce Springsteen and the E Street Band performed in Phoenix, playing for a sold-out crowd at the 10,000-seat Veterans Memorial Coliseum. By this point in his career, Springsteen was well known to audiences on each coast, but largely unknown throughout much of the nation's interior. Phoenix, in fact, was one of the few inland cities where he had a real reputation. Perhaps this is why Springsteen added a new element to a story he told as part of his shows at the time.

He typically told this story as part of his performance of "Growin' Up"—in fact, the version that appears on *Live 1975–85* was recorded the night before the Phoenix show at the Roxy, a fabled L.A. concert hall (his parents and sister had been at that show). During a musical interlude in the song, Springsteen would narrate a monologue about how his parents were worried about his fixation with rock and roll, which they felt was no way to make a living. His father thought he should be a lawyer; his mother thought he should become a writer. Eventually, he tells them they'll have to settle for rock and roll (at which point the crowd usually roars).

In Phoenix, however, Springsteen makes a digression. "My mother, she's very Italian, she says, 'This is a big thing, you should go see a priest,'" he explains. So he goes to the rectory and talks with Father Ray, whose very name implies that he will shed some light on the matter. After hearing his dilemma, however, Father Ray concludes, "'This is too big a deal for me. You gotta talk to God.'"

Springsteen has no idea where to find God. So—part of the humor of the story derives from this being described as a logical, even inevitable step—he asks E Street Band saxophonist Clarence Clemons, his can-do sidekick. Clemons, of course, knows just where God is: in a house at the edge of the woods. Springsteen drives over.

Music blasts through the door of the house as Springsteen approaches it. "Clarence sent me," he says, and the door opens to reveal the Lord himself seated behind a drum set. Springsteen explains his dilemma. The Lord replies:

> What they [his parents—*all* parents] don't understand is that there was supposed to be an eleventh commandment. Actually, it's Moses's fault. He was so scared after ten, he said this is enough, and went back down the mountain.

You shoulda seen it—great show, the burning bush, thunder, lightning. You see, what those guys didn't understand was that there was an eleventh commandment. And all it said was: LET IT ROCK!

With that, Bruce Springsteen receives his confirmation. The show goes on.

Even without the aural and visual cues of a typical rock concert, this anecdote sounds like—indeed, was surely intended to be—an amusing, even silly, story. No one actually believes Springsteen visited God; he's telling a tall tale, not a religious parable. But all stories have morals, whether or not those meanings are obvious, conscious, or straightforward.

One of the things that makes this story striking, for example, is the way in which Springsteen makes subtle jabs at his Catholic upbringing. Although Father Ray seems like a decent man, it is Clarence Clemons, not the priest, who helps the troubled youth find God. Once he does, God informs him that the laws and traditions that have been passed down to him are incomplete, even irrelevant. Far from the humorless, severe figure of parochial school legend, God has adolescent taste in music and likes a good show (the burning bush, the thunder and lightning, etc). The rules we inherited, Springsteen tells 10,000 disciples in Phoenix, can be safely ignored.

And yet this story is more religious, and specifically Catholic, than it initially appears. For one thing, it depicts a person genuinely troubled at the prospect of not honoring his father and mother—one of the commandments that Moses *did* bring back from the mountain. The very imagery Springsteen uses to describe God and his actions has a chummy, even flashy, quality more typical of a Catholic mind than, say, a more abstract, Presbyterian one. In fact, it's helpful to go a step further and point out what *doesn't* happen here: this is not a story in which a young man *denies* the existence of God, or angrily *rejects* him, or is *disappointed* by what he finds.

Instead, this is a story about a man who seeks—and has the good fortune of actually receiving—divine approval for doing what he most wants to do. Which is, in effect, to become a missionary. The happy ending of this story is that the man whose parents fear he does not want to "work" ends up doing the most important work of all: God's work.

This is not an outcome anyone, least of all the boy himself, would have predicted. Though Springsteen is a Dutch name, most of his ancestry is Irish and Italian. Adele Springsteen's maiden name was Zirilli, and it appears that her maternal influence played a large role in shaping his musical personality. Springsteen has described his mother as "real smart, real strong, real creative," and judging from his relatively unfettered, often sexually expressive songs one suspects that the Italian strain of Catholicism suffuses his music more than a more puritanical Irish one.

Though neither had steady jobs, Springsteen's parents found the money to send him to St. Rose of Lima, a parochial school in Freehold. The experience has repeatedly been described as disastrous. "I spent half of my first thirteen years in a trance," Springsteen explained to biographer Dave Marsh. He also (apparently like every single person who has ever recollected a Catholic education) described discipline problems. "In the third grade a nun stuffed me in a garbage can because, she said, that's where I belonged," he recalled. Such experiences were not limited to the classroom. "I also had the distinction of being the only altar boy knocked down by a priest during Mass. The old priest got mad. My mother wanted me to serve Mass, but I didn't know what I was doin' so I was trying to fake it." Throwing in the towel, Springsteen's parents sent him to the public high school in Freehold in the mid-sixties, where his experiences were hardly better, if less costly.

Springsteen's memories of his Catholic education are notable less for their typical content than they are for the clarity with which he described them decades later. There's humor in these stories, but wounded pride as well. Whatever its long-range effect on him, it is clear that by the end of his adolescence Springsteen, like many young people, had largely rejected church teaching and practice. Music (especially soul music, an incompletely secularized African-American idiom) became his religion.

But Springsteen's Catholicism was never far from the surface. Indeed, it was discernible during his audition for Columbia Records in 1972. Asked by talent scout John Hammond if he had written any songs he would not perform live, Springsteen responded by playing the as yet unreleased "If I Was the Priest":

> *Well now if Jesus was the sheriff and I was the priest*
> *If my lady was an heiress and my mama was a thief*
> *Oh and papa rode shotgun for the Fargo line*
> *There's still too many outlaws tryin' to work the same line*

Other lyrics describe the Virgin Mary running the Holy Grail Saloon; the Holy Ghost managing a burlesque show; and the narrator refusing Sheriff Jesus's request to come up to Dodge City. "When he sang that song, I knew he could only be Catholic," Hammond remembered. Perhaps Hammond meant that the satirical, if not actually contemptuous, thrust of such words—which fuse a specifically American mythology with a more broadly Catholic one—could only come from familiarity.

By the time Springsteen was making his first records, however, his stance toward Catholicism had softened somewhat. He seemed more interested in poking fun at religion than in actively demystifying it. This more playful attitude is evident in "It's So Hard to Be a Saint in the City," the final track of *Greetings from Asbury Park*:

> *The devil appeared like Jesus through the steam in the street*
> *Showin' me a hand I knew even the cops couldn't beat*
> *I felt his hot breath on my neck as I dove through the heat*
> *It's so hard to be a saint when you're just a boy out on the street*

Springsteen's Catholic impulses are vividly on display: an instinctive blurring of good and evil (Jesus as devil); a fusion of matter and spirit (Satan emerging from the mist on to the street); and a view of religion as analagous to a police force (which can nevertheless be beaten at its own game). What is most remarkable here, though, is that final line. Directly or indirectly, the singer pleads his case to God; in a kind of mock confessional, he seeks to be excused on the grounds that he's only a boy and can't be expected to have the self-control of a saint—or, at any rate, a man further along in his spiritual development. It's as if he's asking God, as the creator of so much marvelous mischief, to overlook a child's availing himself of it. Note, however, that it's *hard,* not impossible, to be a saint. The overall feel of the song is rhapsodic, but a nagging guilt tugs, almost unnoticed, at the margins. Even as the boy enjoys himself, he knows all the while that he's not supposed to give in to temptation.

"If I Was the Priest" and "It's So Hard to Be a Saint in the City" notwithstanding, Springsteen did not usually engage with specifically religious issues in his early music. More common are reflexive habits of thought that reveal, perhaps unwittingly, his Catholic background. Such habits are clearly in evidence in "Thunder Road:"

> You can hide 'neath your covers
> And study your pain
> Make crosses from your lovers
> Throw roses in the rain
> Waste your summer praying in vain
> For a savior to rise from these streets
> Well now I'm no hero
> That's understood
> All the redemption I can offer, girl
> Is beneath this dirty hood

With a chance to make it good somehow
Hey what else can we do now?

Unlike "If I Was the Priest" or "It's So Hard to Be a Saint in the City," Springsteen has no particular interest here in confronting religious questions. But religious metaphors ("crosses," "roses," "savior") powerfully shape the narrator's understanding of what romantic love with Mary (!) is about, even when he uses those metaphors in a dismissive way.

Conscious or unconscious, hostile or playful, the most salient quality of the young Springsteen's religious character is innocence. With few exceptions, there is no real evil on his early records. Though hardly respected, authority figures like clergy and policemen are generally depicted as humorless rather than malignant. Small-time criminals pepper these songs, but insofar as any judgment is passed on them, Springsteen is usually approving; the hustlers of songs like "Incident on 57th Street," "Meeting Across the River," and "Jungleland" invite identification far more than censure.

The notable departure from this generalization, and one that points to the next step in Springsteen's moral development, is "Lost in the Flood," an antiwar precursor to "Born in the U.S.A." "Lost in the Flood" features profane imagery (pregnant nuns, a congregation drinking unholy blood, etc.), but not as a playful joke.

And I said, "Hey gunner man, that's quicksand
That's quicksand, that ain't mud
Have you thrown your senses to the war
Or did you just lose them in the flood?

Later in his career, war veterans like the "gunner" this narrator describes would receive a good deal of Springsteen's sympathy and philanthropic support. The tone here, however, is skeptical, even judgmental. (It seems safe to say that Springsteen's ongoing opposition to the war and experiences with the draft did not promote imaginative identification with soldiers.) What "Lost in the Flood" does document, however, is Springsteen's growing penchant for using Old Testament imagery to suggest a harsh or corrupt social order.

This tendency is especially obvious in *Darkness on the Edge of Town*. Some of these allusions are obvious, almost clichéd, as the very title of "The Promised Land" suggests. But others are more sustained and direct. One such example is "Adam Raised a Cain," in which a young man compares his situation to one in the Book of Genesis:

> *In the Bible Cain slew Abel*
> *And East of Eden he was cast*
> *You're born into this life payin'*
> *For the sins of somebody else's past*

The singer's father is an Adam figure, condemned to mortal misery. But what may be even more alarming is that he is the father of—i.e., is raising—Cain, a man destined for still more misery ("You inherit the sins, you inherit the flames," he explains). The song evokes a severe, even vindictive, God who makes little allowance for personal aspiration, and a world in which sin becomes a way of life.

In "Prove It All Night," another song from *Darkness*, sin takes on an almost feral allure. "I've been working real hard trying to get my hands clean," asserts the singer of "Prove It All Night," his voice almost menacing in its determination. Suspicions that his hands *aren't* clean are confirmed in the final verse:

> *Baby, tie your hair in a long white bow*
> *Meet me in the fields behind the dynamo*
> *You hear their voices tell you not to go*
> *They made their choices and they'll never know*
> *What it means to steal, to cheat, to lie*
> *What it's like to live and die*

So speaks an avowed sinner. There's no attempt here to excuse or understand stealing, cheating, and lying, the way a liberal Protestant (or an atheist) might. Note also the inversion of the pastoral impulse: the only pure thing in the field takes the form of evil. As he moved into maturity, Springsteen's work took on a much tougher, yet more ambiguous, moral edge.

NEW TESTAMENT

You don't make up for your sins in church. You do it in the
streets. You do it at home. The rest is bullshit and you know it.
—CHARLIE (HARVEY KEITEL), IN MARTIN SCORSESE'S
Mean Streets (1974)

In religious terms, *The River* marks a major turning point in Springsteen's career. In the seventies, religion was a matter of metaphor, used as a source of playful humor or as a means to describe dilemmas that were perceived as essentially secular, like heterosexual romance in "Thunder Road," or strained parent-child relations in "Adam Raised a Cain." In the eighties, however, it became a subject of increasingly self-conscious exploration in its own right.

One oblique but powerful hint of this emerging sensibility can be glimpsed in the black-and-white photograph on the back cover of *The River*, shot by Frank Stefanko with art direction from Jimmy Wachtel. The photo depicts a store-window bride, groom, and four bridesmaids made from prefabricated cardboard figures (the women wear 3-D paper dresses). The backdrop for these figures includes paper cups, a package of glow-glitter, and other party goods. Cardboard patriotic symbols are also prominent: an eagle, a Liberty Bell, and an unfurled flag (a furled cloth flag stands in the far left of the photo). In another context, such a picture could be used as camp, a mock commentary on shopworn working-class aspirations, especially those of women. This image could also be used as a pathetic illustration of the way in which capitalism packages symbols into disposable commodities. Here, however, the message seems much more empathetic: even the humblest, paperthin materials can be vessels of meaning and dignity.

On the album itself, Springsteen largely drops the playful mockery that characterized his early work. "I wish God would send me a word/Send me something I'm afraid to lose," says the anguished narrator of "Drive All Night," lamenting a lost love. There's no humor or anger here, nor is there subversion or irony in

CATHOLIC TASTES: The back cover of *The River* (1980). In its willingness to endow common, even clichéd, iconography with transcendental meaning, this image, like Springsteen's work generally, is marked by what theologian David Tracy calls "the analogical imagination."

his description of the "fallen angels" (i.e., other lovelorn people) who haunt the song. But not all of this man's religiosity is cast in negative terms; in fact, one of the more striking aspects of the song is the way ordinary objects are endowed with sacred intensity, similar to the manner of that back cover. When the narrator of the song sings the chorus—"I swear I'll drive all night/just to buy you some shoes"—the ragged, anguished quality of Springsteen's voice forcefully endows a piece of clothing with an almost religious aura.

But the most obvious and important indication of Springsteen's religious evolution on *The River* is his more direct confrontation with the psychological dimensions of sin and human mortality. While the characters of *Darkness* wrestle with burdensome legacies in the struggle to realize their aspirations, many of those on *The River* actually lose the fight. For the characters of the title track, this is an unexpected and uncontrollable event resulting from an unplanned pregnancy and a collapsed economy. In the case of "Hungry Heart," this is part of an ordained (and unpunctuated) order: "We fell in love I knew it had to end." In "Point Blank," the fatal blow is administered by another individual, in this case a former lover.

In early Springsteen songs, characters respond to such adversity with renewed determination. The truly scary songs of *The River* are those, especially on the last half of the album, in which individuals realize that they've come up against something much larger than they can handle. Whereas in "Prove It All Night," sin is an option, a way of asserting one's autonomy in a blandly conformist society, "Stolen Car" depicts an impoverished soul for whom sin is a compulsion, proof of lost control:

I'm driving a stolen car
Down on Eldridge Avenue
Each night I wait to get caught
But I never do

Like a character in a Dostoyevsky novel, it seems that this man *wants* to be caught. He's also comparable to the narrator of "Drive All Night" in that losing something—in this case, a disorienting freedom—might somehow restore meaning in a life thrown into crisis since his marriage failed. Lacking direction, he veers toward a void more frightening than any punishment:

> *I'm driving a stolen car*
> *On a pitch black night*
> *And I'm telling myself*
> *I'm gonna be alright*
> *But I ride by night*
> *And I travel in fear*
> *That in this darkness*
> *I will disappear*

The muted bass drum that has appeared sporadically through the song becomes incessant during this last verse. It's not loud or obvious, which only increases its ominousness. A dirgelike organ rises after the word "disappear," and one hears a last ripple of piano notes before they fall off, like the last leaves of autumn.

The last song on the album, "Wreck on the Highway," suggests the illusory nature of control even for those who are not spiritually ill. The very title of the song, an allusion to the Roy Acuff tune of the same name, suggests Springsteen's growing receptiveness to country music, one of the more fatalistic genres of American musical styles. In the song, a man driving home from work on a rainy night encounters an accident scene, and gets out of his own car to help. He sees blood and glass, and hears a pitiful voice ask for help. Eventually, an ambulance comes to take the victim away—a sign of hope—but the narrator remains haunted by the image of a state trooper knocking on a door in the middle of the night to inform a girlfriend or wife about the death of a loved one. Lest there be any doubt, the final verse spells out the implications for his own life:

Sometimes I sit up in the darkness
And watch my baby as she sleeps
Then I climb in bed and hold her tight
I just lay there awake in the middle of the night
Thinkin' 'bout the wreck on the highway

There's nothing specifically religious about "Wreck on the Highway" (or, for that matter, many of the other tracks of *The River*). An atheist or agnostic can hear and appreciate the message of the song—that life is fleeting and unstable, and that one must attempt to live it in the fullest, most committed way—without drawing a doctrinal moral. At the same time, however, considered within the context of his career as a whole, the song is part of a broader transition from indifference to such broad existential questions that lead toward deep engagement (and specifically Christian engagement) with them.

Nebraska represents the next step in this process. If the characters of *The River* veer toward a spiritual abyss, those of this album plunge into it. Nowhere is clearer, appropriately enough, than in the title track, whose protagonist (based on Charlie Starkweather, a man who went on a notorious murder rampage in the 1950s) reveals much about the mood of the album. Tried, convicted, and sentenced to death, he is informed that his soul will be hurled into "that great void." Unlike the characters of "Stolen Car" or "Wreck on the Highway," however, he receives this news with an almost unnerving lack of affect. Asked why he has committed such monstrous crimes, he offers an explanation that looms over the album as a whole: "Well sir I guess there's just a meanness in this world."

The disembodied quality of "meanness" is crucial. At the time of its release during the worst recession since the Great Depression, reviewers of *Nebraska* wrote a great deal about the political critique embedded in the album. Far less has been said about the religious foundation of that critique, which rests on a confrontation with the problem—and nature—of evil. While some might project their darkest impulses on to a particular group of people (blacks, Jews, immigrants) and others single out more abstract, socially determined institutional forces (inequality, economic dislocation, homophobia), Springsteen posits evil as a force that defies demographic specificity or rational explanation. So when convicted murderer Johnny 99 asks whether you can take a man's life for the thoughts in his head, the question is largely rhetorical: you can, but then you become implicated in the very act you seek to purge.

And evil is everlasting. This is the message of "My Father's House," Springsteen's most conventionally pious song. An adult son dreams of being lost in the woods with the devil snapping at his heels. He desperately seeks, and finds, his father—only to awaken to a powerful sense of guilt and longing over their broken relationship. Impulsively, he dresses and drives to the house, only to learn he no longer lives there. The concluding verse sounds a collective indictment:

> My father's house shines hard and bright
> It stands like a beacon, calling me in the night
> Calling and calling, so cold and alone
> Shining 'cross this dark highway where our sins lie unatoned

The imagery here is resolutely simple, even archetypal. Biblical language suffuses the song (most obviously in its very title), but is no longer a mere stand-in for secular concerns as it was in previous Springsteen songs. In a sense, his heritage has finally caught up with him.

Fortunately, that heritage is not unrelievedly grim. Springsteen suggests that there is a flip side to transcendental sin, one he offers in the immediate aftermath of "Nebraska." "Everything dies baby that's a fact/But maybe everything that dies some day comes back," speculates the narrator of "Atlantic City." The hope here is tempered, but not without a certain plausibility: if sin permeates every action, so, too, may grace. Ironically, it's the very tentativeness of this proposition, asserted amid unmistakable civic corruption, that gives the song its psychological and moral credibility.

Moreover, neither damnation nor grace is wholly independent of individual will. *Nebraska* features a number of songs in which the actions or intentions of particular people can make a difference in each other's lives. In the case of "Johnny 99," such possibilities are defined by their absence: an immoral economic system leaves him with "debts no honest man can pay," and no one steps forward to save him from his damnation. In "Highway Patrolman," by contrast, Joe Roberts repeatedly faces difficult choices in dealing with his wayward brother, Franky. He explains his stance in a pointedly allegorical line, "I try to catch him when he's strayin', like any brother would/Man turns his back on his family well he just ain't no good." This does not prevent the prodigal Franky from committing more crimes, and there's no indication that Joe really expects otherwise. But he lets him escape across state lines nonetheless, because he chooses to obey a code of family loyalty.

It's significant that the secular social order of these songs is portrayed as immoral or rigidly indifferent toward human life. Thus the narrator of "State Trooper" tells the policeman who pulls him over, "License, registration, I ain't got none/But I got a clear conscience 'bout the things that I done." The very skepticism about justice that marks these songs also translates into a reluctance to invest too much credulity in official behavior or explanations. Under certain circumstances, then, a revolt against the status quo is both possible and morally defensible.

But the hopes animating "Atlantic City" or "Highway Patrolman" offer, at best, partial solutions to worldly dilemmas. As often as not, human actors are forced to confront mysteries that are more trying than reassuring. Nor, despite the hopes of some believers (and, perhaps, the assumptions of some nonbelievers) does faith always make matters any easier to understand or accept.

Springsteen addresses this last point in "Reason to Believe," which closes *Nebraska*. The song is a litany of dead dogs, abandoned lovers, baptisms, and funerals, each punctuated by an assertion that "at the end of every hard earned day/People find some reason to believe." Far from the hard-won affirmation many observers took it to be, "Reason to Believe" is the work of a man more troubled than inspired by the irrational faith of the sufferers he observes. But its very rigor, its refusal to accept simple answers, in itself represents the degree to which a man who started out by poking fun at religion was now fiercely wrestling with it.

FAMILY VALUES

Tunnel of Love *may be a more important Catholic event in this country than the visit of Pope John Paul II. The Pope spoke of moral debates using the language of doctrinal propositions that appeal to (or repel) the mind. Springsteen sings of religious realities—sin, temptation, forgiveness, life, death, hope—in images that come (implicitly perhaps) from his Catholic childhood, images that appeal to the whole person, not just the head, and that will be absorbed by far more Americans than those who listened to the Pope.*
                                        —FATHER ANDREW GREELEY, 1988

Far more than its predecessors, *Tunnel of Love* is an intimate record. Ever since *Born to Run*, Springsteen had been widening his scope to take into account social forces that affected his characters' lives—their family histories, their country, and in the case of *Nebraska*, their faith. Now, in the aftermath of the international hoopla surrounding *Born in the U.S.A.* and *Live 1975–85*, he turned inward. "I was interested in personalizing my music," he explained shortly after the album's release. "It's just a natural thing you want to do. You put something out there, it gets pulled in and taken up, and becomes part of the culture and part of people's lives. And then you have to reinvent yourself."

This reinvention was not simply artistic. Springsteen married model/actress Julianne Phillips in 1985 and settled down for the first time since his childhood. This was not to be a happy experience, however, and one did not have to be a pyschoanalyst or a tabloid newspaper reader to wonder if the marriage was going well, because *Tunnel of Love* conveyed clear signs of distress. As we know, Springsteen and Phillips divorced in 1989 amid, at the least, the appearance of adultery on his part, news that rippled outward from those tabloids. Again judging from his music, in this case *Human Touch* and *Lucky Town,* Springsteen's subsequent marriage to Patti Scialfa has been far happier.

The relevant point here is that the major reorientation in Springsteen's personal life in these years seems to have had direct consequences for his religious sensibility. "I wanted to make a record about what I felt, about really letting another person in your life and trying to be a part of someone else's life," he said in 1988. "That's a frightening thing, something that's always filled with shadows and doubts, and also wonderful and beautiful things." Springsteen is talking about Phillips here, but he could just as easily be talking about the nature of religious experience. Marriage, after all, is a sacrament.

Andrew Greeley put his finger on the spiritual orientation that was taking place. "Religion is more explicitly expressed in *Tunnel of Love* than in any previous Springsteen album. Prayer, heaven and God are invoked naturally and unselfconsciously as though they are an ordinary part of the singer's life and vocabulary." He adds, "The piety of these songs—and I challenge you to find a better word—is sentient without being sentimental, an Italian-American male piety not unlike that found in some of the films of Martin Scorsese (especially *Mean Streets*). It is, perhaps, not Sunday Mass piety, but it is, if anything, much richer and deeper and more powerful. It is the piety of symbol rather than doctrine."

Actually, in "Walk Like a Man," there *is* an element of Sunday Mass piety. For the first time in a Springsteen song, a church scene is described in a manner he might have actually seen as a child:

By Our Lady of the Roses
We lived in the shadow of the elms
I remember Ma draggin' me and my sister up the
*   street to the church*
Whenever she heard those wedding bells . . .

More often, however, a state of grace is experienced outside church walls. For the insouciant narrator of "All That Heaven Will Allow," a dance club is a cathedral. In "Valentine's Day," timber-wolves, jukeboxes, and cold river bottoms, like wives and children, are signs of "God's light . . . shinin' on through."

What's especially significant about these songs is the way in which popular culture is not simply a *symbol* of spiritual awareness but an actual *means* toward achieving it. In "Tunnel of Love," a man involved in a roller-coaster relationship takes his beloved to an amusement park, where many of their dilemmas seem to be dramatically reenacted, even embodied: "the lights go out and it's just the three of us/you, me and all that stuff we're so scared of." At the end of the song, though, the narrator describes what he's learned from riding an actual roller coaster, and does so in language that closely resembles religious teachings. Compare

God grant me the serenity to accept the things that I cannot
*   change*
The courage to change the things that I can
And the wisdom to know the difference

in the prayer of St. Francis to

You've got to learn to live with what you can't rise above
If you want to ride on down through this tunnel of love

Springsteen's emphasis here is on the first half of the prayer, which within the context of his career as a whole is especially significant. In his work leading up to *Darkness on the Edge of Town*, his focus was almost exclusively on characters who sought to make change on their own terms ("Honey I want the heart/I want the soul/I want control right now," declares the young narrator of "Badlands"). Here, however, a man learns that there are some things you "can't rise above," and that love—in the most specific and transcendental senses of the term—requires a measure of acceptance of things as they are.

These are the "wonderful and beautiful things." But *Tunnel of Love* is filled with—and finally dominated by—"shadows and doubts." The second half of the record in particular portrays people who are wrestling with demons. In "Brilliant Disguise," a husband begins by accusing his wife of infidelity, but as the song proceeds he reveals his own waverings, finally confessing that he, too, wears a mask. This is less a matter of comeuppance than a costly confession. "God have mercy on the man/Who doubts what he's sure of," he concludes. This is meant to be ironic, of course, but like so much else in Springsteen's work, doubt is finally couched in the language of faith, suggesting a powerful sense of struggle.

This sense of struggle often clouds the album's "happy" songs. Bill Horton of "Cautious Man" overcomes the temptation to flee his sleeping wife, returning to her and "the beauty of God's *fallen* light." As the narrator explains, the words "love" and "fear" will always be tattooed on his knuckes. *Tunnel of Love* ends with the epiphanal "Valentine's Day," but the narrator's joy is laced with fear: "I woke up scared and breathin' and born anew."

To be scared and breathing, however, is to be vitally alive, and perhaps the most powerful feeling the characters of *Tunnel of Love* project is a strong, even fierce sense of life itself as a sacramental gift. "Now some may wanna die young man/Young and gloriously/Get it straight now mister/Buddy that ain't me," reports the singer of "All That Heaven Will Allow." This is less an expression of hostility to larger commitments than a vivid assertion that even though there may be limits on what is "allowed," love makes mortal life eminently worth living.

This message is communicated most forcefully in "Spare Parts," precisely because the value of life is seriously called into question. "Spare Parts" features a lean, bluesy arrangement and a storyline that unfolds like an Old Testament story (Abraham's near sacrifice of Isaac and Moses's being hidden in the rushes come to mind). Impregnated and abandoned, young Janey gives birth to a son and lives with her mother. She pines after her lost life while her lover, down in Texas, vows never to return. Before long, she comes to a crucial crossroads, one that corresponds to the bridge of the song—and, not so coincidentally, the entrance of an organ:

> *Janey heard about a woman over in Calverton*
> *Put her baby in the river let the river roll on*
> *She looked at her boy in the crib where he lay*
> *Got down on her knees cried till she prayed*
> *Mist was on the water low run the tide*
> *Janey held her son at the riverside*
> *Waist deep in the water how bright the sun shone*
> *She lifted him in her arms and carried him home . . .*

The place name "Calverton" evokes Calvary, the site of Christ's crucifixion, and underlines the agonizing quality of Janey's struggle. But her situation stabilizes in the penultimate line, whose very diction suggests why: her entrance into the water suggests a kind of baptism (her own as well as her child's), while the shining sun could be the face of God (or, perhaps more accurately, Jesus Christ). In any case, she pulls herself back from the brink of damnation and immerses herself back in the world. She goes home, gets her wedding dress and engagement ring, and takes them down to a pawnshop for "some good cold cash." Her (literal as well as figurative) immersion in the material world becomes a kind of salvation.

The Springsteen albums that follow *Tunnel of Love* evince a commitment to materialism of a different kind: sexual expression. The very title of *Human Touch* suggests such an emphasis. Nevertheless, the pleasures of the body, like other kinds of worldly creation, are valued not in themselves, but in the way in which they open windows to something beyond. This connection between a corporeal state and a spiritual one is spelled out with unusual clarity in *Lucky Town*'s "Leap of Faith": "your legs were heaven, your breasts were the altar/Your body was the holy land." While Springsteen has never been a prude, his sexual imagery has never been quite so graphic. Given the stereotype of Catholic priggishness, it's ironic that his more deeply engaged religious heritage appears responsible for this relative openness.

Sexuality is not altogether drained of a sense of sin, however. Adultery looms over "Cross My Heart" (from *Human Touch*) and "The Big Muddy" (from *Lucky Town*). In the latter, Springsteen offers a maxim that captures his basic philosophic stance since at least the time of *Darkness:*

> *Well you may think the world is black and white*
> *And you're dirty or you're clean*
> *You better watch out you don't slip*
> *In those places in between*

This is not really advice, however, because neither this character or the others on these two albums seem to think it is possible to avoid slipping "in between." Thus, to cite another example, the man of "With Every Wish" learns that with fulfillment "comes a curse."

The hard ambiguity of everyday life is made explicit in "Souls of the Departed," a latter-day version of "Lost in the Flood." This time, the Persian Gulf War takes the place of Vietnam, and the walls the narrator builds around his home to protect his children replace an abandoned shooting victim in the Bronx. Here, however, Springsteen's sense of irony and self-awareness is sharper. "Now I ply my trade in the land of king dollar/Where you get paid and your silence passes for honor," this character observes. For what it's worth—and this character knows it isn't much—he is *not* silent. What difference that makes is not clear. Hypocrisy is a hardy perennial, but it is also possible that a seed of justice may yet take root.

Yet even in the murkiest terrain lies the possibility for epiphany, as "Living Proof," the most remarkable track on *Human Touch*, makes clear. "Living Proof" is a celebration of the body—in this case, of birth. But like other Springsteen songs, it derives its power from his ability to convey a deep intimacy with the very desecration characters wish to overcome. His voice here sounds utterly ravaged, never more so than when he says, "You do some sad, sad things baby/When it's you you're trying to lose," as if he's reliving the banality of past evil. And yet the gnarled guitars that dominate the song also suggest a kind of flesh-and-blood immediacy, a heightened sense of living in the moment. The birth of this child represents a transfigurative moment, but it is one that is enacted in a material (and still cynical) world:

> *Well now all that's sure on the boulevard*
> *Is that life is just a house of cards*
> *As fragile as each and every breath*
> *Of this boy sleepin' in our bed*
> *Tonight let's lie beneath the eaves*
> *Just a close band of happy thieves*
> *And when that train comes we'll get on board*
> *And steal what we can from the treasures, treasures of the Lord . . .*

"The treasures of the Lord," conferred in mysterious ways, make questions of worldly justice irrelevant. Since no one is ever truly deserving, they should be accepted humbly and with great gratitude, which is exactly what the narrator of "Living Proof" does.

Conscious or unconscious, sarcastic or sincere, Springsteen's religious imagination has always been marked by a clear tendency to explore spiritual subjects in the most concrete terms, as "Living Proof" makes clear. But in one final layer of development and complexity, he closes *Lucky Town* with "My Beautiful Reward," which moves him into a frankly mystical dimension: in the final verse, the narrator has been transformed into a soaring bird. "I'm flyin' high over gray fields/My feathers long and black," he explains. Even here, however, an air of realism suffuses the magic; "cold wind," "gray fields," and "black feathers" both ground the imagery and maintain the dappled quality of Springsteen's religious imagination. Such a move seems consonant with the desert landscapes featured in the lyric booklet. Now a southern Californian, Springsteen has moved closer to the Latin Catholicism that thrives beyond the border.

BROTHERLY LOVE

That belief in Christ is to some a matter of life and death has been a stumbling block for readers who would prefer to think it is a matter of no great consequence.
—FLANNERY O'CONNOR, *Wise Blood* (1952)

There is a particular kind of artistic integrity that prizes following one's own muse, of producing from an absolute desire to do the work one wishes without consciously taking into account the tastes or needs of a wider community. This has been Springsteen's model, and he has had the discipline and good fortune to make a successful living at it. There is another kind of integrity, though, that comes from trying to produce within a larger framework, whether it be the strictures of a particular artistic genre or as part of a larger collective enterprise. Such situations call for a special kind of mastery, and, paradoxically, afford otherwise impossible expressive possibilities.

Bruce Springsteen's music has been recorded by a number of other artists, and has been used in a number of feature films. But he had never been commissioned to write a song until director Jonathan Demme approached him in 1992 with such a request for *Philadelphia,* a 1993 film about a man with AIDS who wrongly loses his position with a law firm. Given the strongly personal flavor of even his least biographical songs, Springsteen may well have regarded tailoring a piece of music for someone else's purposes beneath him at an earlier point in his career. But whether it was his esteem for Demme, a desire to take new risks, or a sense of impulsive generosity, Springsteen agreed to see what he could do.

The result, of course, was "Streets of Philadelphia," which won multiple Grammy Awards, a 1994 Oscar for Best Original Song, and enjoyed tremendous commercial success as part of the *Philadelphia* soundtrack and as a video that Demme himself directed. Among people inside as well as outside the entertainment industry, the song solidified Springsteen's good-guy credentials, clearly signaling his sympathy for AIDS victims, his social open-mindedness, and his generally left-wing politics. Perhaps more than any other record he had ever produced, "Streets of Philadelphia" ratified his entrance into the nation's cultural establishment.

Whatever else this song may be, however, it is also a profound religious statement. "There was a certain spiritual stillness that I wanted to try and capture," he later told *The Advocate,* a magazine oriented toward a gay and lesbian readership. Springsteen represents an experience outside his own immediate frame of reference—that of a sick, dying, presumably homosexual man—by drawing on the resources of his Catholic heritage. The way this alchemy of the unfamiliar and the distinctive resolves itself is perhaps the greatest accomplishment of his career.

"Streets of Philadelphia" depicts a *presumably* homosexual man because, unlike the movie, the protagonist's sexual orientation is never forthrightly stated. Springsteen in effect universalizes this man's situation by not fixing his sexuality or his disease. To some, this may seem like an evasion. Another artist may have insisted on a specific gay/AIDS setting, especially because there seems to be so much room for denial of both in this society, with dreadful consequences. Such a choice would be legitimate, honorable, and powerful. But not as powerful, one suspects, as the way in which Springsteen chose to write this song, which in quietly inviting identification may be more rhetorically effective.

It begins with percussion, eight measures of a syncopated rhythm that runs through the whole song. This rhythm reminds one of the kind of beat one hears on rap records: its metronomic quality, produced by a drum machine, calls attention to its very artifice. But while in the case of rap this technique is a source of the genre's vitality, the drumming of "Streets of Philadelphia" is notable for its flatness. It sounds, quite literally, like a broken record—or an irregular heartbeat sustained by technological means. The very continuity of this irregularity has a paradoxical effect, though, because it suggests a will to persist, however imperfectly.

The next instrument one hears (Springsteen plays all of them) is an organ. The key is minor, the tone somber. The overwhelming feeling is one of grayness, like very heavy cloud cover. By the time the narrator sings the first verse, then, a funereal mood is firmly established. In this case, though, it's the music, specifically that organ, that will reveal this man's fate more accurately than his words will.

Those words are marked by a potent sense of alienation that operates on a number of levels. First, this man is cut off from himself:

> *I was bruised and battered and I couldn't tell what I felt*
> *I was unrecognizable to myself*

I saw my reflection in a window I didn't know my own face
Oh brother, are you gonna leave me wastin' away

The final line here reveals a different kind of alienation. The "brother" here could be a family member, a lover, or simply a fellow man. Whoever it is, this character feels a deep loneliness in his despair. He hasn't given up—he wouldn't ask his question if he had—but he has his doubts. These become clear in the final verse when he tells this "brother" to receive him with his "faithless kiss," which links Judas's betrayal of Christ with a more specifically erotic betrayal.

This sense of estrangement intensifies, even multiplies, in the bridge of the song:

Ain't no angel gonna greet me
It's just you and I my friend
My clothes don't fit me no more
I walked a thousand miles
Just to slip this skin

These words are marked by what is now a familiar duality in Springsteen's recent work. On the one hand is the concreteness of his descriptions. (The mournful way Springsteen sings "clothes" bespeaks yet another kind of alienation: that of separation of the material world of objects.) On the other are habitual invocations of spiritual terms and images, in this case of angels. Even the descriptions themselves suggest a kind of internal division. We already know by this point in the song that "friend" is an ambiguous term. Walking a thousand miles to shed a skin suggests simultaneous endurance and exhaustion. Also, while humans walk, it's typically reptiles—specifically, snakes, an icon of evil—who shed their skins. At the same time, shedding a skin is also a sign of healing and renewal.

The most important form of alienation in the song is spiritual: this man denies a belief in the afterlife. The saving paradox here is that this man denies Christ in the language of faith. The angels, the invocation of Judas, that desire to shed his skin—and through it all, that organ, which brightens noticeably during this bridge—all bespeak an almost overwhelming longing for transcendence. At the end of it, that irregular heartbeat stops for the only time in the song. It's as if he's just about to let go.

But not yet. He turns one last time to his earthly veil, lying awake in the darkness. In a subtle shift, however, he turns his concern outward. In the first verse, he was afraid of being left alone. Now, including his partner in his concerns, he wonders if they will leave *each other* that way. The question is left unanswered as the narrator sings the words "Streets of Philadelphia" for the last time.

But the song is not over. In fact, it goes on for about another minute. The chanting harmonies and drumbeat gradually fade as the organ increasingly dominates the song. The same phrase—the chord progression is one often used for "Amen" during church hymns—is played repeatedly, rising in steps. Finally, the lower notes fall out as the organ notes peak and disappear. He has risen.

CATHOLIC INTERESTS

The point of being Irish is knowing the world will break your heart.

—An old saying

Written between 1835 and 1840, Frenchman Alexis de Tocqueville's *Democracy in America* is required reading for students of American history not only because it offers a vivid portrait of the early American republic, but also because many of the essential characteristics of his subject are still in evidence a century and a half later. His impressions of American Catholicism are one of many examples. In their clarity and acuity, they are worth quoting at some length:

I think that the Catholic religion has erroneously been regarded as the natural enemy of democracy. Among the various sects of Christians, Catholicism seems to me, on the contrary, to be one of the most favorable to equality of condition among men. In the Catholic Church the religious community is composed of only two elements: the priest and the people. The priest alone rises above the rank of his flock, and all below him are equal.

On doctrinal points the Catholic faith places all human capacities on the same level; it subjects the wise and ignorant, the man of genius and the vulgar crowd, to the details of the same creed; it imposes the same observances on the rich and the needy; it inflicts the same austerities upon the strong and weak; it listens to no compromise with mortal man, but, reducing all the human race to the same standard, it confounds all the distinctions of society at the foot of the same altar, even as they are confounded in the sight of God. If Catholicism predisposes the faithful to obedience, it certainly does not prepare them for inequality; but the contrary may be said of Protestantism, which generally tends to make men independent more than to render them equal.

In this passage, de Tocqueville identifies the great paradox of American Catholicism: it is simultaneously the most hierarchical and the most egalitarian of sects. "Catholicism is like an absolute monarchy," he continues. "If the sovereign be removed, all the other classes of society are more equal than in republics."

In an important sense, however, a large portion of the American laity, especially in recent decades, has behaved as if the papal "sovereign" has indeed been removed. While one should not ignore the deeply conservative, even reactionary, elements of U.S. Catholicism since the nineteenth century, one should be equally careful to note a powerful reformist, egalitarian stream that courses through the religious history of Catholics in the United States, one that runs from Orestes Brownson's denunciations of slavery in the 1850s to Dorothy Day's Depression-era Catholic Worker movement in the 1930s. If this has never been a dominant stream, it is surely one worth tracing—and preserving.

This is particularly true when one considers the relative mildness of American Catholicism compared to some varieties of American Protestantism. Take, for example, this (fairly typical) invocation from Jerry Falwell to his Lynchburg, Virginia, congregation in 1979: "I am speaking to Marines who have been called of God to move in past the shelling, the bombing, the foxholes and, with bayonet in hand, encounter the enemy face-to-face and one-on-one bring them under submission to the Gospel of Christ, move them into the household of God, put up the flag and call it secured. You and I are called to occupy until he comes." This is an American Dream gone curdled and sour, an imagined destiny that frightens and divides many more people than it inspires and unites. In fact, it is precisely this attitude which led to "Born in the U.S.A.," a critique of a manifest destiny that conquered a continent and lost countless souls.

Of course, fundamentalist Christians have no monopoly on intolerance and bigotry. Millions of American Catholics listened to the anti-Semitic broadcasts of Father Charles Coughlin, the so-called "Radio Priest" of the 1930s. Eventually, Coughlin's excesses (which included attacks on the New Deal as "communistic") discredited him even in the eyes of his followers. We can wish that the same will happen of Pat Robertson's supporters even as we recognize historical, geographic, and other ties—some reluctantly, some not—that bind us to them.

Indeed, nonevangelicals can agree with people like Jerry Falwell that we live in a fallen world. We can agree as well that sins may be redeemed; if the point in being Irish is knowing that the world will break your heart, the point in being American is believing that the world can nevertheless be made better. At its best, U.S. Catholicism offers believers and nonbelievers alike a combination of confidence and modesty that serves as a kind of ballast for imperfect, but worthwhile, American Dreams.

A failed altar boy whose religious observance has been erratic at best, Bruce Springsteen is no one's idea of a saint. But in listening carefully to his music, one hears a series of acquired as well as inherited values—an emphasis on egalitarianism; an instinctive compassion; a pragmatic skepticism toward utopian solutions; and, especially recently, a bracing humility about human endeavor—worth emulating in sacred as well as secular life. These are the values of a good conservative. These are the values of a great people.

CONCLUSION

Better Angels

"I am loth to close," Abraham Lincoln told the crowd assembled to witness his inauguration on March 4, 1861. He referred not to his speech, which he was concluding, but to the Union he was elected and constitutionally bound to preserve. Seven states had already left that Union rather than remain with Lincoln as president of it; four more would follow. His address represented a last-ditch effort to allay Southern fears and prevent war. "We are not enemies, but friends," Lincoln told the South. "We must not be enemies." He then ended with what might be called his profession of faith:

> Though passion may have strained, it must not break our bonds of affection. The mystic chords of memory, stretching from every battlefield, and patriot grave, to every living heart and hearthstone, all over this broad land, will yet swell the chorus of the Union, when again touched, as surely they will be, by the better angels of our nature.

Lincoln's appeal was unsuccessful; the war came. And yet while "better angels" did not always prevail—indeed were rare—they never quite disappeared, either. Lincoln himself has come as close as any American ever has in embodying them in the dignity he brought to his office, his lack of vindictiveness in public or private life, and most important, his decision to do the right thing and end slavery, the great scourge of American life and ideals.

INAUGURATING GREATNESS: Matthew Brady's portrait of Abraham Lincoln, February 23, 1861, eight days before he took the presidential oath of office.

In the almost 150 years since the Civil War, numerous politicians, artists, activists, and others have called on our better angels. More often than not, such calls have fallen on deaf ears. One might even say that our most notable achievements, ranging from the passage of child labor laws to defeating the Nazis, have cynical explanations. But no nation can function at all without some faith in its intentions, and it is the American faith—a faith that gains at least some support from empirical analysis and comparisons with other nations, as well as mystic chords of memory—that the republican democracy of the last 200 years can claim more success than failure, more progress than regress.

Honorable people can disagree as to the degree of success or regress, and can disagree as to what exactly constitutes better angels. My own answers, described at some length in this book, were formulated with the help of a rock and roll singer with little in the way of formal education. It may seem unlikely to think of him in such Lincolnian terms (though Lincoln himself had little in the way of formal education), but it seems to me that part of our American faith is a willingness to look for—and the confidence that we will find—answers to our most important questions in relatively humble quarters.

Indeed, the value of Bruce Springsteen's art resides not in some vast, Promethean talent (though I do hope I have convinced a few skeptics that he is an unusually talented man), but rather in his acuity in representing the people who populate his songs, people who have foibles and failings, but people who in the end constitute our last best hope for making this society work. At the same time, considered as a whole, Springsteen manifests a series of tendencies—his republicanism, his accommodation of personal and collective failure, his hope for his country, and his belief in something larger than it—which really do reveal better angels that at least coexist with lesser ones.

These tendencies are not Springsteen's alone; that is precisely why he is important. His art bears a strong resemblance to that of a number of other important figures in our history, from the expressive poetry of Walt Whitman to the humorous prose of Mark Twain. His politics reflect an egalitarian spirit that brings Jefferson's plowman to FDR's fireside. His moral fervor resonates with that of Lincoln and Martin Luther King. Springsteen may not be as accomplished as any of these people. But *they* attained the status they did in large measure for the degree to which embodied *common* values spread across American society at large.

The core of Springsteen's achievements in American culture resides less in providing new visions of national identity (the way, say, the Founding Fathers did) than in his talent for rearticulating older ones. This is the thread that connects his stance toward subjects as varied as politics, aesthetics, race relations, war, work, gender, and religion. Yet such rearticulations are not mere restatements; there is genuine originality in the way Springsteen revitalizes traditions by shifting (and in some cases, expanding) their parameters—in applying the lessons of the Civil Rights movement to Asian immigrants; in recognizing the homoeroticism that has always animated "normal" friendships; in rejecting the hidebound conventions of his religious heritage but reaffirming the vitality of its core tenets. In his hands, history is not an inert mass that weighs us down. Rather, it becomes the raw material for making history anew.

In January 1993, inaugurating a presidency that has been a disappointment to many of us, Bill Clinton told his fellow citizens that "there is nothing wrong with America that can't be fixed by what's right with America." This, it seems to me, is the core of our national creed and the essence of Springsteen's music, nowhere more so than when he and others convincingly demonstrate that many of those things—equality, freedom, or, simply faith in the creed itself—show signs of diminished vitality. It is the job of the historian to remind us that, for better and worse, our way of life is neither inevitable nor immortal. Amid this impermanence, it is the job of the artist to remind us of who we are. When I listen to Bruce Springsteen, I remember how to be an American.

Sources and Notes

There has been no shortage of commentary on Bruce Springsteen. Most of it has taken the form of reviews in newspapers and magazines too numerous and ephemeral to list here except for specific articles cited in the ensuing notes.

Springsteen has been the subject of over a dozen books, many of which are now out of print. The most important are two biographical works by Dave Marsh: *Born to Run: The Bruce Springsteen Story* (New York: Dell, 1981) and *Glory Days: Bruce Springsteen in the 1980s* (New York: Pantheon, 1987; both books were reissued with new introductions by Thunder's Mouth Press in 1996). Less informative, but often incisive, is *Los Angeles Times* writer Robert Hilburn's *Springsteen* (New York: Scribner's, 1985). Also of note is *Backstreets Springsteen: The Man and His Music,* edited by Charles Cross (New York: Crown, 1988; updated in 1990). This is a collection of articles from *Backstreets,* a high-quality fanzine published by Cross in the 1970s and '80s.

For discographies, histories, rare photographs, and other data, the definitive (though by now dated) work is probably *Springsteen: Blinded by the Light* by Patrick Humphries and Chris Hunt (New York: Holt, 1986). A similarly useful reference tool, this one for those seeking a compendium of Springsteen's remarks on a variety of subjects, is *In His Own Words: Bruce Springsteen,* edited by John Duffy (London: Omnibus, 1992). Also of note is Marc Eliot's *Down Thunder Road: The Making of Bruce Springsteen* (New York: Fireside, 1992), a book written with the participation of former Springsteen manager Mike Appel. While it has something of a polemical tone—Appel clearly seeks vindication in the wake of his bruising legal battle with his former client—the book features a revealing collection of depositions, letters, and other materials that vividly document the legal and financial mechanics of the entertainment industry.

Notable essays on Springsteen include Anthony DeCurtis's piece in *The Rolling Stone Illustrated History of Rock & Roll,* third edition (1976; New York: Random House, 1992) and Springsteen's unattributed entry into *The New Rolling Stone Encyclopedia of Rock & Roll* (1983; New York: Fireside, 1995). As this book was being completed in late 1996, Hyperion published *Bruce Springsteen: The Rolling Stone Files,* a collection of previously published articles on Springsteen edited by Parke Puterbaugh. A number of these pieces are cited below by their original date of publication. Finally, the *New York Times Magazine* published a cover story on Springsteen, "Steinbeck in Leather," on January 26, 1997. The story, by reporter Nicholas Dawidoff, discusses recent developments in Springsteen's career.

INTRODUCTION: A BIG COUNTRY

xiii–xiv Springsteen in Denver: This account draws on Springsteen's later recollection in *Glory Days,* pp. 19–20.

xiv *"if I'm doing my job right":* In His Own Words, p. 91.

xiv *Springsteen's impact on American culture:* Elizabeth Wurtzel, *Prozac Nation: Young and Depressed in America* (Boston: Houghton Mifflin, 1994), pp. 37–56, passim. See also her largely critical, but deeply engaged, reviews of *Human Touch* and *Lucky Town* in *The New Yorker,* August 17, 1992, pp. 55–59.

xv *"knew exactly what she was feeling":* Bobbie Ann Mason, *In Country* (1985; New York: HarperPerennial, 1993), p. 138.

xvii *"Victory Culture":* See Tom Engelhardt, *The End of Victory Culture: Cold War America and the Disillusioning of a Generation* (New York: Basic Books, 1995).

ONE: THE GOOD CONSERVATIVE

My understanding of the term "republican" as sketched out in this chapter draws on a number of works. Among the most important are those of Gordon Wood: *The Creation of the American Republic, 1776–1787* (1969; New York: Norton, 1972) and *The Radicalism of the American Revolution* (1991; New York: Vintage, 1992). Also important is Sean Wilenz, *Chants Democratic: New York City and the Rise of the American Working Class* (New York: Oxford University Press, 1984). Those seeking an overview of the concept, its trajectory, and exponents are advised to see *American Quarterly* 37:4 (Fall 1985), a special issue devoted to republicanism. See also Daniel Rodgers, "Republicanism: The Career of a Concept," *Journal of American History* 79:1 (June 1992), pp. 11–38.

Anyone familiar with this literature will readily note that I am stretching the term—both in suggesting it has persisted far longer than most of these historians indicate, and in projecting it into the cultural realm as much as, even more than, the political realm. But as I hope the ensuing discussion indicates, republican ideas have continued to echo, however partially and diffusely, in U.S. society long after the early nineteenth century.

1 *Nixon in that election:* Francis X. Clines, "President Heaps Praise on Voters in the Northeast," *The New York Times,* September 20, 1984, p. B20. The *Washington Post, Los Angeles Times,* and *Christian Science Monitor* issued that day

were also consulted. Reagan's memoir, *An American Life* (New York: Simon and Schuster, 1990) makes no mention of the Springsteen affair.

2 *"what this job of mine is all about":* "President Heaps Praise," p. B20; Jon Wiener, "Rockin' with Ron," in *Politics, Professors and Pop* (New York: Verso, 1991), pp. 297–298. Wiener's piece originally appeared in the October 6, 1984, issue of *The Nation.*

3 *"'Born in the U.S.A.!'":* The Reagan/Will/Springsteen affair is discussed in *Glory Days*, pp. 254–266. Will's column was widely published; the version I've used ("Bruce Springsteen's U.S.A.") ran on the op-ed page of the September 13, 1984 edition of the *Washington Post.*

4 *Reagan listened to Springsteen's records all the time: Glory Days*, pp. 255–256; "President Heaps Praise," p. B20; Wiener, pp. 297–298.

5 *"an obscenity": Glory Days*, p. 258.

5 *"honorable title of republic":* Alexander Hamilton, James Madison, and John Jay, *The Federalist Papers*, edited by Garry Wills (New York: Bantam Books, 1982), p. 190.

7 *"artificial rules":* Jefferson quoted in *Radicalism*, p. 240.

9 *hate and fear of black people:* For more on this point, see Eric Foner, *Free Soil, Free Labor, Free Men: The Ideology of the Republican Party Before the Civil War* (New York: Oxford University Press, 1970).

11 *railroad tracks that ran through it: Glory Days*, pp. 85–88.

11 *"always inside of you": Glory Days*, p. 36.

12 *"reasonably prosperous":* Franklin Delano Roosevelt, radio address of July 24, 1933, in *Fireside Chats* (New York: Penguin, 1995), p. 24.

12 *"a very long time":* Roosevelt, p. 31.

13 *"my own ideas about them":* Neil Strauss, "Springsteen Looks Back but Keeps Walking On," *New York Times*, May 7, 1995, Section 2, p. 30.

14 *"character reference": Glory Days*, p. 260.

16 *"small sums to the people themselves":* Andrew Carnegie, "Wealth," in the "Documents Set" to *Out of Many: A History of the American People* by John Faragher, et al. (Englewood Cliffs, NJ: Prentice-Hall, 1992), p. 260.

17 *better pay and working conditions:* For a good brief treatment of the Homestead strike, see Herbert G. Gutman, et al., *Who Built America: Working People and the Nation's Economy, Politics, Culture and Society* (New York: Pantheon, 1992), pp. 132–137.

17 *"listening to this one":* Springsteen quoted in Wiener, p. 295.

20 *"adherence to the Union and the Constitution":* Abraham Lincoln, "Address to the New Jersey General Assembly," in *Speeches and Writings 1859–1865*, ed. Don Fehrenbacher (New York: Library of America, 1989), p. 210.

20 *hometown of New Salem:* David Donald, *Lincoln* (New York: Simon & Schuster, 1995), p. 46.

21 *won a seat in the legislature handily:* Donald, p. 52.

21 *"boss":* On the etymology of this term, see David R. Roediger, *The Wages of Whiteness: Race and the Making of the American Working Class* (London: Verso, 1991), p. 54.

22 *experience in adversity:* I'm thinking of Roosevelt's polio. For a good brief assessment of its effect on him, see Richard Hoftstadter's essay on Roosevelt in *The American Political Tradition* (1948; New York: Vintage Books, 1954), pp. 322–324.

22 *"don't ever call me boss":* Down Thunder Road, epigraph; *Glory Days*, p. 347.

TWO: REPUBLICAN CHARACTER

23 *"a scholar's idle times":* Ralph Waldo Emerson, "The American Scholar," in *Selected Essays, Lectures and Poems of Ralph Waldo Emerson*, edited by Robert D. Richardson (New York: Bantam, 1990), p. 87.

23 *"hobgoblin of little minds":* Emerson, "Self-Reliance," in *Collected Essays*, p. 155.

23 *"man is a god in ruins":* Emerson, "Nature," in *Collected Essays*, p. 53.

24 *"the poet I describe":* Emerson, "The Poet," in *Selected Essays*, pp. 212, 221.

25 *"anywhere, at any time":* Whitman quoted in Gay Wilson Allen, *Waldo Emerson: A Biography* (New York: Viking, 1981), pp. 400–401. One should note that Emerson and Whitman had something of a rocky relationship, Emerson at first praising Whitman's early poetry but then moderating his ardor after Whitman publicized a private letter Emerson sent him. Whitman, for his part, tended to minimize Emerson's influence late in life. Nevertheless, it does seem clear that Whitman's work was at least consonant with Emerson's aesthetics, and that the two shared a powerful cultural kinship.

25 *"song of myself":* Walt Whitman, "Song of Myself," in *Leaves of Grass* (1855; annotated edition, ed. Sculley Bradley [New York: Norton, 1973]), pp. 43–44.

26 *"you may enjoy":* Whitman, 1855 Preface to *Leaves of Grass*, p. 719.

26 *"monologue" songs:* For more on the role of monologues in Springsteen's work, see Alan Rauch, "Bruce Springsteen and the Dramatic Monologue," *American Studies* 29:1 (Spring 1988), pp. 29–49.

29 *"circles of New-York":* Royall, Tyler, *The Contrast: A Comedy in Five Acts* (1790; Boston: Houghton Mifflin, 1920), p. 20.

29 *literature, "in its nature, must be aristocratic":* J. Q. Adams quoted in Russel Blaine Nye, *Society and Culture in America, 1830–1860* (New York: Harper & Row, 1974), p. 79.

29 *"Nothing is better than simplicity":* Whitman, p. 719.

30 *"position in the world":* Alexis de Tocqueville, *Democracy in America,* Part II (1840; New York: Vintage, 1990), p. 169.

31 *"Blue-Tail Fly":* lyrics quoted in Lawrence W. Levine, *Black Culture and Consciousness: Afro-American Thought From Slavery to Freedom* (New York: Oxford University Press, 1977), p. 194.

31 *influenced* by *them:* On Whitman's passion for popular song, see David Reynolds's chapter on music, oratory, and theater in *Walt Whitman's America: A Cultural Biography* (New York: Knopf, 1995). My view of Whitman's, Emerson's, and other nineteenth-century writers' receptiveness to the popular culture of their time has also been influenced by Reynolds's *Beneath the American Renaissance: The Subversive Imagination in the Age of Emerson and Melville* (Cambridge: Harvard University Press, 1988).

32 *"blood and air through my lungs":* Whitman, "Song of Myself," in *Leaves of Grass,* p. 29.

34 *"as long as we live?":* Whitman, "Song of the Open Road," in *Leaves of Grass,* p. 159.

36 *"changeable longings elsewhere":* de Tocqueville, p. 136.

36 *"comfortable on a raft":* Mark Twain, *The Adventures of Huckleberry Finn* (1885; New York: Signet, 1959), p. 119.

36 *"to be a steamboatman":* Mark Twain, "Old Times on the Mississippi," in *Great Short Works of Mark Twain,* edited by Justin Kaplan (New York: Harper & Row, 1967), p. 1. This essay was first serialized in *The Atlantic Monthly* in 1875. A longer book version was published in 1883.

38 *"spirit in which they are won":* Whitman, "Song of Myself," in *Leaves of Grass,* p. 46.

39 *"fasten words again to visible things":* Ralph Waldo Emerson, "Nature," in *Collected Essays,* p. 30.

39 *"I'll go to hell":* Huckleberry Finn, p. 210.

40 *"bruis'd feet":* Whitman, "Song of Myself," in *Leaves of Grass,* pp. 37–38.

40 *"weeds and stones":* Whitman, "Song of Myself," in *Leaves of Grass,* p. 66.

40 *"to give his message":* Truth quoted in Reynolds, p. 148.

41 *biography of Guthrie: Glory Days,* p. 29.

43 *"healthy attitude of human nature":* Emerson, "Self-Reliance," *Selected Essays,* p. 150.

43 *"they know supper's ready"*: John Steinbeck, *The Grapes of Wrath* (1939; New York: Penguin, 1976), p. 537. This line is also spoken by Henry Fonda in the 1940 film version of the novel.

43 *"sings People's Ballads"*: On Guthrie at the Forrest Theater, see Joe Klein, *Woody Guthrie: A Life* (1980; New York: Ballantine, 1986), p. 145.

44 *change in the system:* For more on this point, see Warren French, *Filmguide to "The Grapes of Wrath"* (Bloomington: University of Indiana Press, 1973), pp. 24–27.

44 *"community of the human spirit"*: See *Past Imperfect: History According to the Movies*, edited by Mark C. Carnes, et al. (New York: Henry Holt, 1995), p. 226.

45 *"I'll be there, too"*: For Steinbeck's version, see *The Grapes of Wrath*, p. 537.

45 *spring of 1944:* Klein, pp. 144, 285.

46 *"He's a musical Steinbeck"*: Maharidge quoted in Tom Schoenberg, "Professor's Research Inspires a Rock Star," *Chronicle of Higher Education*, January 19, 1996, p. A7.

48 *"we keep going"*: Springsteen quoted in Steve Pond, "Bound for Glory," *Live*, February 1996, p. 51.

THREE: VISIONS OF KINGS

50 *"which I was"*: On the Springsteen at Graceland episode, see *Born to Run*, pp. 193–194.

50 *rock artists of succeeding generations:* One example of this can be seen in Presley's 1968 television special, in which he grudgingly pays tribute to newer artists—"the Beatles, the Beards"—while subtly undercutting them at the same time (there were no "Beards," only acts like the Beatles whose hair was conspicuous—to Presley, perhaps the most noteworthy thing about them).

50 *"wanting to be Elvis Presley"*: *Born to Run*, p. 27.

52 *Baby in dreams:* These lyrics, which have not been released on any official Springsteen recording, appear in *Glory Days*, p. 28.

52 *"change the world a little bit, you know?"*: Kurt Loder, "The Rolling Stone Interview: Bruce Springsteen," *Rolling Stone*, December 6, 1984, p. 21.

53 *"city upon a hill"*: John Winthrop, "A Model of Christian Charity," in *The Puritans in America: A Narrative Anthology*, ed. Alan Heimert and Andrew Delbanco (Cambridge: Harvard University Press, 1985), p. 91.

54 *"success unexpected in common hours"*: Henry David Thoreau, *Walden; or, Life in the Woods* (1854; New York: Mentor Books, 1942), p. 215.

55 *"more Christlike"*: Rev. William Wallace, "The Relation of Wealth to Morals," in *Democracy and the Gospel of Wealth*, ed. Gail Kennedy (Boston: D.C. Heath and Company, 1949), p. 73.

55 *"capacity for wonder":* F. Scott Fitzgerald, *The Great Gatsby,* the authorized text, ed. Matthew J. Bruccoli (New York: Collier, 1992), p. 189.

56 *"That's all a man can ask for":* Presley quoted in Greil Marcus, *Mystery Train: Images of America in Rock 'n' Roll Music,* third ed. (1975; New York: Plume, 1990), pp. 133–134.

57 *"Colonel" Tom Parker:* Parker's officer status was not earned during his stint in the army, but was rather an honorary commission he finagled with his carnival connections from Louisiana governor (and country singer) Jimmie Davis. See Peter Guralnick, *Last Train to Memphis: The Rise of Elvis Presley* (Boston: Little, Brown, 1994), p. 167.

58 *"demeaning to apply it":* Marcus, pp. 125–127.

58 *"a cult of personality":* Mikal Gilmore, "Bruce Springsteen," *Rolling Stone,* Nov. 5–Dec. 10, 1987, p. 26. For an informative history of the rise (and, to some minds, anyway, the fall) of *Rolling Stone,* see Robert Draper, *Rolling Stone Magazine: The Uncensored History* (1990; New York: HarperPerennial, 1991).

58 *"you cannot live inside that dream":* Gilmore, p. 26.

58 *"Mr. Lincoln and the Black Republican party":* *Abraham Lincoln: Speeches and Writings 1832–1858,* edited by Don Fehrenbacher (New York: Library of America, 1989), p. 504.

It should be noted that Douglas's description of Lincoln's position was a distortion—the very phrase "Black Republican" had pejorative overtones much in the way "welfare queen" did in the Reagan era. Lincoln himself made this point in his fourth debate with Douglas in heavily proslavery Charleston, Illinois, a month later, when he declared, "I am not, nor have ever been in favor of bringing about in any way the social and political equality of the black and white races" (p. 636). In part, such a comment represented typical, even cynical electioneering; even a whiff of antislavery doctrine in southern Illinois was political suicide for someone seeking a seat in the U.S. Senate in 1858. There can be no doubt, though, that Lincoln meant what he said, or that he was in late twentieth-century terms a racist. At the same time, however, it is also clear that Lincoln had a lifelong antipathy to slavery, sought to limit it before the Civil War, successfully destroyed it via the Civil War—and in so doing set in motion the very result Douglas warned about in his speech. In that regard, Douglas was prophetic.

59 *"Heartbreak Hotel":* Chart position from *The* Billboard *Book of Top 40 Hits* edited by Joel Whitburn. *Billboard* is a weekly trade magazine and the most widely cited authority on the sales and airplay of American music.

59 *"Man in the News":* Taylor Branch, *Parting the Waters: America in the King Years* (New York: Simon & Schuster, 1988), p. 185.

59 *"content of their character":* Martin Luther King Jr., "I Have a Dream," in *A Testament of Hope: The Essential Writings and Speeches of Martin Luther King Jr.,* ed. James M. Washington (New York: HarperCollins, 1986), p. 217.

61 *"God is just":* Thomas Jefferson, *Notes on the State of Virginia,* ed. William Peden (1781; New York: Norton, 1982), p. 163.

61 *"the destiny of this country":* Frederick Douglass, "Hope and Despair in These Cowardly Times," an address delivered in Rochester, NY, April 28, 1861, in *The Real War Will Never Get in the Books: Selections from Writers During the Civil War,* edited by Louis Masur (New York: Oxford University Press, 1992), p. 101.

61 *"degrades and impoverishes everyone":* Martin Luther King Jr., "Who Speaks for the South?" in *Testament,* p. 93.

62 *"the best of the American Dream":* Martin Luther King Jr. "The Time for Freedom Has Come," in *Testament,* p. 165. King paraphrased these remarks in "I See the Promised Land," a speech he gave the night before his death on April 4, 1968. See *Testament,* p. 286.

62 *"the spiritual discipline against resentment":* Christopher Lasch, *The True and Only Heaven: Progress and Its Critics* (New York: Norton, 1991), chap. 9. This is a somewhat idiosyncratic book, marred by Lasch's penchant for large, unsupported generalizations. I nevertheless find much of his description of the Civil Rights movement in this chapter persuasive, and it has influenced my presentation of it here.

63 *"That's frightening":* Springsteen quoted in *The Rolling Stone Files,* p. 330.

63 *"the evil among themselves":* Harriet Beecher Stowe, *Uncle Tom's Cabin; or, Life Among the Lowly* (1851; New York: Bantam, 1981), p. 442.

65 *too dependent on black culture to reject it completely:* For one contemporary example of this phenomenon, see the analysis of Lynyrd Skynyrd in Jim Cullen, *The Civil War in Popular Culture: A Reusable Past* (Washington D.C.: Smithsonian Institution Press, 1995), pp. 123–128. For a good discussion of the origins of racist appropriation of black culture—and the ambivalence surrounding it—see David Roediger's discussion of blackface minstrelsy in *The Wages of Whiteness: Race and the Making of the American Working Class* (London: Verso, 1991), pp. 115–131. Other examples (and suggestions for further reading) are discussed in Jim Cullen, *The Art of Democracy: A Concise History of Popular Culture in the United States* (New York: Monthly Review Press, 1996).

70 *the last Springsteen wrote for the album:* "Springsteen on the Edge of Darkness," *Boston Globe,* December 15, 1995, p. 74.

71 *violations of civil rights and antitrust statutes:* Morris Dees with Steve Fiffer, *A Season for Justice: The Life and Times of Civil Rights Lawyer Morris Dees* (New York: Charles Scribner's Sons, 1991), pp. 6–49.

72 *"and his slaves":* Michael Lind, *The Next American Nation: The New Nationalism and the Fourth American Revolution* (New York: The Free Press, 1995), p. 288.

73 *"intermarriage between the races":* This and the subsequent quote from Douglass are cited in Lind, p. 380.

73 *"but a prophet":* Lind, p. 380.

73 *"behavior can be regulated":* Martin Luther King Jr., "An Address Before the National Press Club," in *Testament,* p. 101.

FOUR: BORNE IN THE U.S.A.

77 *"a holler of impotent desperation":* Jon Pareles, "Hard Times and No Silver Lining," *New York Times,* December 14, 1995, p. C11. I did not attend this or any other performance of *The Ghost of Tom Joad* tour, my description of it here relying on published accounts and a conversation with someone who did.

77 *this and all other offers:* For a discussion of the Iacocca affair, see *Glory Days,* pp. 424–426.

77 *"the* spirit *of his music":* Glory Days, p. 426.

78 *"it's back, you know?":* Glory Days, p. 426.

78 *"another chance to get it right":* Steve Pond, "Bound for Glory," *Live,* February 1996, p. 48.

79 *"It had nothing to do with you":* Bobbie Ann Mason, *In Country* (1985; New York: HarperPerennial, 1993), p. 57.

80 *"cornerstone" of the Southern way of life:* On Stephens's shifting justification for secession, see the excerpts from his speeches in *The Causes of the Civil War,* ed. Kenneth Stampp (1959; New York: Touchstone, 1990), pp. 63–65, 152–153.

81 *difficult, sticky, or repellent:* For a fuller elaboration of this point (and numerous suggestions for further reading), see my chapter "Reconstructing Dixie" in *The Civil War in Popular Culture: A Reusable Past* (Washington, D.C.: Smithsonian Institution Press, 1995), pp. 108–138.

81 *one Vietnam film came out during that conflict:* "F.Y.I.," *Premiere,* May 1991, p. 15.

82 *"a dark room full of deadly objects":* Michael Herr, *Dispatches* (1977; New York: Vintage, 1991), p. 71.

83 *"noble-grunt film":* Pat Aufderheide, "Good Soldiers," in *Seeing Through Movies,* edited by Mark Crispin Miller (New York: Pantheon, 1990), pp. 81–111.

83 *"having felt so bad for so long":* Aufderheide, p. 111.

88 *"of really loving":* Clinton quoted in David Maraniss, *First in His Class: The Biography of Bill Clinton* (1995; New York: Touchstone, 1996), p. 180.

89 *"guys who did come back were not the same"*: Kurt Loder, "The Rolling Stone Interview: Bruce Springsteen," *Rolling Stone,* December 6, 1984, p. 21.

89 *"It just didn't seem right"*: Loder, p. 21.

92 *"there would be no Vietnam veterans movement"*: Glory Days , pp. 66–77. Muller's quote appears on p. 75.

92 *"is gettin' manipulated and exploited"*: Loder, p. 21.

92 *"where your audiences come from?"*: Loder, p. 21.

93 *"smart enough to know that much"*: Herr, pp. 206–207.

93 *considered naming:* Arlen Schumer, "Cover Me: Behind the Design of Born in the U.S.A.," in *Backstreets Springsteen,* p. 114.

93 *Springsteen put the song aside:* On the origins of "Born in the U.S.A.," see *Glory Days,* pp. 104–106.

94 *"that turbulence and that scale"*: *Glory Days,* pp. 115–116.

94 *"the most exciting thing that ever happened in a recording studio"*: *Glory Days,* p. 116.

95 *"a situation destructive of morale overall"*: Colin Powell with Joseph E. Persico, *My American Journey* (1995; New York: Ballantine Books, 1996), p. 49.

96 *a long, dishonorable tradition of "orientalism"*: For a fuller elaboration of this point, see Edward Said, *Orientalism* (New York: Knopf, 1978) and *Culture and Imperialism* (New York: Knopf, 1993).

98 *"a lasting peace, among ourselves, and with all nations"*: Lincoln: *Speeches and Writings, 1859–1865,* ed. Don Fehrenbacher (New York: Library of America, 1989), p. 687.

FIVE: THE GOOD LIFE

99 *"the work ethic is undergoing some changes"*: Nixon quoted in Herbert G. Gutman, *Work, Culture and Society in Industrializing America* (New York: Vintage, 1977), p. 4; Puritan maxim quoted in Daniel T. Rodgers, *The Work Ethic in Industrial America 1850–1920* (Chicago: University of Chicago Press, 1979), p. 7. Both books are major works in the historiography of the work ethic.

100 *"ascetic Protestantism"*: Max Weber, *The Protestant Ethic and the Spirit of Capitalism,* trans. Talcott Parsons (New York: Charles Scribner's Sons, 1930).

102 *"a pretty wonderful thing for a record to do"*: In His Own Words, p. 38.

102 *major urban slave revolts:* David R. Roediger, *The Wages of Whiteness: Race and the Making of the American Working Class* (London: Verso, 1991), p. 24. Roediger's work, like that of virtually all scholars who have investigated this subject since the sixties, is indebted to that of Winthrop Jordan. See *White Over Black: American Attitudes*

Toward the Negro, 1550–1812 (Chapel Hill: University of North Carolina Press, 1968). Jordan emphasizes the racism at the roots of the very first white/black encounters, but he and others note that the institutionalization of this attitude was a process that took place over a long period of time and was not monolithic.

104 *"the folklore of industrial society":* Lawrence Levine, "The Folklore of Industrial Society," in *The Unpredictable Past: Explorations in American Cultural History* (New York: Oxford University Press, 1993). See especially p. 295, where Levine explains the position of popular culture relative to folklore. Much of what is here and follows draws from my previous book, *The Art of Democracy: A Concise History of Popular Culture in the United States* (New York: Monthly Review Press, 1996).

106 *"People never sold out by buying something":* In His Own Words, p. 90.

108 *"That's fucking triumph, man":* Townshend quoted in *In His Own Words,* p. 94.

109 Springsteen in Seattle: Charles Cross, "Reason to Believe," in *Backstreets Springsteen,* pp. 12–15.

110 *"I mean every date, too":* Jackson quoted in *In His Own Words,* p. 94.

110 *"the work ethic is alive and well":* George Will, "Bruce Springsteen's USA," *Washington Post,* September 13, 1984.

110 *"a purely magical object":* Roland Barthes, *Mythologies,* translated from the French by Annette Lavers (1957; New York: Noonday Press, 1972), p. 88.

111 *"beyond intellectual distinctions":* Johan Huizinga, *Homo Ludens: A Study of the Play Element in Culture* (1938; Boston: Beacon Press, 1955), p. 213.

111 *"that felt good":* In His Own Words, p. 38.

113 *canonical works of early rock and roll:* For an insightful reading of Berry's automotive imagery, see Warren Belasco, "Motivatin' with Chuck Berry and Frederick Jackson Turner," in *The Automobile and American Culture,* edited by David L. Lewis and Laurence Goldstein: (Ann Arbor: University of Michigan Press, 1983), pp. 279–282.

115 *automotive statement of choice:* Peter Marsh and Peter Collett, *Driving Passion: The Psychology of the Car* (Boston: Faber and Faber, 1986), p. 97.

115 *the road became a tired cliché:* Belasco, p. 277.

115 *"like detective movies":* In His Own Words, p. 58.

115 *"saddest songs I've ever written":* Born to Run, p. 256.

121 *"play as frivolous":* Jackson Lears, *Fables of Abundance: A Cultural History of Advertising in America* (New York: Basic Books, 1994), p. 7.

122 *three key terms:* Hannah Arendt, *The Human Condition* (Chicago: University of Chicago Press, 1958). See especially parts III, IV, and V, where Arendt gives a taxonomy of these categories.

122 *"the greedier and more craving his appetites":* Arendt, p. 133.

SIX: MODEL MAN

124 *"Dancing in the Dark," his first video:* On the making of the video, see *Glory Days*, pp. 190–193.

125 *"dance with her in the dark":* Bobbie Ann Mason, *In Country* (1985; New York: HarperPerennial, 1993), pp. 97, 190.

126 *"he don't care":* Zeitvogel quoted in Merle Ginsberg, "The Fans," *Rolling Stone,* October 10, 1985, p. 31.

126 *a real working-class person would be:* Simon Frith, "The Real Thing: Bruce Springsteen," in *Music for Pleasure* (New York: Routledge, 1988), p. 96.

126 *the population at large:* For examples of celebrations of sex role violations or inversions in eighties popular culture, see, for instance, Camille Paglia's discussions of Madonna in *Sex, Art and American Culture* (New York: Vintage, 1992) and John Fiske's take on her in *Reading Popular Culture* (Boston: Unwin/Hyman, 1989). The second half of Simon Reynolds's and Joy Press's *The Sex Revolts: Gender Rebellion and Rock 'n' Roll* (Cambridge: Harvard University Press, 1995) explores the varied ways in which women have explored—and exploded—gender expectations. For critiques of exaggerated masculinity, see James William Gibson, *Warrior Dreams: Violence and Manhood in Post-Vietnam America* (New York: Hill and Wang, 1992), and especially the work of Susan Jeffords, including *The Remasculinization of America: Gender and the Vietnam War* (Bloomington: University of Indiana Press, 1991) and *Hard Bodies: Hollywood Masculinity in the Reagan Era* (New Brunswick, NJ: Rutgers University Press, 1994).

127 *"stick by them as best as possible":* In His Own Words, p. 92.

128 *"that night I was happy":* Walt Whitman, *Leaves of Grass,* ed. Scully Bradley and Harold W. Blodgett (1855/1892; New York: Norton, 1973), p. 123.

128 *the boys of Clary's Grove:* This account of the Lincoln-Armstrong match relies on David Donald, *Lincoln* (New York: Simon & Schuster, 1995), pp. 40–41; Stephen B. Oates, *With Malice Toward None: The Life of Abraham Lincoln* (1977; New York: Mentor, 1978), p. 20; and Carl Sandburg, *Abrham Lincoln: The Prairie Years and the War Years,* a one-volume edition of the six-volume biography published in 1926 and 1939 (1954; New York: Galahad Books, 1993), p. 25.

129 *"boy culture":* E. Anthony Rotundo, *American Manhood: Transformations in Masculinity from the Revolution to the Modern Era* (New York: Basic Books, 1993), pp. 31–55.

131 *sharing a bed with his friend Joshua Speed:* For details on this arrangement, see Donald, p. 66.

131 *"he did not assume he had them"*: Rotundo, pp. 83–88; 274–279. Donald makes a similar point about the commonplace nature of men sleeping together in *Lincoln,* p. 70. Gore Vidal draws on this convention when he has Lincoln's secretaries John Hay and John Nicolay share a bed in his novel *Lincoln* (1984; New York: Ballantine, 1985), p.69. For a fuller treatment of the intensifying interest—and anxiety—about masculinity at the turn of the century, see Gail Bederman, *Manliness and Civilization: A Cultural History of Gender and Race in the United States, 1880–1917* (Chicago: University of Chicago Press, 1995).

132 *sharing a microphone throughout any given evening:* For a perceptive reading of the homoerotic strains in Springsteen's performances, see Martha Nell Smith, "Sexual Mobilities in Bruce Springsteen: Performance as Commentary," *South Atlantic Quarterly* 90:4 (Fall 1991), pp. 833–854.

139 *a time of traditional sex roles:* For more on perceptions of women and sex roles in the fifties, see Elaine Tyler May, *Homeward Bound: American Families in the Cold War Era* (New York: Basic Books, 1988).

142 *"something people rarely are in life":* Born to Run, p. 163.

142 *"keep Candy safe":* Smith, pp. 842–844.

145 *"It wasn't gonna be any good without her":* In His Own Words, p. 73.

146 *gay couples fleetingly interspersed with straight ones:* This point is made by Smith in her perceptive reading of the song. See "Sexual Mobilities," p. 845.

153 *"make sure the world don't fall apart":* Glory Days, p. 87.

154 *"so much bitterness":* In His Own Words, p. 11.

154 *"a six-pack and a cigarette":* Born to Run, p. 24.

156 *John Steinbeck's* East of Eden: *Born to Run,* p. 209.

162 *"what both men and women* might *be":* Barbara Ehrenreich, *The Worst Years of Our Lives: Irreverent Notes from a Decade of Greed* (New York: HarperPerennial; 1984, 1991), p. 137.

162 *"man is or could be":* Robert Bly, *Iron John: A Book About Men* (1990; New York: Vintage, 1992), p. ix.

SEVEN: INHERITED IMAGINATION

In this chapter, I use the terms "religion" generally and "Catholicism" specifically less to refer to systematic theology or church doctrine than to the phenomenon anthropologist Clifford Geertz described in his famous 1966 essay "Religion as a Cultural System." For Geertz, religion is "a system of symbols which acts to establish powerful, pervasive, and long-lasting moods and motivations in men by formulating conceptions of a general order of existence and clothing these conceptions with such an aura of factuality that the moods and motivations seem uniquely realistic." Geertz's definition is well-suited to explore how religion has functioned in Springsteen's music. See Geertz, "Religion as a Cultural System" in *The Interpretation of Cultures* (New York: Basic Books, 1974), p. 90.

I have also benefited from perusing a growing literature on the cultural dimensions of Catholicism. The definitive general history is Jay Dolan's *The American Catholic: A History from Colonial Times to the Present* (New York: Doubleday, 1985). Two works of decisive importance in shaping my ideas about Springsteen's Catholicism are Paul Giles's superb *American Catholic Arts and Fictions: Culture, Ideology, Aesthetics* (New York: Cambridge University Press, 1992) and David Tracy, *The Analogical Imagination: Christian Theology and the Culture of Pluralism* (New York: Crossroad Publishing, 1981), especially the final chapter. Tracy's ideas were popularized by Andrew Greeley—a kind of patron saint of this chapter—in *The Catholic Myth: The Behavior and Beliefs of American Catholics* (New York: Collier, 1990), especially chapter 3. See also John E. Tropman, *The Catholic Ethic in American Society* (San Francisco: Josey-Bass, 1995).

My source for information on Springsteen's Phoenix concert and God's dialogue in the story he told there comes from a 1978 *Rolling Stone* article by Springsteen biographer Dave Marsh. It is reprinted in *The Rolling Stone Files*, pp. 78–93.

164 *"to imagine a destiny rather than inherit one":* Fiedler's *Playboy* essay, "Cross the Border, Close the Gap," was included in his essay collection of the same name (New York: Stein and Day, 1972), p. 73. In retrospect, it's amazing that the musings of *any* literary critic were deemed to be of interest to readers of *Playboy* (or, for that matter, any general-interest magazine). Readers of this chapter may also perceive more than a little irony in Fiedler's remark given *Playboy's* mission of purveying sexual fantasy—a form of imagined destiny in its own right.

I first became aware of this quote when I read Greil Marcus's *Mystery Train: Images of America in Rock & Roll Music*, 3d edition (1975; New York: Plume, 1990), p. 5. Like Fiedler, Marcus has relatively little to say about it. Nevertheless, its presence in the book is only one of the many reasons my work is indebted to his.

167 *"cafeteria" Catholics:* My understanding of this term (and the less pejorative "cultural" Catholics) has been influenced by the work of Catholic sociologist Andrew Greeley. See, for example, *The Communal Catholic: A Personal Manifesto* (New York: Seabury Press, 1976); *The American Catholic: A Social Portrait* (New York: Basic Books, 1977); as well as *The Catholic Myth*.

167 *"Once a Catholic, always a Catholic":* For a compendium of personal responses to Catholicism, including those of apostates like *Penthouse* publisher Bob Guccione and rock composer Frank Zappa, see Peter Occhiogrosso, ed., *Once a Catholic: Prominent Catholics and Ex-Catholics Discuss the Influence of the Church on Their Lives and Work* (Boston: Houghton Mifflin, 1987).

168 *"a Quaker meetinghouse cannot":* Greeley, *The Catholic Myth*, pp. 56–57.

169 *"Some people pray, some people play music":* Springsteen quoted in *Born to Run*, p. 23.

172 *"real smart, real strong, real creative":* *Glory Days*, p. 87.

172 *"I was trying to fake it":* *Born to Run*, p. 22.

173 *"I knew he could only be Catholic":* "If I Was the Priest" lyrics and Hammond quoted in *Born to Run*, p. 60.

173 *a specifically American mythology with a more broadly Catholic one:* James T. Fisher has also noted the "mystically concrete sensibility" of "If I Was the Priest." See "Clearing the Streets of the Catholic Lost Generation," *South Atlantic Quarterly* 93:3 (Summer 1994), pp. 616–617. This essay was part of "Catholic Lives/Contemporary America," a special edition of the journal under the editorship of Thomas J. Ferraro.

174 *reflexive habits of thought:* See Giles, p. 70.

177 *furled cloth flag:* "Curiously enough, a great many flags tend to be waved around in the work of Catholic authors—one thinks of all the icons of national myth in Robert Altman's films—and while this might be attributed to the insecurity of aliens wishing urgently to display their patriotic allegiance, it may also be the case that Catholics tend to have a cultural predilection for seizing upon and investing significance in emblems of communal iconography." See Giles, p. 156.

184 *more troubled than inspired:* I was one of a number of people who once saw "Reason to Believe" as an affirmative song. That I now think otherwise is

attributable to an interview I conducted with Dave Marsh in 1985 and his own reading of the song. See *Glory Days*, pp. 137–139.

184 *"more Americans than those who listened to the Pope"*: Andrew M. Greeley, "The Catholic Imagination of Bruce Springsteen," *America* 158:5 (February 6, 1988), p. 110.

185 *"you have to reinvent yourself"*: *In His Own Words* p. 52.

185 *"wonderful and beautiful things"*: *In His Own Words*, p. 53.

185 *"symbol rather than doctrine"*: Greeley, "The Catholic Imagination of Bruce Springsteen," pp. 112, 114.

191 *"a matter of no great consequence"*: Flannery O'Connor, author's note to the second edition of *Wise Blood* (1952; New York: The Noonday Press, 1962). Springsteen read some of O'Connor's short stories after seeing a film version of *Wise Blood* in the 1980s. See *Glory Days*, p. 97.

192 *"spiritual stillness that I wanted to try and capture"*: Judy Wieder, "Bruce Springsteen: The Advocate Interview," *The Advocate*, April 2, 1996, p. 48.

195 *"Amen" during church hymns*: For this observation, I am indebted to Harvard student Aaron Montgomery of Detroit, Michigan, who noted it when I played the song for a class in November 1996.

195 *"the world will break your heart"*: quoted in Fisher, p. 623. Thomas Cahill attributes the aphorism to Daniel Patrick Moynihan in the aftermath of John F. Kennedy's assassination. See *How the Irish Saved Civilization: The Untold Story of Ireland's Heroic Role from the Fall of Rome to the Rise of Medieval Europe* (1995; New York: Anchor, 1996), p. 97.

196 *"render them equal"*: Alexis de Tocqueville, *Democracy in America*, vol. I (1835; New York: Vintage, 1945), p. 311.

196 *"more equal than in republics"*: de Tocqueville, pp. 311–312.

197 *"occupy until he comes"*: Falwell quoted in Frances Fitzgerald, *Cities on a Hill: A Journey Through Contemporary American Cultures* (New York: Simon & Schuster, 1986), p. 164. Fitzgerald notes Falwell's and other evangelicals' fondness for military metaphors, partially attributable to the prominence of military traditions in the South. Nonetheless it's hard to ignore the imperial overtones of such language. "Nowhere in this sermon does Falwell mention Satan," Fitzgerald observes. "The enemy here is quite clearly human; it is quite clearly everyone who does not subscribe to his own particular brand of fundamentalism." (I myself find the very name of Lynchburg frighteningly evocative.)

197 *the New Deal as "communistic"*: See Alan Brinkley, *Voices of Protest: Huey Long, Father Coughlin and the Great Depression* (1982; New York: Vintage, 1983), p. 257.

CONCLUSION: BETTER ANGELS

199 *"I am loth to close":* Abraham Lincoln, "First Inaugural Address," in *Speeches and Writings, 1859–1865,* edited by Don Fehrenbacher (New York: Library of America, 1989), p. 224.

202 *"what's right with America":* "Transcript of Address by President Clinton," *New York Times,* January 21, 1993, p. A15; Todd Purdum, "What Kind of Democrat?" *New York Times Magazine,* May 19, 1996, p. 78.

Select Discography

Given the sheer volume of material he has released in the last twenty-five years, and the plethora of unauthorized recordings in circulation around the world (the Grateful Dead is probably the only act that has generated more bootlegs than Bruce Springsteen), it would be difficult and impractical to compile a complete discography here. Though now dated, the best such discography is Chris Hunt's, included in *Springsteen: Blinded by the Light,* the book he wrote with Patrick Humphries. Parke Puterbaugh's discography (and videography) in *The Rolling Stone Files* is less comprehensive but includes material produced through 1995.

This document is simply a list of Springsteen's albums for Columbia between 1973 and 1995, and the individual songs that appear on each. While Springsteen has released a number of EPs and singles, it seems clear that he regards his albums as his major artistic productions, and the songs included on them to be the focal point of his work. The primary purpose of this discography is to function as a kind of index that allows readers of this book to know which of those songs appear on the most commonly available Springsteen albums.

All songs were written by Springsteen unless otherwise noted. The figures that appear in parentheses after the titles are Columbia Records catalog numbers, followed by the year of release.

Greetings from Asbury Park, NJ (31093), 1973

Blinded by the Light
Growin' Up
Mary Queen of Arkansas
Does This Bus Stop at 82nd Street?
Lost in the Flood
The Angel
For You
Spirit in the Night
It's So Hard to Be a Saint in the City

The Wild, the Innocent and the E Street Shuffle (32432), 1973

The E Street Shuffle
4th of July, Asbury Park (Sandy)
Kitty's Back
Wild Billy's Circus Story
Incident on 57th St.
Rosalita (Come Out Tonight)
New York City Serenade

Born to Run (33795), 1975

Thunder Road
Tenth Avenue Freeze-Out
Night
Backstreets
Born to Run
She's the One
Meeting Across the River
Jungleland

Darkness on the Edge of Town (35318), 1978

Badlands
Adam Raised a Cain
Something in the Night
Candy's Room
Racing in the Street
The Promised Land
Factory
Streets of Fire
Prove It All Night
Darkness on the Edge of Town

The River (36854), 1980

The Ties That Bind
Sherry Darling
Jackson Cage
Two Hearts
Independence Day

Hungry Heart
Crush on You
Out in the Street
You Can Look (But You Better Not Touch)
I Wanna Marry You
The River
Point Blank
Cadillac Ranch
I'm a Rocker
Fade Away
Stolen Car
Ramrod
The Price You Pay
Drive All Night
Wreck on the Highway

Nebraska (38358), 1982

Nebraska
Atlantic City
Mansion on the Hill
Johnny 99
Highway Patrolman
State Trooper
Used Cars
Open All Night
My Father's House
Reason to Believe

Born in the U.S.A. (38653), 1984

Born in the U.S.A.
Cover Me
Darlington County
Working on the Highway
I'm on Fire
No Surrender
Bobby Jean
I'm Goin' Down
Glory Days
Dancing in the Dark
My Hometown

Live 1975–85 (40558), 1986

Thunder Road
Adam Raised a Cain
Spirit in the Night
4th of July, Asbury Park (Sandy)
Paradise by the "C"
Growin' Up
It's Hard to Be a Saint in the City
Backstreets
Rosalita (Come Out Tonight)
Raise Your Hand [Steven Cropper, Eddie Floyd, and Alvertis Isbell]
Hungry Heart
Two Hearts
Cadillac Ranch
You Can Look (But You Better Not Touch)
Independence Day
Badlands

Because the Night [Springsteen and Patti Smith]
Candy's Room
Darkness on the Edge of Town
Racing in the Street
This Land is Your Land [Woody Guthrie]
Nebraska
Johnny 99
Reason to Believe
Born in the U.S.A.
Seeds
The River
War [Barrett Strong and Norman Whitfield]
Darlington County
Working on the Highway
The Promised Land
Cover Me
I'm on Fire
Bobby Jean
My Hometown
Born to Run
No Surrender
Tenth Avenue Freeze-Out
Jersey Girl [Tom Waits]

Tunnel of Love (40999), 1987

Ain't Got You
Tougher Than the Rest
All That Heaven Will Allow
Spare Parts
Cautious Man
Walk Like a Man

Tunnel of Love
Two Faces
Brilliant Disguise
One Step Up
When You're Alone
Valentine's Day

Human Touch (53000), 1992

Human Touch
Soul Driver
57 Channels (And Nothin' On)
Cross My Heart [Springsteen and Sonny Boy Williamson]
Gloria's Eyes
With Every Wish
Roll of the Dice [Springsteen and Roy Bittan]
Real World [Springsteen and Roy Bittan]
All or Nothing at All
Man's Job
I Wish I Were Blind
The Long Goodbye
Real Man
*Pony Boy [traditional; arrangement and additional lyrics by
    Springsteen]*

Lucky Town (53001), 1992

Better Days
Lucky Town
Local Hero
If I Should Fall Behind

Leap of Faith
The Big Muddy
Living Proof
Book of Dreams
Souls of the Departed
My Beautiful Reward

Greatest Hits (67060), 1995

Born to Run
Thunder Road
Badlands
The River
Hungry Heart
Atlantic City
Dancing in the Dark
Born in the U.S.A.
My Hometown
Glory Days
Brilliant Disguise
Human Touch
Better Days
Streets of Philadelphia
Secret Garden
Murder Incorporated
Blood Brothers
This Hard Land

The Ghost of Tom Joad (67484), 1995

The Ghost of Tom Joad
Straight Time
Highway 25
Youngstown
Sinaloa Cowboys
The Line
Balboa Park
Dry Lightning
The New Timer
Across the Border
Galveston Bay
My Best Was Never Good Enough

A Springsteen Chronology

1949

Bruce Frederick Springsteen is born on September 23 in Freehold, New Jersey, to Douglas Springsteen, a bus driver (among other occupations), and Adele Zirilli Springsteen, a legal secretary. The couple later have two daughters, Pamela and Virginia.

1966

Springsteen enters the Castiles, a local rock band. It is the first of a number he will lead, join, or form over the next five years, including Steel Mill, Child, and Dr. Zoom and the Sonic Boom.

1971

After playing in ensembles that include future E Street Band drummer Vini Lopez, organist Danny Federici, pianist David Sancious, saxophonist Clarence Clemons, and guitarist Steve Van Zandt, Springsteen decides to pursue a solo career as a singer/songwriter.

1972

Springsteen signs a management contract in March with independent producers Mike Appel and Jim Crecetos on the hood of a car in the unlighted parking lot of a bar. Appel, who later buys out Crecetos's interest, lands Springsteen an audition with John Hammond, the legendary talent scout who discovered and worked with Billie Holiday, Count Basie, Miles Davis, Aretha Franklin, and Bob Dylan. "The kid absolutely knocked me out," Hammond later says of Springsteen's May 2 audition. "I only hear somebody really good once every ten years, and not only was Bruce the best, he was a lot better than Dylan when I first heard him."

1973

Greetings from Asbury Park, NJ is released in January. Though it gains critical attention, early sales are poor. Some critics are repelled by a Columbia Records marketing campaign that hails Springsteen as "the new Dylan." The label arranges for Springsteen to perform as the opening act for the highly successful jazz-rock band Chicago, which proves disastrous.

The Wild, the Innocent and the E Street Shuffle is released in September. Much more of a rock and roll record than its predecessor—it features the E Street Band—this album also gets some good reviews, but is a commercial disappointment.

1974

Rolling Stone record review editor Jon Landau attends a Springsteen show at the Harvard Square Theater in Cambridge,

Massachusetts, in May. "I saw rock & roll's future and its name is Bruce Springsteen," he writes in a column for a Boston newspaper and that becomes the most famous line in rock criticism. Landau befriends Springsteen, and ultimately gives up his journalism career to become his manager and coproducer.

1975

In August, Springsteen makes a series of acclaimed performances at New York's fabled Bottom Line nightclub (one show is broadcast live on a Manhattan radio station). A review by music critic John Rockwell makes the front page of the *New York Times*.

The following week, *Born to Run* is released, creating a national sensation. Springsteen is the cover story for both *Time* and *Newsweek* in their October 27 issues. A media debate ensues over whether the Springsteen phenomenon is a matter of genuine talent or hype.

STAR-MAKING MACHINERY: Springsteen appeared on the covers of *Time* and *Newsweek* simultaneously in 1975, precipitating a national discussion of whether he actually had any talent or was in fact a commercially fabricated flash-in-the-pan.

1976

Springsteen's relationship with Appel is increasingly tense; the two file countersuits against each other in July. Appel wins an injunction from a judge preventing Springsteen from producing an album with Landau while the matter is pending.

1977

Springsteen and Appel settle their differences out of court in May. Landau is now officially Springsteen's manager and producer.

1978

Darkness on the Edge of Town is released in July. It is respectfully reviewed and sells well, but does not attract the attention *Born to Run* did.

1979

Springsteen performs in the Musicians United for Safe Energy (MUSE) benefit concerts held at Madison Square Garden in September. His appearance there and in the subsequent concert film raise his national profile, especially as a live performer.

1980

In March, a New Jersey state assemblyman, picking up on the suggestion of a New York disc jockey, introduces a successful resolution to make "Born to Run" the state's "Unofficial Youth Rock Anthem."

The River, a double album, is released in October, and becomes Springsteen's first album to reach number one on the *Billboard* magazine album chart. One song, "Hungry Heart," becomes Springsteen's first top-ten single on the *Billboard* singles chart (all subsequent chart references are from *Billboard*). When Springsteen's management announces that he will perform at New York's Madison Square Garden, the 18,000-seat arena receives enough ticket requests to fill it for sixteen nights.

1981

Springsteen organizes a benefit concert for the Vietnam Veterans of America in Los Angeles on September 20, part of his intensifying interest in veterans' issues that reaches full flower in *Born in the U.S.A.*

Late in the year, the New York Chapter of the National Organization for Women (NOW) instigates a letter- and phone-call appeal demanding that he stop referring to women as "little girls" in his music. A spokeswoman in Springsteen's office defends his use of "little girl," calling it "a rock & roll term." She is quoted in *Rolling Stone* magazine as saying that no calls or letters had been received, except from NOW members wishing to disassociate themselves from the project.

1982

Nebraska, a stark, solo acoustic album, is released in September. Defying expectations, the album is a relative success, reaching number three on the album chart.

1984

Born in the U.S.A. is released in June. Besides making it to number one on the album chart (it remains in the top ten for the next two years), it spawns seven hit top-ten singles in the ensuing eighteen months: "Dancing in the Dark," "Cover Me," "Born in the U.S.A.," "I'm on Fire," "Glory Days," "I'm Goin' Down," and "My Hometown." The album goes on to sell over 20 million copies domestically (and another 10 million abroad), making it the best-selling album in Columbia Records history. The accompanying videos for these songs and his world tour make Springsteen an international superstar and icon of the Reagan era.

In September, the president himself invokes Springsteen. "America's future rests in a thousand dreams inside our hearts. It rests in the message of hope so many young people admire: New Jersey's own Bruce Springsteen. And helping you make those dreams come true is what this job of mine is all about."

1985

Springsteen performs (singing a duet with Stevie Wonder) on the "We Are the World" single and album to benefit hunger victims of the Ethiopian famine. He also works with E Street Band alumnus Steve Van Zandt on *Sun City*, a benefit song and album to combat apartheid in South Africa.

Springsteen marries model/actress Julianne Phillips in May.

1986

Bruce Springsteen Live 1975–85, a forty-song multialbum set is released in November, precipitating a run on record stores. Springsteen's top-ten version of "War," the 1970 Edwin Starr hit, explicitly attacks Reagan administration policy in Latin America.

1987

Tunnel of Love, Springsteen's most low-key album since *Nebraska*, is released in September. A collection of love songs, it tops the album chart, and contains three hit singles—"Brilliant Disguise," "Tunnel of Love," and "One Step Up."

1988

Springsteen headlines the six-week, international Amnesty International Human Rights Now! tour, which includes Sting, Peter Gabriel, Tracy Chapman, and Youssou N'Dour. Springsteen releases *Chimes of Freedom,* a four-song, extended play record of the event, and donates over $200,000 in the royalties it generates, the largest single gift ever made to the organization.

During the tour, tabloid newspapers report that Springsteen is having an affair with Patti Scialfa, a backup singer who joined the E Street Band during the *Born in the U.S.A.* tour.

1989

Springsteen and Julianne Phillips divorce.

Springsteen breaks up the E Street Band, though he will continue to play with assorted members on an ad-hoc basis, and the group will periodically reunite.

1990

A son, Evan James, is born to Springsteen and Scialfa.

1991

Springsteen and Scialfa marry. A daughter, Jessica Rae, is born.

1992

Human Touch and *Lucky Town,* Springsteen's first albums in almost five years, are released simultaneously in April. The title track of the former is a hit, but both are relative disappointments commercially and critically. Springsteen uses session musicians to record the album and in live performances, which include his first appearances on *Saturday Night Live* and MTV's *Unplugged* (in which he played with electric instruments, despite the show's acoustic format).

1993

Springsteen writes "Streets of Philadelphia" at the request of director Jonathan Demme for his film *Philadelphia*. A top-ten single, it becomes one of his biggest hits.

1994

"Streets of Philadelphia" wins an Oscar for Best Original Song at the Academy Awards ceremony in Los Angeles in March.

A son, Sam Ryan, is born to Springsteen and Scialfa.

1995

Greatest Hits, featuring four previously unreleased songs, is released in January, and debuts at number one on the *Billboard* album chart. Springsteen reunites the E Street Band for a club performance filmed by Jonathan Demme and later broadcast on VH1 and MTV.

The Ghost of Tom Joad is released in November. Like *Nebraska,* this is a solo, largely acoustic album. Springsteen launches his first club tour in twenty years.

1996

Upon learning that a bus for the Bob Dole campaign is blaring "Born in the U.S.A." as it drives through Red Bank, New Jersey, in October, Springsteen sends a fax to the *Asbury Park Press.* "Just for the record, I'd like to make clear that [the song] was used without my permission and I am not a supporter of the Republican ticket," he writes.

Blood Brothers, a documentary video, is released with a five-song compact disc in November.

1997

The Ghost of Tom Joad wins a Grammy Award for Best Contemporary Folk Album. Despite the album's (and Springsteen's) low-key profile, it sells over 2 million copies.

ACKNOWLEDGMENTS

Like many books, this one has a long history. I'd like to briefly recount it as a means toward thanking the many people who have aided and shaped the realization of a durable dream.

I have been at least peripherally aware of Bruce Springsteen since about 1975, when as an early adolescent I spotted a copy of *Born to Run* at my older cousin Lisa Palatella's house one Christmas and was struck by its elegant cover design. Anything Lisa (or another cousin, Rick Montani) liked was good enough for me; I picked up a copy. Nevertheless, I didn't listen to the album much, regarding it more as a means of rounding out my collection than as a cherished possession. It was only during my senior year of high school, in the fall of 1980, that I began to get really excited about Springsteen, an excitement that intensified upon the release of *The River.* In retrospect, I feel as if a kind of baton was passed from John Lennon, who was murdered that December, to Springsteen, a man whose music I was growing up with. Now that I have grown up, I can only hope that mere words *can* express my gratitude. In a fundamental sense, that's what this book is all about.

My parents, Grace and Jim Cullen, accepted my musical obsessions as part of the price they paid for raising happy children. Mom typically asked me to turn the stereo down; Dad would stick his head in my bedroom and wonder how I could possibly do homework with music on. Of a different time, they had little appreciation of Springsteen. But Springsteen helped me appreciate them, two people with difficult childhoods, limited educations, and a remarkably focused and successful commitment to giving my beloved sister, Cathy, and me opportunities they never had. I have thanked them before, in print and elsewhere, but it seems apropos to do so again.

I first got the idea of writing a book about Springsteen on a Greyhound bus to Boston in the spring of 1983, when, as a sophomore at Tufts University, it occurred to me that there were some affinities between what Springsteen sang about and what Mark Twain wrote about. Until that point, my intellectual orientation had been largely European; reading James Joyce's *Ulysses* and T. S. Eliot's "The Waste Land" constituted my idea of what it meant to be an educated person. I returned from a semester abroad in 1984 to spend my senior year writing a senior honors thesis on Springsteen. I am grateful to the English department at Tufts for even allowing such a project, and especially to Jeff Titon (of the English and music departments) and Jeanne Dillon (then of the Italian department and the American studies program) for providing me with supervision and the encouragement to undertake that enterprise, one which bears little direct—but much indirect—resemblance to this one.

Shortly after my graduation in 1985, Professor Titon left Tufts to chair the ethnomusicology program at Brown University. When I applied to graduate school the following year, he made me aware of Brown's American civilization doctoral program, to which I was admitted. Under the tutelege of great teachers like Mari Jo Buhle, Bill McLoughlin, Jim Patterson, Susan Smulyan, and Jack Thomas,

I learned how to write history. Though I have strayed from some of the precepts of these people, I remain indebted to the examples, personal as well as professional, that they established for me at a formative period in my life.

In these years, Springsteen's music remained an important backdrop. My graduate school years are bounded by the release of *Tunnel of Love* in 1987 and *Human Touch/Lucky Town* in 1992. My first seminar paper and last academic article were on Springsteen, though my dissertation and the second book I wrote after it was completed were on other subjects. I hoped to finally write a book on Springsteen, but I wasn't sure when, how, or if I would ever do so.

The opportunity presented itself in the fall of 1994, when I came to Harvard University to teach in the history and literature and expository writing programs. In hiring and/or supervising me, Dan Donoghue, Jan Thaddeus, and Vince Tompkins of history and literature, and Nancy Sommers, Gordon Harvey, and Linda Simon of "expos" provided me with not only a livelihood, but also access to some very fine colleagues. Dirk Killen, my co-lecturer in our course "The Political Culture of the United States," reacquainted me with—and introduced me to—figures ranging from John Winthrop to Maxine Hong Kingston, many of whom found their way into these pages. The informal history and literature writing workshop my wife founded during her own stint at Harvard afforded me great pleasure and insight when I participated in 1994–96. I'd particularly like to thank Steve Biel, Ruth Feldstein, Kristin Hoganson, Kim Hamilton, Joseph Lease, John McGreevy, Alison Pingree, and Vince Tompkins for their contributions.

Since 1994, my institutional home away from home has been Sarah Lawrence College, where my wife works with colleagues and staff who have personally and professionally extended themselves to me. I would particularly like to thank library staffers Judy Kicinski and Barbara Hickey, and computer lab administrators Sarah Allen and Philip Wachtel for treating me as one of their own.

I would also like to acknowledge some purely intellectual debts. Not all of these are academic. I was particularly influenced, for example, by some of the remarkable pop music criticism written in the 1970s, much of it for *Rolling Stone* and the *Village Voice*. Many of these writers went on to write distinguished books. Among them are Robert Christgau, Simon Frith, Peter Guralnick, Geoffrey Stokes, Ken Tucker, Ed Ward, and Springsteen biographer Dave Marsh, whose work was indispensable. Of particular note is Greil Marcus, whose *Mystery Train: Images of America in Rock & Roll Music* showed me that it was possible to write an intelligent, engaged book on rock music. Anyone familiar with Marcus's work will readily see his influence on my own. Anyone who isn't is urged to seek out *Mystery Train*.

Within the academic community, I have been inspired by some gifted historians, among them John William Ward, Warren Susman, Lawrence Levine, and in an imprecise but real way, Laurel Thatcher Ulrich, whose brilliance in breathing life into tiny historical fragments in *A Midwife's Tale* provided me with an imaginative model for my own work. Gordon Wood's studies of republicanism provided me with a usable past I employed in ways I suspect neither he nor many of his colleagues would comfortably sanction (the blame for any excesses here and elsewhere is my own). And Garry Wills has written books whose excellence I aspire to emulate, if not actually realize.

I am indebted to Mr. Wills for another reason: his limited, but surely important, role in making his daughter Lydia Wills the terrific agent that she is. An incisive reader, a talented negotiator, and (most important of all) a patient soother of anxious authors, she navigated this project from unwieldy proposal to finished manuscript. I would also like to thank Betsy Lerner of Doubleday for her own role in shaping my work and in connecting me with Lydia.

This project was acquired for HarperCollins by Eric Steel, who more than any other person helped me shape a dense collection of observations into a book. It is a measure of his character that he continued to work on the manuscript after leaving Harper to return to the movie business, an act of generosity I did not deserve but humbly accepted. I was doubly blessed in that official responsibility for the book passed on to my new editor, Eamon Dolan, who amplified Eric's suggestions and helped me stitch my ideas more tightly together. I only wish every writer could have such incisive, encouraging editorial direction. I also wish every writer could have some of the other forms of support I received from assistant editor Sarah Polen, who took calls and gave comfort (and good advice); David Cohen, who designed the elegant and evocative jacket; Natalie Goldstein, who researched and collected the photos; Victoria Mathews, who copyedited the manuscript; and Joseph Rutt, the skilled craftsman who designed the book.

Born in the U.S.A. is dedicated to my dear friend and longtime roommate Gordon Sterling. In ways too countless to enumerate here, he and his family have shared—and supported—the passions that animate this book. I feel similar admiration, gratitude, and affection for Theodore and Nancy Sizer, whose work has enriched my own. I'm even more grateful to them for the youngest of the four fine children they raised, the one I had the good sense to want as my wife. My final thanks go to that wife, Lyde Cullen Sizer, who threads through these acknowledgments much in the way she threads through this book and the soul of the man who penned it. Mate, muse, mother of my beloved son, she is the greatest of my blessings. There is no luckier husband on God's good earth.

Jim Cullen
Bronxville, New York
March 1997

COPYRIGHT ACKNOWLEDGMENTS

The author would like to express his gratitude to Barbara Carr of Jon Landau Management for her cooperation, on behalf of Bruce Springsteen, with photographs, permissions, and other matters pertaining to the publication of this book.

PHOTOGRAPHY CREDITS

INDEX